Dutch–Australian Jill Koolmees grew up on a flower farm in the hills east of Melbourne. After graduating in Politics, Literature and Education, she took to the road, working as a Jill-of-all-trades to fund her travels to places as far flung as Morocco, India, Japan and the USA. Upon her return to Australia at the start of the 1990s, she became an English language teacher. She lives with her husband in North Melbourne, where she tends a rampant garden and dreams of her next journey.

CANCELLED

CANCELLED

My Desert Kingdom

Finding a life in Saudi Arabia

My Desert Kingdom

Jill Koolmees

BANTAM
SYDNEY • AUCKLAND • TORONTO • NEW YORK • LONDON

Extract from *Arabia Phoenix* © 1946 Gerald de Gaury used by permission of Chambers Harrap Publishers Ltd. Extract from *Arabian Sands* © 1959 Wilfred Thesiger used by permission of HarperCollins Publishers Ltd. From *Sandstorms: Days and Nights in Arabia* by Peter Theroux. Copyright © 1990 by Peter Theroux. Used by permission of W.W. Norton & Company, Inc.

Every effort has been made to identify copyright holders of extracts in this book. The publishers would be pleased to hear from any copyright holders who have not been acknowledged.

MY DESERT KINGDOM
A BANTAM BOOK

First published in Australia and New Zealand in 2004
by Bantam

Copyright © Jill Koolmees, 2004

All rights reserved. No part of this publication may be reproduced, stored in a retrieval system, transmitted in any form or by any means, electronic, mechanical, photocopying, recording or otherwise, without the prior written permission of the publisher.

National Library of Australia
Cataloguing-in-Publication Entry

    Koolmees, Jill.
    My desert kingdom.

    ISBN 1 86325 437 4.

    1. Koolmees, Jill – Journeys – Saudi Arabia. 2. Women – Saudi Arabia – Biography.
    3. Australians – Saudi Arabia – Biography. 4. Women – Saudi Arabia – Social conditions.
    5. Saudi Arabia – Description and travel. 6. Saudi Arabia – Social life and customs.
    I. Title.

    915.38

Transworld Publishers,
a division of Random House Australia Pty Ltd
20 Alfred Street, Milsons Point, NSW 2061
http://www.randomhouse.com.au

Random House New Zealand Limited
18 Poland Road, Glenfield, Auckland

Transworld Publishers,
a division of The Random House Group Ltd
61-63 Uxbridge Road, London W5 5SA

Random House Inc
1745 Broadway, New York, New York 10036

Cover design by Darian Causby/Highway 51
Cover photographs: Sand dunes © Austral International Photo Library; Carved sandstone © Jake Causby/Blue Cork
Maps by Caroline Bowie
Typeset by Midland Typesetters, Maryborough, Victoria
Printed and bound by Griffin Press, Netley, South Australia

10 9 8 7 6 5 4 3 2 1

To the best of the author's knowledge and research, all information in this book was correct at the time of publication.

To my good and kind father, John Koolmees,
and to my own true love, Geoff.

CONTENTS

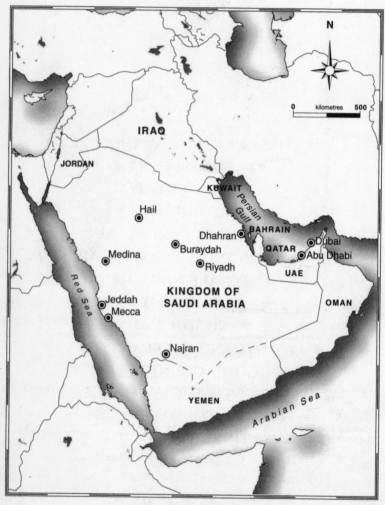

Map 1: Kingdom of Saudi Arabia

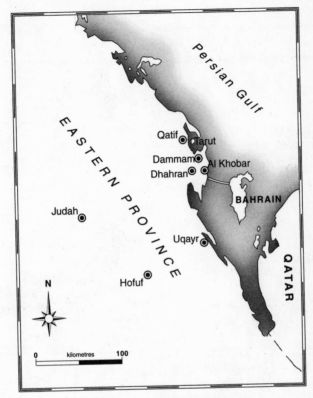

Map 2: The Eastern Province

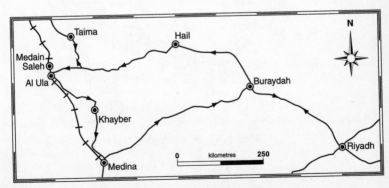

Map 3: Journey to the north

FOREWORD

I began writing this book just after September 11, 2001, a time when many were asking what sort of country could have produced Osama bin Laden and his suicide bombers. This seemed then to be a question worth trying to answer; the passage of time and subsequent events have only made it more so. The War on Terror and the actions of America and her allies in Afghanistan and Iraq have polarised Muslim opinion and forever changed the power equation in the Middle East. A new, confrontational era of East–West relations has been engaged, and is being played out within the borders of Saudi Arabia.

At first the assaults against Westerners were small in scale. In June 2002 an Australian working in the northern city of Tabuk narrowly escaped death in a sniper attack, the third that had taken place in Saudi cities over the preceding months. Several expatriates were killed or injured by bombs exploding under their cars, placed outside shops or tossed over compound walls. By late 2002 there had been eleven such incidents.

In 2003, events took a more sinister turn. On May 12, truck bombs exploded outside three foreign compounds in Riyadh, killing thirty-five people and injuring as many as two hundred. In August, British Airways announced that it was suspending flights to the Kingdom, based upon intelligence reports that militants planned to launch missile attacks on their aircraft near Riyadh. On November 8, another massive explosion at a compound in Riyadh killed eighteen. This time most of the victims were not Westerners, but expatriate Muslims.

Meanwhile, the Australian Department of Foreign Affairs has advised its citizens to defer all non-essential travel to Saudi

Arabia. Many foreign workers have already left; many more have sent their families home.

Although it is easy to read these events in terms of their effect on the relatively small expatriate community, their true significance can be understood only in relation to the tremors now shaking the power balance in Saudi Arabia. The country has entered a new era of instability. Whether the House of Saud manages to retain its grip on power, and whether the scales tip towards tolerance and openness or towards an even deeper conservatism, the outcome will affect us all.

This book is my attempt to make sense of the Saudis and their world. Most of the events I have described took place between October 1997, when I first arrived in the Kingdom, and June 2000, when I returned to Australia. In fact, I had two sojourns amongst the Saudis: the first was a visit of three months; a year later, I returned for a stay of nineteen months. For narrative purposes, I have compressed these two visits into one. Also, because I have followed a partially thematic approach, events are not presented in strict chronological order.

In Riyadh, a Parisienne friend told me a story that highlights a serious concern for anyone attempting to write about Saudi life. She conducted a French conversation class for a group of Saudi women, and during their weekly meetings the women's conversation would usually stray into chatter and gossip. They talked about travel and shopping and clothing. They talked about their children, their husbands and their lives. Sometimes . . . often . . . they complained. One day, said my friend, she found the group in an uproar. Their previous teacher had, upon her return to Paris, published a tell-all account of their lives in a *Marie Claire* article with a title that translates roughly as 'Women imprisoned by the veil'. The magazine was not available in the Kingdom, and perhaps the writer believed that the women would never see her report. If so, she was mistaken, for two of them bought copies on trips abroad, and were horrified to recognise themselves in the article. They were outraged that their private confidences, the idle chatter of unguarded moments, had been betrayed, and dreaded what might happen to them if their husbands should find out. Eventually some of the men did indeed come across the article, but, to the relief of their wives, chose to see the funny side of it. A happy outcome to an incident that had the potential for real harm.

The Saudis are such a reserved and private people that it is hard to write about them at all without the feeling that one is betraying their trust, especially when so much that has been written is sensationalist, prurient and one-dimensional. Because I have no wish to compromise the people I encountered, the names of most of the characters and certain key details have been changed. I hope that I have captured something of the complexity and variety of their world.

One evening when I was teaching an English lesson to a group of young Saudi women, a student started to talk about a trip to America she had made with her parents the previous year. 'Do you know,' she said indignantly, 'people in the West are so ignorant about us. We know all about them. At school we study their history and their culture. We read about them and see them on television. But they know nothing about us. They think that Arabia is just sand and camels!'

I tried to suggest that the reason for our ignorance was that it was difficult for outsiders to find out anything about her country; that the Saudis did not welcome foreign visitors and actively discouraged foreign scrutiny.

'Then tell them about us,' she insisted.

I

THE PRICE OF ADMISSION

Tell me, said he . . . what moved thee, or how couldst thou take
such journeys into the fanatic Arabia?
CHARLES DOUGHTY, Travels in Arabia Deserta

Dawn in Riyadh. The terminal at King Khalid Airport was a
frozen oasis rendered in glass and pale marble. Inside,
fountains splashed and trickled under a vaulted ceiling. Outside
on the tarmac, lines of private jets were parked side by side.
Behind them, a molten red sun was oozing over the horizon
through an ominous purple haze.

The call to prayer had sounded. The men had withdrawn to
the mosque. Men in military uniforms, men in white robes and
red-chequered head cloths, men in baggy cotton shirts and
trousers. They had come gliding up silent escalators and then disappeared down carpeted halls, strolling companionably to their
morning devotions.

In the air-conditioned chill of the domestic departure lounge,
I sat shivering on a cold metal bench. Huddled around me were
eight small figures draped in black: young Indonesian women
bound for the homes of Arabian families and jobs as housemaids.
They slept, exhausted, still clutching their little bundles of
possessions.

As for me, I was hyper-awake. I had come 11,000 kilometres

and crossed seven time zones to be here. My last real sleep was over forty hours ago. I had reached that state of jittery, crazed tiredness where nothing seemed real, least of all my immediate surroundings.

Fifteen hours earlier, fresh from the cheerful bustle of the streets of Singapore, I had hesitated outside another airport lobby, and asked myself if this journey was one I really wanted to take.

The vast room had been buzzing with people. Tour leaders clutching stacks of passports scurried about herding their charges into tight clusters. The men wore matching batik shirts; the women's faces were framed in white, lace-trimmed scarves wrapped low on their foreheads and pinned demurely under their chins. A joyful hubbub arose from the surrounding crowds, gathered there to farewell them and to bless their journey.

For this was to be a flight of pilgrims, all bound for Mecca. Some of the men moving through the throng had already donned the traditional garb of the pilgrim: one white towel slung sarong-style around their hips and another draped across their shoulders. Some individuals sat devoutly reading their Qurans, silently mouthing the holy words that Muslims believe were directly transmitted from Allah to his prophet Mohammad. Everywhere, faces filled with a rapt intensity.

Against their eager anticipation I had measured my own feelings of trepidation. I was no pilgrim, and this was not my world. I felt that I stood poised on a threshold between two hemispheres. Behind me, the familiar West: progressive, secular, commercial, spinning on an axis that in my imagination passed through the earth somewhere in the vicinity of New York. In front of me, the world of Islam: traditional, separate, reclusive, twirling around the Kaabah, a mysterious black cube in the centre of a square in Mecca. It was a world I knew little about.

I had taken a deep breath, and plunged into the crowd.

It wasn't my idea to go to Saudi Arabia. In fact, I would have placed it near the bottom of my list of possible travel destinations. When I thought about it, if I thought about it at all, I pictured a place where black-veiled women suffered appalling repression, a place of public amputations and beheadings, a place with a climate from hell. Even before the horrors of September 11, I found its conservative brand of Islam confronting.

The truth was that having recently returned to Melbourne after a long stint in the USA, I wasn't really keen to go anywhere. I was getting used to living back in my own home city amongst family and friends. I liked Melbourne. I was comfortable there. Then I met Geoff, and before long he and I were talking about spending the rest of our lives together.

We hadn't known each other for very long when he mentioned his dream of going to Saudi Arabia. 'No way,' I said. 'Last place on earth,' I said, and, 'Are you mad?' I suggested alternatives. Japan. Hong Kong. Wonderful places with intriguing cultures where a pair of English teachers would be welcomed; where there was good money to be made. He was unmoved. We agreed to defer our discussion. In my heart, I hoped he would lose interest.

But like some latter day Lawrence, he was drawn to Arabia. True, he had a rational reason for going there: the chance to put away some serious savings. The salary that he was offered for teaching at a Saudi university was modest, and no better than he would have earned in Australia, but his contract promised to cover almost all of our expenses, including accommodation and return annual airfares. There would also be no Saudi taxes on his earnings, and he would receive a generous end-of-service bonus. But despite the allure of Saudi money, it was the mystique of the place that drew him in. In the end, after holding out for more than four years, my resistance crumbled. Signing the contract seemed almost a sensible thing to do.

Against all expectations, Arabia began to work its charms on me. The desert peninsula has for much of its history been off limits, even hostile, to non-Muslim travellers, yet somehow its very inaccessibility has proved a fascination. What is it about the curiosity of Westerners? Wherever we are told we cannot go, wherever a seraglio screen hides a world from our eyes, our imaginations run wild. Bewitched by the possibility of a different reality, we thrill to exotic/erotic fantasies of luxury and indolence. We want to lift a corner of the veil, to peek inside.

Once we had decided to go, I gave free rein to my imagination. Geoffrey of Arabia may have had his 'hoof beats over the burning sand' fantasies. I became lost in the enchantments of Scheherazade and the Arabian Nights: tales of genies, magic lanterns, treasure chests and hidden doors leading to unknown destinies.

But then, just as we started making plans to depart, I was offered a job I simply could not refuse: the chance to transform myself from a mere English teacher into a university lecturer. Two pictures presented themselves to me. In the first, I was a successful, independent career woman; in the second, an expat wife: restricted, repressed and frustrated. Suddenly Geoff and I found ourselves drawn in opposite directions. We had heated discussions. Each of us felt betrayed. Finally we compromised. He would go to Saudi Arabia alone. I would join him after a year. Secretly I hoped that by that time he would be over it.

And then he was gone. Weeks were to pass before I heard from him again. Arabia seemed to have swallowed him up, leaving me anxious, angry. When he finally called, it was on a line that crackled and hissed and sent my voice echoing back to me. He spoke of money troubles (he hadn't been paid), of delays in getting his work permit, of the difficulty of getting to a telephone, and of how hard it was to control a class full of young Saudi men ('boy wrangling', he called it). But he sounded more alive than he had in years. In the wake of his enthusiasm, and because I missed him so very badly, I began to make plans for my own journey.

Announce that you are about to visit Saudi Arabia, and the reaction of most people is predictable. A sudden intake of breath, a raising of the eyebrows, and a pursing of the lips. 'Saudi Arabia!' they exclaim.

'Will you have to cover up?' my female friends asked in alarm. 'Will you be able to get a drink?' the men fretted. Everyone had misgivings about repression, safety and terrorism, and so did I. To my surprise, almost everyone had some connection with the Kingdom: a cousin or a brother who had worked there, or a friend who had visited on business. Invariably, their reports were negative.

I asked a colleague who had spent several years teaching there what he thought of my travel plans. He was non-committal in his reply, but advised me to speak to his wife. Maryanne was not encouraging. 'Even now, when I think of that place, I get angry,' was the first thing she told me.

In 1997 when I began my journey, the newspapers were full of the story of two British nurses arrested for the murder of an Australian colleague, and widely seen as victims of an arbitrary Saudi justice system. At this time, too, in yet another reprise of the 'Mother of All Wars', tensions were rising between Saddam Hussein and the Americans and their Saudi allies. It did nothing for my confidence to learn that I would be living wedged between an American consulate and a Saudi military air base, and I seriously considered packing a gas mask in my luggage.

Thoughtful family members spent the weeks before my departure sending me newspaper clippings, even videos, that detailed the horrors of life in the desert Kingdom. Friends simply rolled their eyes.

And it wasn't as if Saudi Arabia was extending a warm welcome to me. The Kingdom is not an easy place to visit. Non-Muslims can go there on contract as expatriate workers, or on business or diplomatic visas; Muslims can obtain travel permits for their *haj* or *umrah* pilgrimages. Until quite recently, however, there was no such thing as a tourist, or even a transit, visa. Foreigners are unwelcome, and those who do manage to get in find themselves subject to strict controls. Effectively, the price of admission is freedom.

In the past, would-be visitors have gone to elaborate lengths to penetrate the secrecy of Arabia. The nineteenth-century explorer Sir Richard Burton, for example, learned to speak flawless Arabic, disguised himself as a doctor from Afghanistan, and joined a pilgrim camel train for his journey to Mecca.

I, too, would have many tests to pass. First, I had to present my marriage certificate – the original, not a copy – to prove that Geoff and I were legally wed. Then there were the medical exams. By the time the Saudi Embassy in Canberra had issued me with a visa, I had been tested for bilharzias, tuberculosis, syphilis, gonorrhoea, hepatitis A, B and C, AIDS and pregnancy. Not only was I pure, I had the papers to prove it.

I began my journey in a confusion of ideas: of deserts and oases, of oil and wealth, of repression, hostility and danger. Quite unable to say what was truth and what was not, I resolved to keep an open mind; to see how Saudi Arabia would reveal itself to me.

Flying Saudia, the Saudi national airline, was an experience in itself. There was an initial kerfuffle as seating arrangements were adjusted. Those in the know immediately set to work on the flight attendants to get themselves upgraded to first class. For those of us left in economy, it was important to ensure that no woman was placed next to an unrelated man. The old Malay gentleman in the seat next to mine did not relax until he had been moved over to the aisle, and his wife brought up from where she had been comfortably ensconced with the women in her group to sit between us. Once the proprieties had been met, however, he was friendliness itself. He leaned over in front of his wife to chat, and translated my replies back to his curious cronies in the seats behind us. His name was Ibrahim.

'I teach Quran,' he told me. 'Every year I take people from my village to make *umrah*.'

'How many times have you been to Mecca?' I asked.

He flashed his fingers at me once, twice, three times, grinning proudly.

'Fifteen times!'

As we taxied down the runway, the chief steward's voice welcomed us aboard, and in seductively guttural Arabic intoned a prayer for travellers. I was not reassured, and muttered a silent prayer of my own that all would go well for me. The rising plane settled into its flight, and the drink carts were wheeled out. They were stacked with an astonishing array of juices, mineral waters,

sodas, milk, and hot tea and coffee. A gin and tonic would have
settled my nerves, but I knew better than to ask for one. Alcohol
was strictly off the menu.

The male flight attendants all looked like Omar Sharif, and the
women wore pillbox hats draped with gauze, just like Barbara
Eden in 'I Dream of Genie'. The flight data screens displayed the
usual tiny plane edging across a map, and told us our speed, our
height above sea level and the temperature of the air outside.
For the convenience of the faithful there was also a screen with
an arrow that pointed constantly in the direction of Mecca.

And that's where we were headed: out across the night-time
glitter of Singapore; out past the burning flares of Sumatran oil
refineries on the Straits of Malacca; onwards over the horn of
India all a-sparkle with a magical network of fairy lights; over the
cities of the Arabian Gulf – Dubai, Manama, Dhahran – ablaze
with sulphur street lights etching the shape of boulevards and of
highways curving away into the surrounding blackness.

We touched down in Riyadh just before midnight. My
Malaysian friends, who were flying on to Jeddah, roused themselves from their slumber to wish me well. 'Have a good *umrah*,'
I told them, not quite sure how to express the idea. It seemed to
do the trick. They smiled and waved cheerfully.

I followed a small crowd to passport control, where the entire
passenger load of a recently landed Air Pakistan jumbo jet was
waiting to be processed. The men (there were no women) stood
in four long, densely packed, jostling lines, anxiously bobbing and
craning around each other to see what was happening at the head
of each queue. From time to time the supervising security guard
grabbed one of the front-runners and shoved him unceremoni-
ously up to the counter, shouting all the while at the others to
stand back. I hesitated, unsure which of the lines to attach myself
to, but the guard suddenly noticed me and waved me up to the
desk reserved for arriving diplomats. It's not all bad news for
women in Saudi Arabia.

'Your husband is waiting for you outside, yes?' the immigration
officer said confidently as he stamped my passport. Well, no. I was
in transit to Dhahran, and my connecting flight was eight hours
away. The officer winced. The hand that was about to return my

passport to me was quickly withdrawn. A hasty conference of uniformed officials followed. It was obviously unthinkable that I could be left to my own resources in the airport for the night, or worse, that I might try to disappear into the city unescorted. No, it was clear that someone would have to take responsibility for me.

And that is how I came to be attached to the Indonesian housemaids contingent: twenty or so young women who were busy swathing themselves in black *abayas* and helping each other to wrap long black scarves around their heads until only their hands and faces were visible. They looked bemused as I joined them and as my passport was added to the stack in the hands of the resentful-looking junior officer who was in charge of them.

'Yala!' said the officer. 'Let's go.' And off we went, marching from one end of the huge terminal to the other, and down an escalator into the basement. We pulled up at a pair of latticed saloon doors painted in fading turquoise: the Women's Transit Lounge (expatriate wags know it as the 'Unclaimed Wives Department'). At a shout from our escort, a fierce-looking woman in maxi-skirted khaki emerged. She took control of my passport, looked me up and down, snapped at a couple of nearby janitors who were gazing at us, and ushered me briskly inside. As I walked through the swinging doors I tried hard to imagine that I was entering an exotic oriental seraglio. It was a passing fancy.

A succession of rooms ranged down two sides of a shabby corridor, each one labelled in descending order of prestige. I was directed into 'Medical Workers', second only in status to 'Doctors'. No doubt my companions were being delivered to a room somewhere named 'Domestic Servants'.

'Medical Workers' was an airless room with peeling wall paper. On low couches covered in faded mustard plush velvet, about 20 sleeping women were stretched out. They had draped their shawls over their faces to shield their eyes from the fluorescent glare. I found a space for myself and settled down to doze, pulling my own scarf over my face. By the clock on the far wall, it was one-thirty in the morning, Saudi time.

A shout of 'Australia' close to my ear brought me back to dazed consciousness – a summons to get up. It seemed that only moments had passed. My bleary eyes strained to focus on the clock. Two-fifteen. It *was* only moments. I staggered into the washroom, splashed some cold water onto my face, and then, wincing in the light, made my way back out into the corridor and through the saloon doors.

There I found the Indonesian girls already assembled. Under the supervision of a young soldier, they were tucking into a breakfast of curried chicken and rice. Served in disposable aluminium tubs, it looked and smelled suspiciously like the dinner on last night's Saudia flight, a meal that even then had not rated highly in the airline dinner stakes. I gagged as the guard held out a portion to me, and waved it away with the hand that was not covering my mouth.

Breakfast and a role call completed, we were formed into pairs and marched like schoolchildren on an excursion back through the empty terminal. At security, bored, uniformed women ran metal detectors over our bodies. Another role call (our guard was taking no chances), and we were deposited in the departure lounge.

As the night wore on, housemaids were detached one after another from our group, and dispatched on flights to Jeddah, to Taif, to Hail, to Medina. Finally only eight were left.

We had progressed to exchanging smiles. Now a fit of nudging, whispering and giggling broke out amongst them, and one tiny figure was pushed forward.

'What . . . iss . . . your . . . name?' she asked, and her companions dissolved into laughter.

Her name was Annie, and that was all her English. I had picked up a few words of Bahasa on a backpacking trip around Indonesia, and now I struggled to bring them to the surface of my tired brain.

'Jakarta?' was the best I could do.

''Noooo,' the girls chorused.

'Java?'

'Yes! Java, yes!'

'*Saudara . . . tahun?*' I managed. 'You . . . years?' I wanted to know how old they were. They seemed to be very young: eighteen perhaps.

The girls were amazed. 'Bahasa!' they trilled.

'*Dua tahun*,' said Annie, holding up two fingers. Two years. I guessed that she was telling me the length of her contract.

Annie had a jaunty air about her. She radiated optimism and excitement, as if she were embarking on a great adventure. Her high spirits buoyed up her nervous friends, but I could not help but wonder what the future held for them.

As dawn approached, their chatter gradually became softer. One by one, heads drooped onto companionable shoulders. Soon I was the only one still awake.

Gradually the airport came to life. Men returned from the mosque and took up their positions at the counters. Businessmen with briefcases appeared, suit jackets over their white *thobes*. One had fallen asleep on the bench behind us – too close. When a security guard roughly shook him awake and ordered him away, he went without a murmur. The first women appeared, escorted by their sons and husbands, although 'appeared' is not quite the right word. They were concealed completely, right down to their long black gloves. The maids woke up, and now even Annie was subdued.

Our flight left at seven a.m. – an uneventful journey over a parched brown landscape. One hour later we stepped out into a warm Dhahran morning, and were shepherded onto a bus for the short drive to the arrivals shed.

Geoff stood out from the crowd of Arab and Subcontinental men waiting there, and not just because of his Western-style clothing. His face was lit up in a huge welcoming grin. I was glad to see him too! I broke ranks and hurried over, and we wrapped each other up in an enthusiastic embrace. And then I thought: Hold on, this is Saudi Arabia – we're not meant to be doing this in public. I looked about nervously. The men who surrounded us had all averted their eyes. They were looking at the floor, at the ceiling, and off into space, but, to my surprise, they were all smiling.

A few more formalities at the immigration desk, then the

official held out my passport. As I reached out to take it, he snatched it back. Then he extended his hand again – to Geoff – leaving me simmering under my own little cloud of chagrin.

My companions had also changed hands: given over into the care of another uniformed official who was marching them away. As they disappeared through a door marked 'Domestic Servants', Annie turned and waved to me.

She looked very small.

Geoff handed my passport back to me. 'Welcome to the Magic Kingdom,' he said, 'where anything can happen.'

2

PARADISE

So, when you ask Allah, ask for Al Firdaus which is the middle
and highest part of Paradise.
HADITH 48, Volume 4

G eoff's sunny mood was short lived. As we drove out of the
airport, I glanced across at him. He seemed tense. His
jaw was set hard and his hands were gripping the steering wheel
so tightly that his knuckles had turned white. Then we were on
the freeway, and cars were hurtling past us like missiles that left
us rocking and gasping in their wake. They were roaring up the
on-ramps and into the traffic beside us, or swerving without
warning in front of us across three lanes to exit, all without a
glance in our direction. Soon my own bloodless hands were
gripping the armrest and my foot was pumping up and down on
a phantom brake pedal. It would be weeks before I could get into
a car without a feeling of panic.

Despite my terror, I was doing my best to assist Geoff by
pointing out any dangers that I thought he may not be aware of.

'Watch out for this guy on the left,' I told him. 'Look out!
There's a truck right up your . . .'

'Would you just let me do the driving,' he snapped. And then
'Damn! I've missed our exit.'

Eventually we made it off the freeway and onto a quieter street.

We were driving through a bleached, ragged moonscape.

'You're lucky to get here in the cool season,' said Geoff, relaxing slightly. 'See how green everything is!'

I looked at him in disbelief. Was he referring to the light fuzz of grey vegetation that sprinkled the desert? I put my hands over my eyes to shield them from the glare ricocheting off the pale sand.

It was a mercifully short ride to the nation's top university, the King Fahd University of Petroleum and Minerals (KFUPM), where Geoff was employed as a teacher, and where we were to live. We drove up through a paved forecourt, skirted a large fountain and arrived at an impressive entrance where security guards glanced at our papers and waved us through. Inside, sprinklers were playing over hillocks of green lawn, and marigolds and periwinkles were blooming in formal beds under groves of date palms. The university proper sat high on a rocky hill to our right. We turned to the left and rolled down an avenue of carefully trimmed trees, past leafy enclaves of flats and townhouses; past tracts of open desert.

Our compound, about a kilometre away at the far end of the campus, was built to house the families of the university's lesser academics. It was named, with no intended irony, Ferdaws, or Paradise. We had been allocated Number 5231, a single-storey dwelling tacked onto the end of a larger group of apartments. A collection of skinny calico cats sized us up with a mixture of hope and wariness as we took possession.

Behind a heavy wooden door was a living room crammed with seventies-vintage, Danish-style furniture. The mix of dining table, sofa, desk and assorted chairs told me that this room was intended to be all things to us. It was impossible to move about without bumping into a coffee table or a lampshade or each other. Sliding glass doors opened onto a small courtyard whose high, mud-coloured walls had the unfortunate effect of making me feel as if I was trapped inside a cardboard box, but at least there was light in this part of the flat.

In the bedroom the only source of natural light was that which came through a glass panel in a door that led to another boxed courtyard. In the small bathroom and galley kitchen there were no windows at all.

The shower rose in the bathroom was rusty, and the hot and cold taps in both kitchen and bathroom were encrusted with a white powder. The cause was soon clear: the water that they dispensed was salty. It had the power to turn any soapy lather into an oily scum, and to corrode every metallic surface it touched. Our only drinking water came from a single tap in the kitchen. It tasted flat and unpleasant.

Until my arrival, Geoff had been living in the accommodation set aside for bachelors. This apartment was new for him too, and later he confessed that his heart had fallen when he had first come to inspect it. Now he was watching me nervously, trying to gauge my reactions.

But I was determined to stay positive. The last thing I wanted to do was make a habit of blaming Geoff for the shortcomings of my surroundings: we had bridges enough to mend after our long separation.

'It's a bit small,' was all I said, 'but it'll be fine.'

Besides, right then the only thing that mattered to me was sleep. I collapsed into bed and Geoff went off to work. I slept through the day and into the night. The hissing and wailing of cats punctuated my dreams. They were fighting each other for lordship of our courtyard.

My first morning alone and awake at Ferdaws. With Geoff off at work again, what better for me to do than a load of washing? It was a short, hot walk through a series of paved courtyards to the communal laundry.

The architecture of Ferdaws captured something of the mood of a traditional Arabian village: a suggestion of rendered mud-brick walls and labyrinthine pathways. The apartments were arranged in one-, two- and three-storey configurations; endless variations on a building-block theme. Here and there children's playgrounds dotted the grounds; sturdy jungle gyms of slides, pipe tunnels and climbing equipment embedded in large sandpits, and shielded from the sun under huge, white polypropylene tents. Along its access roads fingers of desert penetrated the compound. Some residents had fenced off plots of the unpromising sand with high, leafy hedges, behind which they had managed to coax improbably green private gardens.

The initial effect was pleasing. Ferdaws was well conceived and solidly built. Interesting patterns of light and shade formed as the sun played on the sand-coloured walls. Palms, eucalyptus trees and a species of ornamental fig grew in the open spaces, and in the courtyards, there were flowers: yellow trumpet vines, red hibiscus, pink and white oleander, rambling lantana, sweet-smelling frangipani, and everywhere the vivid magenta of tumbling bougainvillea.

It was only on closer examination that I noticed the cracked paving, the crumbling masonry and the stucco flaking from the walls. Despite the efforts of a small army of maintenance workers, the effects of age and a harsh climate had combined to give Ferdaws a shabby, down-at-heel air.

On the other side of the border fence there was a highway, and just beyond that Dhahran's busy international airport and a military air base. Ferdaws sat almost directly beneath the path of a constant stream of 747s, either lumbering into flight or thundering into a landing, and of fighter jets that took to the skies with a sound like ripping canvas and pounding sonic booms. The mist of fuel that they ejected drifted down to mingle with the acrid smell of desert dust and with cooking smells emanating from the compound's kitchens: whiffs of the ubiquitous chicken curry.

In the laundry, only a few of the battered washing machines were in working order. Half concealed behind them, a tangle of pipes encrusted with roses of copper and iron corrosion dripped salt water into a dark, stagnant pool. I loaded my clothes into tubs caked with greasy soap scum, suspecting that they would end up dirtier than they had begun, and abandoned them to their cycle.

Half an hour later, as I walked back to the laundry, I found familiar underpants, bras and other bits of my clothing hanging from shrubs and scattered over the ground. As I gathered them up, I heard muffled giggling and the sound of scampering feet.

This was my first encounter with the neighbourhood children. It was not to be my last.

The greatest luxury in travel is to have as little baggage to encumber you as possible. I had learned this lesson the hard way, soon after I graduated from university, when I trudged off to Indonesia and places beyond under the weight of a monstrous orange backpack stuffed with things meant to see me through every eventuality. Cooking equipment, sleeping bag, books, flashlight, warm clothing, a formal dress, toilet paper: I had it all. I only really started to enjoy my trip after a thief had relieved me of most of my worldly goods. Reduced to a small shoulder bag containing a toothbrush, a cake of soap, a sarong and a change of clothes, I travelled with a delicious sense of lightness and freedom.

And yet, when faced with packing for my Arabian journey, I felt that there were things I could not do without – things I needed to comfort and divert me throughout what would surely be a period of intense deprivation. This was despite being assured that everything I could possibly desire (outside of a ham sandwich) would be available for me to purchase in the Kingdom. Amongst the things I packed were my computer (not, alas, a laptop) and printer, my exercise mat, a raft of books, magazines and CDs, a year's supply of my favourite shampoo and cosmetics, a large cooking pot, my best carving knife, a salad spinner, a good tablecloth. I limited myself to five cartons, and was rather pleased with my restraint. That was until I had to retrieve them from Saudi customs.

This was no job for a woman. In the Kingdom, women have fathers, husbands, brothers and servants to take care of such things, and I expected that Geoff (he of the single small suitcase) would be able to do the same for me. But his work schedule co-incided almost exactly with the opening hours of the customs office, and I soon realised that if I wanted my treasures, I would have to get them myself.

Farouk, the shipping agent I had been advised to call to check that my boxes had arrived, was specific in his instructions: 'Leave your taxi at the security gate. Tell him to wait. Proceed on foot. Submit your shipping number. Pay the fee of 60 riyals. Collect your goods. Call your taxi in and load it.'

How long would all this take? 'Oh, fifteen minutes to two hours,' he said airily. It should have been a warning.

Customs was comprised of a large warehouse and sorting yard, and an accretion of aging prefabricated buildings, each with an air-conditioner pasted onto its side and held there with duct tape. The whole complex was surrounded by a high mesh fence.

Things went smoothly as far as the 'proceed on foot' stage. I proceeded into the first building, marked 'Cargo Office'. Inside, a rabble of men were crushing themselves three and four deep against a counter, each waving a fistful of official papers aloft and shouting for attention. Behind the counter a few clerks were dealing with the throng, all in their own good time. My heart sank, but to my surprise, the shouting stopped, the crowd parted, and I was ushered courteously up to the counter – only to be told that I was in the wrong place.

In the next office a clerk and a cashier were caged behind a wall of wood and glass panels: the sort of wall you might find in an old-fashioned bank. There were only three clients, but they were trying simultaneously to wedge their entire upper bodies through a single narrow opening in the glass as they pleaded with the clerk. Once again the miraculous happened. Noticing my presence, the three extricated themselves from the window, and waved me forward.

I found myself wondering if this deference was a mark of respect and courtesy towards me, or whether these men felt that having a woman (any woman) present in their midst was simply intolerable, and wanted to get rid of me as quickly as possible. Perhaps both answers were true. Whatever the reason, it was to happen again and again, so much so that I soon got into the habit of walking to the front of all queues as if it was my birthright.

I gave the clerk my shipping number, he handed me a sheaf of documents, and I paid the cashier my 60 riyals (US$16). Not bad, I thought to myself. Now to collect my goods and summon my taxi. But the cashier sent me back to the cargo office, where my papers were checked, signed and stamped. The clerk handed them back to me, and added a few more to the pile.

'You fill this form,' he said, pointing to one of them, 'and take to warehouse.'

'But it's in Arabic!' I protested.

He shrugged expressively. Then two polite but highly amused young men nudged each other forward and told me what to write, and off I went, clutching my papers, to the warehouse.

This was a huge open shed filled with piles of crates and boxes. A lone forklift was zipping back and forth between them, and Bangladeshi porters were trotting around toting bundles on their heads. Everywhere hopefuls like myself were waving handfuls of documents at the sole customs officer. I found my cartons and settled down beside them to wait.

The customs officer was a distinguished-looking Arab dressed impeccably in a spotless white *thobe* and *ghutra*. He was attended by a Pakistani clerk with a clipboard and pen, and a Bangladeshi labourer to take care of the manual work. Obviously a man of importance, the customs officer moved slowly about, gesturing for this or that box to be opened.

Eventually it was my turn. My boxes were sliced open, the customs officer took a perfunctory look inside, and looked at my papers.

'You must pay duty of 200 riyals (US$53),' he said. My face registered shock – Farouk hadn't said anything about duty, and I didn't have much cash on me. 'OK,' the officer took pity, 'you can pay 185 riyals (US$49). Go to the customs office for a stamp.' The clerk scribbled something on one of my papers, and handed them all back to me.

But it was eleven a.m. Doors were slamming, windows were closing, and the customs office was empty. Prayer time. Clearly there was nothing more to be done. I summoned my taxi and proceeded home without my goods.

At twelve-thirty I was back in the customs office presenting my papers to be stamped. But the customs officer had forgotten to sign them, and was no longer on duty.

As I stood wondering what to do next, a Pakistani clad in customs khaki came up and offered me his assistance, which

I gratefully accepted. This kind gentleman gave up his afternoon to traipse through a series of shabby offices with me. In each one we collected another form to add to our already alarming pile, and in each one we had to wait patiently for the resident Saudi manager to notice us and to sign and stamp it. The process went on and on.

Feeling uncomfortable and increasingly sorry for myself, I stood in the corner of one office and buried my face in my hands. Immediately the manager, who I had assumed to be quite indifferent to my existence, looked up.

'I am so sorry, madam,' he said with an expression of the utmost courtesy. 'Soon all will be done.'

And soon I realised that we were indeed going back to offices we had already visited, this time in reverse order. Now we discarded forms as we progressed, until at last we arrived at the customs office and collected our stamp.

I summoned my taxi and loaded my goods. There was *baksheesh* for the porters, but I'm sorry to say that for my saviour, the Pakistani customs officer, I had only 10 riyals (US$3) left. He deserved far more.

I surrendered my final stamped and signed document to the guard at the security gate, and urged my driver to 'Go, go, go!' as we sped away in a cloud of dust and triumph.

The process took five hours. Later everyone marvelled at how smoothly things had gone for me.

In the weeks before my departure I had endured the stress of winding up my job, arranging my affairs in Australia, making my farewells and preparing for travel – to say nothing of the anxiety I felt about the journey. I arrived in the Kingdom mentally and physically exhausted. Now the pressure was off. With little to do but please myself, I started to unwind. To my surprise, I was in a holiday mood.

I got up late to find the sun shining, and the days pleasantly hot. The air was sticky with a humidity that sapped my energy, and made me happy to drift and go slow.

I strolled around the residential areas of the campus, exploring. It was soon apparent that Ferdaws was at the down-market end of KFUPM housing. Further up the hill, arranged around a large modern mosque, were leafy suburbs full of well-maintained villas and townhouses. Many stood in established gardens behind high green hedges. Apart from a few gardeners and maintenance workers, there was no-one about.

Off to one side of the campus, beyond the housing compounds and the sports fields, stood the staff recreation centre, a low, dark brick building. Once inside, I made my way upstairs to the library. As I walked through the door a tiny African girl of about three rushed over with her arms in the air, demanding to be hugged. I swept her up, glad to find a friend.

'She does that to everyone,' smiled her mother, who was also the librarian. 'You are new here, I think. Welcome to our library.'

I was surprised and reassured to see a woman working there. The only other patrons were a pair of Subcontinental men seated in comfortable armchairs reading the daily newspapers. The shelves were stacked with English-language books on arts and crafts, history, geography, business, economics, literature, psychology, cooking and computers, as well as a collection of Arabic texts. Although few of the books in the library were less than ten years old, I was delighted by it. Here at least I had a resource that would occupy my time. I made plans to visit as often as possible.

The recreation centre also had a cafeteria, a small gymnasium, meeting rooms, indoor basketball courts, outdoor tennis courts and a swimming pool where a notice on the wall announced different schedules for men's and women's bathing. The only sign of life was a group of teenage boys playing ping pong in one of the side rooms. Where was everyone? I wondered.

Leaving the recreation centre, I swung back through a fig orchard and a stand of townhouses towards the main road that bisected the lower campus as it ran down the hill towards Ferdaws. On the other side of the road, I came to the Co-op, our very small supermarket. Here there was more action. A steady stream of shoppers strolled the aisles: for the most part, Arab and Pakistani men, women, and children – so many children! A few

Westerners smiled a friendly greeting as they went past. I stocked up on vegetables, pasta and milk, and headed for home.

It was mid-afternoon. Teenage girls in black robes were spilling out of the gate of the on-campus girls high school, and climbing into waiting vehicles. More cars filled the road that wound from the university down to Ferdaws: staff returning home from their duties. Western men on bicycles and on foot passed me by.

As I cut across the desert, squads of quail scurried from my path. I picked up sparkling quartz crystals from the sandy gravel, and examined the tough little plants growing there. Geoff had been right – the desert was blooming.

At home I cooked our evening meal, my sole task for the day, and welcomed Geoff back from his toils. I felt that I was play-acting at being a housewife, and wondered how long I'd manage to sustain the act. For now, at least, it was pleasant.

Meanwhile, we were getting used to each other's company again. We talked endlessly, exchanging accounts of our separation, trading observations on our surroundings, delighting in simply hanging out together. In the evenings we strolled along the concrete path that ran around the edge of Ferdaws. Our neighbours would be out taking the air too. Sometimes expats stopped to say hello to Geoff and to introduce themselves to me. But each time we saw a Muslim family approaching us – the man in his red and white, his wife in her black, pushing a stroller with one or two small children gripping onto the sides – the husband would step in front of his wife to shield her from Geoff's view. And so we sailed past each other, eyes averted, neither side acknowledging the other by so much as a glance.

Not long after my arrival, we were invited to a Ferdaws party given by one of Geoff's colleagues from the English department. We wandered around, lost in the dark, trying to read the numbers on the buildings, until we arrived, largely by luck, at our host's door. His apartment seemed strangely familiar – as well it might. Although he had added his own decorations, it was essentially identical to our own, down to the Danish furniture, the rug on the floor, and the dinnerware and cutlery in the kitchen. But the air was sweet with sandalwood incense, music was playing on the stereo, and food was laid out on the table. I helped myself to a piece of cheese impaled on a toothpick and accepted the plastic cup of homemade white wine my host was holding out. I complimented him on its quality. I lied.

The fraternity (they were all males) of English teachers were a mixed lot, mostly British and American, with a sprinkling of Australians, New Zealanders, Canadians and Irishmen. The youngest was thirtyish and the oldest was seventy (or at least that was the age that he was prepared to admit to). Some were greenhorns like Geoff; others had spent virtually their whole working lives in the Middle East. Some had been away from the moderating influence of home for a long time – perhaps too long. I had heard stories of the individualism that flourished amongst them, as well as of their tolerance of and support for each other. At this early stage I could see only hints of the eccentricities that would later become so endearingly apparent: the splendidly morose outlook of our host, the old Raj manner of an ancient Englishman, a flamboyant American's propensity for wild exaggeration.

If some of the men were eccentric, the Ferdaws wives tended towards the exotic. The first to arrive were a pair of beaming Africans wrapped in brilliant yellow batik costumes. They were followed in rapid succession by women from Japan, Hong Kong, Malaysia, Thailand and Indonesia. There was a Cuban, a Greek, a Brazilian, an Italian, an Ambonese from Amsterdam, and an Indian from Zaire. Many of the English teachers had spent time working in exotic locations, and more than a few of them had fallen in love with and married local women. As an Australian married to an Australian, I felt decidedly ordinary.

The party was lively. Everyone was friendly, welcoming, and very intent upon relaxing and having a good time. They responded to my new chum questions – Where are you from? How long have you been here? How do you like it? What do you do to amuse yourself? – with kindness. Then they settled down to serious gossip. I helped myself to another cup of wine, and looked around me. Eccentric, exotic, wild or mild, I was beginning to feel that there were possibilities here.

The university proper was perched on top of the highest hill in the area, referred to by everyone as the *jabal*, or mountain. Along the sides of each faculty building ran shady arcades formed by a succession of columns and arches. The arches were pointed in homage to an Islamic architectural motif, but the overall effect, when viewed from a distance, was classical. With only the external columns of their arcades visible, the buildings looked like a group of Greek temples high on Mount Olympus. A huge octagonal concrete water tower with clocks on four of its sides dominated the campus. Each clock showed a different time, and none was correct.

On weekdays the *jabal* was a woman-free zone, but on weekends the university emptied, and Geoff and I would walk up there to get the lie of the land. From this vantage point we could gaze out over the campus and beyond: down over Ferdaws, nestled at the rim of the university; down past the airport with its planes like toys in the distance; and out over the towns strung along the shores of the Arabian Gulf. Virtually everything we saw, including KFUPM itself, was there as a result of oil.

In 1938, only a few kilometres from where the university now stands, American geologists from the Standard Oil company tapped into the world's largest known reserves of oil. Their discovery launched Saudi Arabia into the modern age, and provided the fabulous wealth that has eased its journey forward. Today the oil company, Aramco, is a gigantic monopoly that is wholly owned by the Saudi Government, and is based in the Eastern Province. Its headquarters are in Dhahran. The sprawling Aramco complex with its neat houses and glass towers lay off to the right of our vantage point.

To our left we looked out towards the pale villas of suburban Doha, each guarding its privacy behind high walls. Quiet and affluent, Doha was the suburb built by the oil company to house its first Saudi employees. The minarets that arose here and there from its mosques looked, from that distance, for all the world like church steeples in a Christian village.

Directly in front of us, beyond the airport, lay the town of al Khobar. When the first expatriate workers arrived in the Gulf, al Khobar was a small fishing and pearling village. Most of its inhabitants would never have seen a European or an American. Today the town is a thriving spread of low-rise buildings stretched out along the shore and is inhabited largely by expatriate workers. We could just pick out al Khobar Towers, the apartment block where, in 1996, a bomb blast killed nineteen American GIs who were housed there.

Nearer to the university lay the US Consulate, bristling with armed guards, sentries and mobile patrols. US expats received frequent security alerts from their consulate warning them to be constantly vigilant, and advising them to lay in stores of drinking water and food in case of civil unrest. This seemed like good advice to me, but few of my fellow expats took it seriously. The British Consulate, which took responsibility for all Australians in the Eastern Province, took a more relaxed approach in its missives: a reminder that, in the unlikely event of an emergency, we should be registered with our local warden. I was soon lulled into the belief that, except for the ever-present danger of a traffic accident, there was nothing much to worry about.

Beyond al Khobar, shimmering soft turquoise in a dusty haze, were the shallow, Sinbad waters of the Arabian (or, depending on your point of view, Persian) Gulf. Down by the shore, clouds of white vapour billowed into the air from the tall chimneys of our local desalination plant. The purified water it produced was not for local consumption, but was piped far away to supply the needs of inland towns. In al Khobar, sweet water had to be purchased by the tanker-load, or collected in containers from communal facilities. Our own limited supplies came to us courtesy of Aramco.

In the distance, sweeping out across the Gulf, was the mighty King Fahd Causeway, a span of twenty-five kilometres linking the island emirate of Bahrain to the mainland. The causeway was built by the bin Laden family construction business (kin of the notorious Osama) at a cost of US$1.2 billion, and was finished in 1986.

To expatriates, the causeway represented freedom. We would find ourselves gazing at it longingly, and dreaming of escape.

Security was tight at the Aramco complex. At the first barrier, we presented our papers to the uniformed armed guards. They looked us over sternly, and allowed us to proceed. At the second barrier, an official checked our papers again and telephoned our contact within the complex to confirm that we had an invitation to visit. Only then were we allowed inside.

'They sure like to keep us under tight control,' I remarked, and Geoff laughed.

'It's not us they're worried about,' he said, 'it's the locals.' He explained that the main function of the security system was to maintain a separation between the residents of Aramco and conservative Muslims who might be offended by their lifestyle.

I looked around. It was true that we seemed to have left Arabia behind us. We were driving down a street that could have been lifted straight out of a city in the American Midwest, complete with high-rise buildings and traffic lights.

I had met our host, Gail, a thirty-something Irish nurse who worked at the Aramco hospital, at a Ferdaws party, and had asked her to show us around. We found her waiting for us outside her low-rise apartment block. We began our tour at the commercial hub of the complex, a supermarket where the shelves were stocked with turkey helper, maple syrup and root beer. Nearby were banks, a beauty salon, even an opportunity shop. The notice board at the community centre carried posters for a children's ballet class, a scout troop and a gardening club. At the huge company restaurant, diners were busy helping themselves to salads and cold cuts from the buffet, or tucking into hearty roast dinners with all the trimmings.

We drove through quiet suburbs full of modest houses set in carefully tended lawns and gardens, down streets with names such as Elderberry Lane and Laurel Drive. We saw schools where big yellow American school buses stood parked outside, and a kindergarten with bright finger paintings stuck to the windows.

Gail pointed out swimming pools, tennis courts and basketball courts, fully equipped gymnasiums, baseball fields with tiers of bleacher seats. Joggers pounded past us in shorts and singlets; kids cycled by in T-shirts and baseball caps.

I felt as though I had somehow strayed into a Norman Rockwell painting. It was not just American, it was ultra-American. Surely there was no town in the US quite so wholesome, quite so peaceful as Aramco. Where was the trailer park? Where were the pawn shops and the junkies? At Aramco everything was middle class, white bread, apple pie. Only the golf course struck a jarring note: in place of green turf, it was laid out over acres of sparkling black sand.

We ended our visit at the equestrian centre café, sipping coffee while we watched grooms tending the residents' horses. Life was sweet indeed for the employees of Aramco.

'It is restrictive here in Saudi Arabia,' Gail told us, 'but on the compound you can do what you like. And the money I earn here gives me an independence I would never have on a nurse's wages back at home.'

In one way or another, every expat was working through this same compromise.

I had come to the Gulf prepared for a life of deprivation and austerity. I knew the rules. Drinking alcohol, and eating pork were *haram*, forbidden. There must be no public display of any religion other than Islam – even the wearing of crosses was forbidden. There must be no social mixing of unrelated men and women, and for this reason, cinemas, theatres, and most forms of public entertainment were banned. (Music was considered to be un-Islamic and was disapproved of, although it was not *haram*.) Married couples should not show affection to each other in public; should not even hold hands. Both women and men must dress modestly, covering their arms and legs. Although there was no official requirement that women cover their hair or veil their faces, they could be harassed if they did not. It was prohibited for women to drive.

I arrived in the Kingdom suitably intimidated, determined to keep my nose clean and to stay out of trouble. I was astonished to learn that behind the high walls and security gates of the Western compounds, very few of the rules applied.

On their compounds, foreigners were doing their best to recreate the lives they had left behind. It didn't take long for newcomers to plug into the expatriate network and to learn about the available diversions. There were English pubs where we could drink an ale and play a game of darts. There were pools with mixed swimming and sunbathing. There was a lively and surprisingly professional local theatre scene. For those with religious leanings, a Catholic mass and a non-Catholic service were conducted every Friday, the Muslim equivalent of Sunday in a working week that runs from Saturday to Wednesday. On compounds, women drove cars and wore short skirts, and men and women played mixed tennis doubles. There were thousands of single young women, nurses and secretaries, keen to meet single men for friendship and romance. There were charity balls and dance parties. There was even, somewhere in the wilds of al Khobar, a honky tonk.

Within days of my arrival I was, to my astonishment, part of a hushed expatriate audience at a piano recital given by a visiting professor from the Royal College of Music in London. Not everyone in the sell-out crowd was a classical music enthusiast, but we were all grateful listeners, and the standing ovation we gave the professor went on and on. Perhaps the sense that we were breaking the rules gave an extra frisson to the audience and soloist alike. I, for one, felt like a naughty schoolchild after a successful day of truancy.

A few days later on a different compound we sat down to a candlelit dinner in a restaurant that was as authentically Italian as one staffed entirely by Indians could be. A deferential waiter in white shirt and black bow-tie brought us servings of lasagne and steaming hot garlic bread, then topped up our glasses with fairly decent red wine. I glanced around at my fellow expat diners. They looked relaxed, prosperous and rather smug.

Concerts and mixed dining in restaurants were totally *haram*, but the authorities seemed to be willing to turn a blind eye to the

antics that Westerners got up to out of sight on their compounds. Perhaps this was because Saudis guarded their own
privacy so jealously. In their homes they, too, could get away with
anything, and if rumours were anything to go by, many did.

There were compounds and there were compounds – and then
there was Ferdaws. For better or for worse, at Ferdaws about a
thousand Muslim residents were living alongside a few hundred
non-Muslims, and Westerners mixed with Middle Eastern, Subcontinental, African and Asian neighbours. There were even a
few Saudis.

The mix was not always comfortable. The most devout Muslim
residents kept to themselves. Even their children stayed aloof.
I had expected them to be like kids everywhere, and to react to
me with a mixture of shyness, cheekiness and curiosity. Instead,
as I walked by, they ceased their games and fell silent. Little ones
took shelter behind their older sisters, and eyed me balefully.
They remained stony-faced as I smiled and greeted them, and as
I passed, I often heard a muttered 'Kaffir!' (infidel). I put it all
down to some very serious lessons from their parents about not
talking to strangers, and especially not to strangers like me.

But if relations were not exactly warm, there was little outright
friction. We respected the need for public sobriety, and our
Muslim neighbours did not complain about us, so long as our
rowdier moments were kept behind closed doors. As compounds
go, Ferdaws was a relatively mild-mannered place.

On some compounds, however, things could get very rowdy
indeed. One of the great myths of Saudi Arabia is that there is no
alcohol. In fact, I discovered, nothing could be sadder than the
alcoholic who had come to the Kingdom to dry out. Far from
finding himself in an alcohol-free state, the poor sod was likely to
have found that he had just given up good booze for bad.

Many new arrivals developed a sudden interest in wine-
making. Some supermarkets helped them out by thoughtfully
stocking everything they needed together: cartons of white and
red grape juice, large plastic rubbish bins, lengths of clear plastic
tubing, and the bottles of Ribena that, when emptied, were used
to hold the finished product.

Wine-making was a competitive enterprise; aficionados would

tell you that so and so's vintage was 'just like the real thing'. Perhaps they had been away from the real thing for rather too long. Still, I am assured that the following recipe, which goes by the name of 'XXX Supreme', really is the right stuff.

---

1. Into a 20-litre water jug, add 14 litres of red grape juice (make sure you buy the kind with no preservatives or sugar added).
2. Mix 2½ kilos of sugar with three litres of boiling water, then add to juice.
3. Wait until the mixture cools before adding ½ teaspoon of yeast.
4. Put on the lid. Shake, rattle and roll.
5. Put a carbon dioxide escape valve into the top of the jug – otherwise, the whole thing might blow. Let it stand until the yeast has eaten all the sugar – usually about 14 to 20 days.
6. You should bottle* it at this time so that oxygen doesn't start seeping into the juice, as oxygen is the nemesis of XXX.
7. Don't bother to cellar XXX; it's ready to drink as soon as it's ready to be bottled. At 14 to 20 days old, it could be described as a cheeky young wine.

*Before you bottle, you can siphon XXX into another jug and let it stand for a few days more, with a tight cap on it. This will eliminate some of the yeast 'poop'. Also, you may save the yeast poop and use it again and again and again. It is a good idea to clean your bottles very well before you reuse them (don't use soap).

Siddiqi is the Arabic word for 'my friend'. Affectionately shortened to 'Sid', it was also the name of the locally brewed spirit alcohol. Sid-making could be big business, and more than one bootlegger had made a fortune from it. This clear moonshine, available in four litre plastic milk bottles to discreet purchasers, was strong enough to strip the paint from furniture. With its distinctive sweaty-saddle palate, it was an acquired taste, but did make a very acceptable gin and tonic substitute. When I poured some Sid into my cough syrup to give it more oomph (there are no alcohol-based medicines in the Kingdom) I found that I had created a liqueur of lingering complexity that intrigued my dinner guests.

There was danger involved in Sid-making – so much so that the Western managers of some foreign companies issued new arrivals with printed instructions (the nicely titled 'Blue Flame' information sheet) on how to safely set up and operate a still. Better that than try to explain to the authorities why the compound bathrooms kept exploding.

It all added up to a whole lot of drinking. Expatriate parties could be well-lubricated affairs where the homemade hooch flowed freely, where partygoers could let their hair down and forget about the difficulties of life in the Kingdom, and where vintners with an inferior batch on their hands could offload a few dodgy bottles.

Then there were those who drank at home in sodden isolation – a real danger, especially when the inevitable question arose: 'What am I doing here?' Some binges were legendary. When one lonely Brit decided to combine drinking with taking a bath, he neglected to turn the tap off. His downstairs neighbours called security when water started to drip through their ceiling. Caught naked and raving and ankle-deep in water in his living room, our man quickly found himself with a one-way ticket out of the Kingdom. Another brilliantly self-destructive Englishman showed up at his college to teach an English class after a long, solitary session, and started to tearfully explain to his astounded Muslim students just how f – ed up his life was. Ever resourceful, he managed to avoid deportation, but had to take a few sideways steps in his career.

My favourite story, however, concerns a more sociable binger. He had been hosting a party in his apartment and was feeling more than a little jolly when he decided to visit a neighbour. The neighbour was not at home. Our friend paused just long enough to throw up in his absent mate's pot of mint, before staggering, legless and keyless, back to his own front door. He was outraged to find that a bunch of people were whooping it up in his locked apartment, and indignantly summoned security to evict them.

The penalties for possessing alcohol were no laughing matter, though: jail, flogging, fines and deportation were all possible, and nobody wanted to tangle with local justice. In general, however, the authorities were prepared to ignore expatriate drinking, so long as it was done with discretion. But every now and then a bathroom would explode or someone would behave so outrageously that the police were called in. News of a raid would spread like wildfire around an unlucky compound, initiating a chorus of panicked curses and flushing toilets as a flood of home brew was poured away.

Some expatriates never adjusted to life in Saudi Arabia. They disliked the place from their first contact with it, and each subsequent experience only served to intensify their conviction. Mark and Kelly, a young American couple who we met at a concert one night, fell into this group. They were both teachers at a nearby college.

'How lucky for you,' I said, 'to both have work here.' Joint contracts like theirs were eagerly sought after and extremely hard to find.

They agreed that they were doing well financially, and yet they were full of bitter complaints: of woeful working conditions, of irrational managers, of Saudi ways in general. They announced that they intended to leave at the earliest opportunity, as soon as their contracts were up.

'It's not just about personal dissatisfaction,' said Kelly. 'It's a matter of principle.' Pressed, she said that they simply could not bear the corruption and the oppression they saw about them.

Perhaps the fact that Mark and Kelly lived in town, outside the protective bubble of compound life, had influenced their views. Within the compounds, I was discovering that it was all too easy to maintain an oblivious indifference to the world outside.

Some expats were driven to distraction by the tedium and

the restrictions of life in the Kingdom, and the feeling that their lives had stalled. Several of Geoff's colleagues kept calendars on their walls, and struck off each passing day with a big red 'X', announcing to anyone who would listen that at the end of their contracts they would be on the first flight out, never to return. At least they had only themselves to blame.

For their wives, especially those who were there under protest, it was far worse. While a stint in the Gulf might have been a good career move for a husband, it often meant sacrifice for his wife. I was not the only one to have given up family and friends, a much-loved job, even independence, to be there. It was tougher for us, too; confronting to have to conform to the many restrictions placed upon our dress, our movements and our behaviour. The faces of some of the sisterhood were etched with boredom and misery.

For couples, the expatriate experience could be a trial that strained their marriage to breaking point. Little wonder that many wives refused to join their husbands, or, having tried the experiment, decided to go home alone and attempt to maintain the relationship long distance. Little wonder that some marriages did not survive.

Despite the difficulties, some expats found it hard to leave. Life in the Gulf could be seductive with its combination of easy money, low living costs and ample leisure time, while work back home might be difficult to find. 'It's not so bad,' the stayers told themselves. 'With just one more contract I'll be able to pay off my college loan . . . put down a deposit on a house . . . send the kids to a top school . . . put a shine on my retirement nest egg . . .' Turkish Farah and her husband had been at KFUPM for sixteen years. 'Every time we think it is the end,' she confessed, 'but then we sign on for another two years.'

For Marie and her family, who had lost everything in a coup in their former West African home, Arabia was a refuge that offered them the chance to rebuild their lives. 'We have to live here,' she told me. 'We have no choice. But we make the best of it.'

The Gulf, however, seemed to be a great place for couples with young children, not least because the Saudis themselves place such a high value on families.

'They just adore children,' said American Katy, the mother of two small boys. 'They make a great fuss of them. In fact, it's one of the few opportunities we have to make contact with the locals.'

A family could live more than well on one salary, freeing the other parent for full-time child care. If both parents were working, it was easy to find an excellent nanny at little cost. World-class medical care was available in the Kingdom's hospitals. Expatriate daycare centres and schools were the equal of or better than those back home.

'And it's so safe for children here,' said Marie. 'You can let them roam around freely, and you know that everyone is watching out for them. It's a wonderful life for children.'

It was a different picture for teenagers. There were few diversions for them and, with most of their friends either having returned home or been shipped off to boarding school, those left behind at Ferdaws complained that their lives were lonely and dull. Parents had to balance the desire to keep their families together against the worry that their adolescent children were missing out on the formative influence of their own culture, and that their outlook on life would be badly distorted by their time in Arabia. Many parents planned to leave the Kingdom as soon as their children reached secondary school age.

Life could be particularly hard for teenage girls. At age eleven, Marie's daughter Therese had blossomed into a strikingly beautiful young woman. While her best friend, Rosie, was still playing with her dolls and enjoying a carefree childhood, Therese found her world suddenly changed.

'She has matured very quickly, so that now boys are looking at her,' sighed Marie. 'I have to watch out for her all the time . . . Really, I fear for her safety. We're either going to have to cover her up, or send her away to boarding school – and we hate the idea of covering her.'

I sympathised. How cruel it would be to wrap this young girl up in funereal black at a time when she should be exploring new freedoms, finding new ways of self-expression. The *abaya* struck me as a dirge in cloth, a symbol of the woes and sufferings of women down the ages.

'Poor Therese,' said Marie. 'She's still just a little girl, and it's so hard for her. She's so upset that she just stays in her room and doesn't want to come out anymore.'

Quick, I thought to myself, buy the girl an *abaya*.

But the *abaya* wasn't always a solution. When I first met Alicia, an Englishwoman, she had been in the Kingdom for only a few months. Amongst the many problems she and her family had encountered, she said, the worst had concerned her daughter, an attractive fifteen-year-old blonde. Every time Lizzie went out, she became the target of unwanted male attention. Men and boys followed her about the streets. Cars crawled along the kerb beside her, honking their horns, their drivers inviting her to get in. Eventually she begged her mother to get her an *abaya*. Alicia took her out to buy one on the Dammam Road, but when Lizzie emerged from the shop in her demure black, three lanes of traffic screeched to a halt to look at her. Somehow, with only her face and hair revealed, she was even more alluring.

Some expats were living lives of permanent exile. They were stateless souls, veterans of serial assignments in faraway lands: Japan and Mongolia, the Sudan and the Congo, Papua New Guinea. In spite of its restrictions, Saudi Arabia offered them freedom and romance of a sort, as well as the opportunity for continued adventure. Seated at the controls of their four wheel drive vehicles, they were lords of the desert and the *souk*. They had, in their travels, become exotic birds themselves, and it was clear that they were never going to fit back easily into the world of nine-to-five jobs and a house in the suburbs.

Then there were the lifers; those who had made their careers in the Gulf. On the Aramco compound there were elderly American couples who had arrived in the 1960s, raised their children there, and thought of Saudi Arabia as home. KFUPM, too, had its share of lifers.

Rick and Amy, a sociable English pair, had been at KFUPM for sixteen years: long enough to have graduated from Ferdaws to one of the fine townhouses on campus, and to have set themselves up very, very comfortably. Renowned for their hospitality and surrounded by a huge circle of friends, they seemed to be perfectly happy. Amy proclaimed that she had taken to the expatriate lifestyle from the moment she set foot in Arabia.

More than any other group, the English seemed ready to settle in for the long haul. Perhaps the heritage of empire had given them a taste for foreign climes; or perhaps, as many of them claimed, it was the English weather that kept them far from home. They would speak with dread of the ravages of arthritis and depression in grey old England, then brighten up as they spoke about their Portuguese villa or the flat they were buying in Cyprus.

Finally, perhaps, the expat lifestyle was a perfectly reasonable choice for those with a mind to it. The money was good, the pace of life slow and relaxed, and with everyone having time on their hands to spend with others, it was easy to build strong friendships.

I began to consider the possibility that Geoff and I, too, might become long-term residents. Perhaps, I thought, a visit home once or twice a year was plenty, after all.

Meanwhile, I was busy adjusting to expatriate life. It wasn't too difficult. I had made friends; I had found much to interest me; I had Geoff beside me. Life in Saudi Arabia was strange, but in those early days, it was a strangeness that fascinated more than it appalled. If at times I felt a sense of boredom and unease creeping up on me as I passed my idle days, I pushed it aside. I still had the lingering feeling that I was on holiday.

There were plenty of things I could have complained about . . . the cramped space and the darkness of our apartment . . . the cold showers when the pilot light on the water heater blew out . . . the salt water that gave me perpetual bad hair days . . . the cheap plastic dinnerware in the kitchen. I could have complained, but I had resolved to be positive.

And then, I lost it.

One afternoon as I sat wedged on my couch reading, I heard the sound of muffled giggling, and, looking up, saw the heads of three or four small boys appear above the high wall of the courtyard. They had discovered that, by standing on a ledge just beyond the wall, they could look in upon me. Only slightly annoyed, I chased them away. They came back. I chased them away again. They came back, more of them this time.

Try making friends, I thought, but at my approach they scattered, shrieking with laughter. Now every day after school they gathered on the ledge, yelling out for attention, jeering, egging each other on. Every day there were more of them. This was a game with escalating stakes, a game I couldn't win.

Breaking my resolve, I complained. Bitterly. Geoff listened sympathetically. He consulted the neighbours, a group of men who stood outdoors smoking in the evenings. Talk to the parents, they advised him – but who were the parents? Who, in fact, were the boys? I couldn't have picked any one of them out of a lineup, although I knew that they were part of a gang that roved the residential areas of the campus. Suddenly every boy was my enemy. Whenever I saw a lad out and about, no matter how meek he looked, I would stare fiercely at him as if to say 'I know you, I know your nasty little game'.

I decided to take action. I wrote a firm but polite letter to the campus Housing Committee, asking them to move us to a more private apartment, and expecting an immediate rescue. After all, I thought, this is a society that places an enormous emphasis on privacy, one that declares that a woman in public should not be looked upon, let alone a woman in her own living room. But nothing happened.

The number of boys on the ledge was still rising, and things were getting serious. Reasoning that if they couldn't see me they would lose interest, I tried drawing the blinds, although this meant giving up my only source of natural light. They took to throwing stones into the courtyard: small ones at first, then rocks that shattered on the tiles and could not be ignored. But by the time I had raced outside and circled around to the front of the block to confront them, they had scampered away.

Beside myself with rage and frustration, I wrote another letter. This one had an immediate effect. Geoff was taken aside and told that it really wasn't the done thing for his wife to be writing letters to the Housing Committee.

'You're supposed to be invisible and let me take care of things like this,' he said.

'But obviously I'm not bloody invisible,' I fumed. 'That's the problem.'

'You must call security,' said one of my new woman friends. Others advised against it, saying that it would cause ill-feeling on the compound.

One afternoon I came home to find that my potted plants had been used for target practice and lay dying in the courtyard amidst the rocks that had been thrown at them. I knelt amongst the shards sobbing, defeated, humiliated. My vision of myself as an intrepid adventurer evaporated. I had been brought to my knees by a bunch of kids, not one of them older than twelve.

And so I called security. The guards failed to find my apartment in the confusing jumble of Ferdaws, but they did make enquiries, and the boys took fright. They never bothered me again.

And finally my letters to the Housing Committee had the desired effect. They decided to move us to a new apartment, a larger one in a quieter corner of Paradise. It didn't take long for us to adjust to the extra space. Adjusting to the furnishings was even faster: they seemed strangely familiar.

It was Christmas time in the Gulf. Christmas was forbidden, and passed without mention in the local English language press, except for one reference to the 'European festive season'. This year, however, Christmas coincided with Ramadan, the Muslim month of fasting. The streets were decked with Ramadan lights, not so very different from Christmas decorations, and the shops were full of tinsel. We could even buy cards, the kind that wish you 'Season's Greetings' and have no scenes of the nativity and no mention of the word 'Christ'.

Expats, whether believers or not, were determined to celebrate Christmas in style. Geoff and I took ourselves off to the Aramco compound for the community concert known as the 'December Festival'. It was a wholesome, all-American affair. Excited children, their eyes all aglow, flocked in with their parents to take their seats in the large school gymnasium. The stage was beautifully decorated in red, green and gold. Two choirs sang a selection of Christmas carols, and an enthusiastic barbershop quartet presented the entire known barbershop quartet repertoire. An accomplished lady pianist did a solo number on a grand piano, and some little girls in fluffy tutus performed the 'Dance of the Sugarplum Fairies' from *The Nutcracker*. A narrator read Christmas stories in an unctuous voice, and a squad of bell ringers rang out 'Jingle Bells'. Finally, to the sound of a collective, wistful sigh from the audience, artificial snow fluttered lightly down onto our heads. How strange it was to emerge into the warm humidity of a Gulf evening.

A few days later it was Christmas Eve, and we found ourselves at Rick and Amy's party, a KFUPM institution. A convivial crowd of mainly British guests milled about in the large living room and spilled out into the courtyard. Midway through the evening, songbooks were distributed, and Amy was summoned to the piano. We sang with gusto as she played the old, familiar carols. The climax was that anthem of Englishness, 'Jerusalem'. 'And did those feet in ancient time . . .' roared patriotic British voices. As we came to '. . . in England's green and pleasant land,' eyes grew misty and voices choked.

Perhaps Rick and Amy were feeling misty too, although not for England. They were about to retire, and this was to be their last Gulf Christmas party. If they were feeling nostalgic, it was surely for Arabia.

If Christmas had been on a weekday, Geoff would have had to work: the authorities made no allowance for non-Muslim celebrations. Luckily it fell on a weekend. We spent a quiet day at home in our tinsel-decked apartment. We made our phone calls home to Australia, and grew nostalgic as the voices of our loved ones came crackling down the line to us. We unwrapped the family presents that I had brought with me in my five cartons, and cut into the fruit cake that I'd been hiding since my arrival. It smelt suspiciously, deliciously, of brandy. We raised a mango juice toast to each other, and a toast to adventures to come.

3

THE GULF

A hooded Bedouin, from his distant camp in the bare hills,
rides on his camel through the blazing heat past a camp where
drillers from Texas and California have ice-cooled drinks in
air-conditioned rooms.
To his 'Peace upon you' they reply 'OK, boy'.
GERALD DE GAURY, Arabia Phoenix

Another illegal gathering. The flyer that announced an
evening with the Travelling Naturalists Society bore a
warning: 'Don't let this document fall into the wrong hands.
Destroy it when you have finished reading it.'

The Travelling Nats, as they were affectionately known, were
adventurous souls with a love of the great outdoors. On any given
weekend in the cooler part of the year, small convoys of Land
Cruisers, Range Rovers and Ladas could be seen heading off into
the desert loaded up with Nats and their camping gear.

On this particular night, we had come to see a slide show and
hear a talk by one of the members about his recent trip through
Jordan. The meeting, held in the canteen of a large compound,
was well attended, with about 200 expats in the audience.
Amongst them, conspicuous in their white *thobes*, were two
polite and friendly Saudi gentlemen. They were not welcome
guests.

Small huddles of Nats stood about clucking their tongues in
disapproval. Who invited them? they wanted to know. Probably
some new boy full of enthusiasm for Arabia. Of course, these two

were probably lovely chaps, broadminded, liberal . . . many of them are. But sooner or later you'll have one of them taking offence at something, and spoiling it for everyone. And how the hell can you relax and get loose on a camping trip when there are Saudis along for the ride?

I wondered at their ability to so enthusiastically embrace the landscape, while at the same time rejecting the people who inhabited it. As for me, I wanted to meet the locals. I intended to immerse myself in Saudi culture, to learn the language, to become expert at cooking Arabic food, to study the local crafts, and to make Saudi friends. More than anything, I wanted to explore. I imagined myself nosing around exotic markets, wandering through ancient villages, sitting in sagging tents woven from dark camel hair and drinking coffee with Bedouin women.

Exploration was not going to be easy. I was forbidden to drive, taxis were too expensive for regular use, and it seemed unfair to expect Geoff to chauffeur me around at the end of an exhausting day's teaching. Salvation came in the form of the big yellow American school bus that was supplied by the university to take its resident wives out shopping. I enlisted Yuko, a young Japanese woman whose sweet smile and quiet demeanour belied an adventurous spirit, to act as my guide.

Eight-thirty on a Saturday morning saw me in a small bus shelter on the edge of Ferdaws, teeth chattering in the chill wind that was blowing in from the desert. The bus, when it came rattling around the corner, was already crowded. The portly Arab at the wheel smiled a welcome as I climbed aboard. I looked down the aisle at my fellow passengers: at rows of faces framed in scarves, two black shapes without faces, a few uncovered Western heads, and an astonishing number of babies and small children. The air was abuzz with chatter: friends called greetings to each other, mothers cajoled their children to sit still, and women fussed over babies who beamed toothlessly back at them. And there was Yuko, waving to me from the back. As I took my seat next to her, familiar faces smiled at me and unfamiliar ones asked me where I was from, when I had arrived, how many children I had, and what my husband was doing.

I had been worried about what to wear, fearful of transgressing the local dress code or of drawing the attention of the *muttaween*, or religious police. Happily, my clothing matched that of the other expat women. Although a few had opted to wear *abayas*, most were dressed, like me, in oversized, long-sleeved shirts and baggy trousers or long skirts. None of us had covered our hair in anything more concealing than a sun hat.

Soon we were speeding through the outskirts of al Khobar, through a pale desert landscape strewn with untidy piles of building rubble and dotted with the half-complete concrete shells of huge private villas. We passed glass-fronted showrooms with displays of expensive furniture, glittering chandeliers and marble bathroom fittings; and apartment buildings with billboards that promised prospective tenants 'luxurious accommodation' and 'all modern amenities'.

We turned off a broad, tree-lined boulevard to plunge down through narrow streets where shopkeepers were raising the metal shutters on shops crammed with clothing and haberdashery and baby furnishings and household goods. Behind the shops, dilapidated, low-rent apartment buildings rose up three and four storeys, their balconies festooned with drying laundry.

It was just past nine when we emerged onto a busy thoroughfare and pulled up outside al Shula Mall. The door of the bus opened and the women clambered down to the footpath in a tangle of children and strollers. Around us, buses from other compounds were disgorging their own clutches of women, all intent upon a morning's shopping.

Al Shula took up an entire city block. An ugly, four-storey concrete building covered with advertising hoardings, it was an unlikely place to start looking for the real Arabia.

Inside, all was cool and quiet. A Bangladeshi worker in blue overalls was wiping a wet mop over the pale terrazzo floor. He paused, eyeing us without expression as we went by, then resumed his slow swabbing. We wandered down wide hallways lined with shops, past bars that advertised freshly squeezed fruit juice and cafés offering 'broasted' (roasted, then dipped in batter and deep-fried) chicken. Past shops selling shoes, electrical goods, CDs, and stationery. Past fake brand-name sportswear, designer jeans and T-shirts. Past computer shops and racks of pirated software. Al Shula may not have been the Arabia of my dreams, but it certainly looked like a good place to find a bargain. And amidst the paraphernalia of everyday life, there were unexpected delights.

Smoke was curling from giant horned censers outside the incense shops, filling the air with a musky fragrance. Inside, merchants were weighing out scoops of sandalwood chips and nuggets of frankincense and myrrh. Perfume-sellers waved pretty bottles full of scented oils as we passed, inviting us to dab some onto the back of our hands. The jewellery shops were dazzling, ablaze with displays of glittering necklaces and bangles worked in gold so rich that it looked as soft as sculpted butter.

Best of all were the oriental shops. They beckoned to us with cluttered displays of old brass platters, elaborate Bedouin jewellery, silver daggers, woven saddle bags and studded wooden chests. But, in fact, very little of their merchandise was local. The papyrus scrolls and the leatherwork came from Egypt, the rugs and inlaid wooden backgammon boards from Turkey, the brass from Pakistan, and the papier-mâché ornaments from Kashmir. These artefacts had been assembled with the local expatriate community in mind, to offer them, for a price, an oriental experience that was about as authentic as al Shula's Rolex watches. Even the miniature oil barrels, the fridge magnets with pictures of camels on them, and the 'I ❤ Saudi Arabia' T-shirts had been produced in Taiwan.

When we'd seen enough of al Shula, we wandered out into the street. Although the approach to al Khobar was along broad boulevards fringed with trees, lawns and flower beds, its commercial centre was not a pretty place. The grid pattern of its streets suggested the hand of a civic designer, but the town had grown up in a hurry, and not a single building looked more than twenty years old. There was no suggestion of oriental refinement, and little to suggest the fabulous wealth of this oil-rich province. Instead, most of the buildings were of that bland concrete bunker-style of architecture that is a feature of third world cities everywhere. The construction boom was still underway. On almost every street new buildings were springing up from new piles of rubble, but already they seemed in danger of being overtaken by the forces of disintegration clearly at work in the town, and surrendering to the shabbiness and grime that surrounded them.

Civic planning did not extend to the footpaths, and walking about was a task that required our full concentration as we negotiated height variations of up to half a metre, surfaces that varied from marble to sand, cracked paving stones and loose ones, potholes, rubble and garbage, and stinking spills from blocked drains. We were soon hot and tired.

At this early hour, there were few people in the streets, and fewer still were Saudis. Most of the shop assistants were Asian, and most of the shoppers moving purposefully between their favourite haunts were expat women like ourselves.

Desert Designs was doing a roaring trade in expensive oriental antiques, Persian textiles and Indian jewellery. At the 2 Riyal Shop buyers were snapping up plastic Taiwanese snow domes that contained tiny models of the Prophet's Holy Mosque or of the Kaabah. The most popular shop of all was the craft emporium, testament to the amount of time expat wives have on their hands and their struggles to fill it. It was two floors of quilting fabric, embroidery kits, brocade trims, polystyrene forms, and everything else you might need to create the sorts of treasures that always seem to end up on a stall at the Christmas fete.

Tamimi Market was a magnet that drew affluent shoppers, both Arab and expat. It was all that a supermarket should be, with its shelves stocked with Middle Eastern, American and European products. Even some Australian cheese had found its way into the mix. The produce section displayed an abundance of cheap locally grown fruit and vegetables: oranges, grapes, aubergines, tomatoes and greens priced at only a few riyals per kilo. Exotic items, such as asparagus from the Netherlands, or cranberries and parsnips from the US were available too. They looked limp and travel-weary, although their prices suggested that they had flown first class. The meat cabinets displayed cuts of camel alongside the chicken, lamb and beef. The deli stocked a huge range of imported cheeses, but the salami and bacon were local, with beef substituted for pork. Local yoghurts, fresh cheeses, and milk products filled the dairy section. In the bakery, sweet baklava and other pastries concocted of honey, rose water, nuts and pastry were piled onto vast brass trays, and the smell of freshly baked bread wafted out from the ovens. At the dry goods counter, the complex aromas of dried rose petals, tea leaves, coffee beans and spices, familiar and unknown, filled the air.

Our final stop was a stylish French patisserie just across the street from Tamimi. We made our way past counters full of croissants and cakes to the family room (no bachelors allowed) at the rear. It was full to overflowing with women seated at small tables surrounded by piles of shopping bags. We joined a group from Ferdaws, and settled down to compare purchases and to chat. A waiter brought us cappuccinos.

I asked the others how they passed their days. Yuko said that she read, did housework, visited her friends, went shopping, wrote letters and short stories, and watched TV.

'My life is so busy,' said Marie. 'I teach French lessons, and I organise a badminton contest. I belong to two reading groups and a drama group. Then I have my Bible study group . . . and of course I have my children to look after.'

'Do you ever get bored?' I asked, and Dutch Johanna confessed that she was fed up with having only women to socialise with. 'I've been to far too many morning tea parties,' she said.

Greek Sophia confided that she had been feeling desperately unhappy lately. The others tried to comfort her.

'Look on the bright side,' said Johanna. 'You have your husband and your children here, and lots of time to spend with them.'

'And don't you love having time to spend on yourself?' added English Linda. 'Look at how fit you've become with all that exercise you've been doing. You look wonderful.'

But Sophia was not to be consoled. 'I'm so bored,' she said. 'I hate my life here, and I hate Ferdaws. If only I had a job . . .'

'Couldn't you teach something?' I suggested. 'Your language perhaps.' I had been thinking about doing a little English teaching myself.

'Who wants to learn Greek?' she snorted. 'No-one.'

'You have to stay positive,' said Marie.

'There's nothing for me here,' said Sophia.

I wondered what effect the Kingdom would have on me after

a few more months. Would I prove resilient, like Marie, or would I, like Sophia, allow it to defeat me?

At eleven o'clock the waiters cleared us out into the street. All around us the shutters were coming back down over the shop-fronts, and the streets were emptying. The call to prayer was sounding as we climbed back onto the bus.

I became a regular on the yellow bus. On Sundays it took us to al Rashid Mall, a lavish commercial palace of pink marble set amidst groves of date palms. Inside was pure luxury: sunlight filtering down into spacious atriums from glass domes overhead, green vines trailing from tiered balconies trimmed in brass and chrome, the splash of fountains in mosaic-lined pools. Shoppers floated up and down on long escalators and in gleaming glass elevators, and roved down wide marble halls past exclusive European boutiques. On our morning visits, al Rashid was uncrowded and peaceful. In the evenings it came to life as Saudi families flooded in. An ice cream at Baskin & Robbins or a burger at Elmer Fuddruckers was the closest thing to public entertain-ment in the Eastern Province.

We would make straight for Joffrey's, our favourite café on the third floor, to sit and chat over coffee and bagels. Later we shopped at JC Penneys, Jahrir Bookshop and The Body Shop.

'I look upon Rashid Mall as my spiritual home,' confessed Linda with a sigh as we waited for the bus to take us home. The others nodded in agreement, but I was still too new in the Kingdom to need such an escape from it.

On Tuesdays the bus went to Dammam, a low-rise city of white domes, cubes and minarets spread out along the Gulf to the north of al Khobar. Dammam was a conservative, thoroughly Arabic town, and the *muttaween* were known to be active there.

On my first visit I noted that, although the streets were crowded, there were very few women abroad. The men scowled upon our small, unveiled gaggle as we passed by. We sought refuge and refreshment in the café of an almost deserted shopping mall. The Indian waiter regarded us nervously.

'I am very sorry, you cannot sit in here.' He pointed to a sign that read 'No women allowed inside'. 'We applied for a licence for a women's section,' he explained, flushing with embarrassment, 'but the *muttaween* refused us permission.'

And so we took the drinks that he sold us, and sat with them out in the centre of the mall on the dirty concrete rim of a dry fountain. Its bed was filled with cigarette buts, empty drink cans and lolly wrappers, and was splattered with crimson. The local Subcontinental *paan*-chewers had been using it as a spittoon.

I crossed the Tuesday trip to Dammam off my list of shopping destinations.

On Wednesdays we went back to al Khobar.

It wasn't so much the shopping that drew me to the bus, as the escape it offered: a chance to enjoy a little companionship and to get out of my apartment.

I wandered around the shops looking for . . . I wasn't sure what. Something old, something that wasn't imported, something that spoke to me of the lives of the people. My eye sought out exotic details: graceful Arabic calligraphy in shop windows; a shoemaker working camel leather into traditional sandals; a merchant, seated on a mat outside a mosque, selling little sticks of *mishwak*, the traditional Saudi toothbrush; the courtly gestures of men greeting each other, hands on hearts and kisses on cheeks.

In vain I searched for fulfilment of my oriental fantasies. In place of the arabesques, filigrees and refinements of the Arabian Nights, the cities of the Gulf were modern and utilitarian. As one of my companions remarked, 'It isn't very exotic here, but it certainly is strange.'

I strolled away from the shops, exploring, and found myself picking my way along deserted footpaths, trying to ignore the honks from passing cars, waving away the incredulous taxi drivers who slowed to a crawl beside me. Passing a lone sentry standing guard outside a government office, I greeted him with a friendly '*Marhaba*'. He looked away at the ground, silent, stony-faced.

The harder I looked, the more Arabia seemed to deflect my gaze. The women remained hidden behind their veils, the men resolutely avoided meeting my eye, and the children preserved a wary distance. The very buildings shut me out: breezeblock shields and metal grills covered the windows of the apartment blocks; high concrete walls surrounded the houses. Behind those walls I knew that life was going on, but it was a life inaccessible to me.

Mosques everywhere. Mosques grandiose: the giant domes and soaring minarets of the central al Khobar mosque. Mosques humble: a roadside shack with a crescent moon cut from a sheet of corrugated iron. Mosques ethereal, floating white above the reedy salt marshes along the seashore. Mosques urban, wedged in between shops. Mosques in petrol stations for the convenience of motorists.

The Ferdaws mosque was a converted bus station, a squat, six-metre square building of stucco and smoked glass, where the men and boys of the compound gathered to pray. The congregation often spilled outdoors onto rugs and strips of carpet that had been laid down over the dusty ground.

The days moved to the rhythm of prayer: dawn, midday, mid-afternoon, dusk and nightfall. Set according to the position of the sun, prayer times shifted from day to day, coming closer together as the days grew shorter. The newspapers published the daily prayer schedule, but this didn't allay my feeling that time had somehow come adrift.

By law, every office and business closed for prayers, although they were not precise in their observance. They might close early if not much was happening, or late if there were still customers to deal with. Reopening times were just as uncertain.

No matter what time I headed to the campus Co-op, I managed to arrive just as the doors were closing. 'How can they ever hope to progress?' I grumbled to myself, fresh from the clock-driven precision of my own, punctual world. 'But then, what right do I have to impose my Western standards? Why should the world move to a Western timetable? Is progress all that matters?' And so I tried to cultivate patience.

The Saudi shoppers waiting at the entrance showed no such forbearance. They peered through into the dimly lit store, and when they spotted movement, rattled the metal grill, beat their fists on the frame, and shouted impatiently for those inside to open up.

The mosques were a constant reminder that I was in an alien world; a world where I would have to negotiate deeper and more disturbing matters than wayward time. They were also the symbol of a social order that defined me by my sex, ahead of all my other attributes or flaws.

It was never going to be easy to adjust to life as a woman in Saudi Arabia. I had done enough research to know what I was getting into when I went there: the restrictions, the discrimination, the injustice. I had done my best to prepare myself, resolving to be patient and detached, to take a back seat to my husband, to try to see things from a Saudi point of view. And yet I was completely unprepared for the relentless segregation I encountered.

At the KFUPM clinic I sought treatment for a persistent cough. Respiratory infections were one of the hazards of life in the Eastern Province, nurtured by airborne dust laden with the dried spittle of hundreds of publicly cleared throats. Wheezing up to the reception window, I gasped, 'Can I see a doctor, please?'

The clerk behind the counter froze, then hurriedly indicated that the women's reception window was the next one along. I took five steps to my right, and repeated to the same clerk, 'Can I see a doctor?'

He sent me to the women's waiting room – I found it by following a red line painted on the floor. A black line led to the men's waiting room. Later I filled my prescription at the women's window of the pharmacy. At least I was served before the men waiting at the main window.

In a clothing boutique, a little navy dress caught my eye. 'Can I try it on?' I asked. The shop assistant looked at me as though I was mad.

'You can bring it back if it doesn't fit,' he said.

The modem on my computer would not connect to the university's Internet server. The IT department said that they would look into the matter, so Geoff and I drove up to the *jabal* and delivered the hard drive to them. And although it was my computer, and although Geoff is a complete technophobe, he was the one who had to handle the negotiations. 'Please ask your husband to talk to us,' they begged me. 'Please do not bring your wife here,' they pleaded with him.

It took me some time to realise that whenever we had any business to transact with the Saudis, it was better to let Geoff handle it. At first I could not help myself, I just had to step in: to explain, to clarify, to add important details. And although I was listened to politely, I could tell that such behaviour appeared shamelessly forward. Out of the corner of my eye I could see Geoff looking agitated, conscious that he was losing face; revealed as a man who could not control his wife. I came to the slow realisation that we would get better results if I simply shut up. I learned to bite my tongue and to stay in the background. Only the grinding of my teeth gave me away.

Even our apartment had folding room dividers installed so that, should we choose to do so, we could separate our male and female guests. But at least at home things were on a more equal footing. Geoff was as appalled as I was by my lowly status, and determined to be as supportive as he could possibly be. We made a pastime of trading ever more outrageous observations of the strange relations, both comic and tragic, between men and women in the Kingdom. When one of his colleagues was banned from visiting his four-year-old son's hospital bedside because only mothers were allowed in the ward, Geoff was incredulous. When he himself was barred entry to the family night shopping bus and directed instead to the men's minibus following close behind, he was shocked, and stamped off to it with ill-concealed irritation. Whenever we went out together in public, he insisted upon his own small gesture of defiance. 'We've always held hands,' he said, 'and I'm not going to stop now.' I gave him my hand nervously, touched in more ways than one.

My encounters with Saudi men were fleeting: a neighbour met by chance in the car park at Ferdaws, a doctor at the KFUPM clinic, a shopkeeper in al Khobar. 'Welcome to Saudi Arabia,' they would say, and flash me a smile of such warmth and dazzling charm that I felt as if the sun had chosen that moment to shine its light on me, and me alone. Mostly, however, they remained figures in a landscape, dressed in their impossible whites and their red and white head cloths.

Before my arrival Geoff had existed in a world virtually without women. He lived in bachelor quarters, and spent his days teaching young men and interacting with other male teachers and staff.

Now we had become part of the family scene at Ferdaws, but it was only with Western families that we had any joint contact. Every morning we went off in our separate directions. Every evening we came back together to compare notes, trying to piece together the two halves of this strange new world.

Although gender segregation was intended to protect the honour of women and their families, to me it seemed to warp rather than to protect. Some of Geoff's bachelor colleagues were like flowers wilting in the desert, dying for a sprinkling of female companionship. Others were obsessed: they steered every conversation into lurid speculation about Saudi women and their kinky lesbian antics or their predatory designs on helpless expatriate men.

But worst affected were the Saudi bachelors. Deprived of contact with any female over thirteen years of age except their sisters, their mothers or their grandmothers, it was hardly surprising that they found the very idea of women madly exciting.

The results could be bizarre. Late one afternoon, I was swimming with a friend at the recreation centre. Alone in the pool, we floated on our backs, looking up at a sky criss-crossed with the vapour trails of fighter jets, watching as the planes returned to base. Suddenly one of them was directly above us, tumbling, diving, twisting and swooping in a breathtaking display of virtuosity. At first we could not believe that spectacle had anything to do with us. We watched in amazement as US$30 million of equipment corkscrewed overhead, until the noise and a descending curtain of kerosene vapour drove us out of the water. Surely, we shouted to each other, surely it couldn't be our aging cleavages that had excited this display, and we laughed at the ridiculousness of it all.

Another incident was less amusing. I had taken a taxi into al Khobar in search of equipment for a camping trip, not realising that the town closed down in the afternoon. I found myself in a deserted street as the mid-afternoon call to prayer sounded, first from one loudspeaker, then from another, and then another, until the air was filled with a strange, intense wailing. A car filled with young men cruised past. They tooted, leaned out of the windows, and invited me to come for a ride. I ignored them. They passed me a second time, jeering and honking. Suddenly, although I stood in the stark daylight of a hot afternoon, a cold chill of fear ran up my spine. Up ahead the car started to turn back towards me, and I looked frantically about me for refuge. Finding none at all, I took to my heels and ran to the most Western place I knew, Tamimi supermarket. I spent the rest of the afternoon huddled on a bench behind a pillar, wishing that I had an *abaya* to disappear into.

'But of course,' said Geoff's friend Claude, an old Saudi hand. 'Didn't you know that the Saudis consider the sight of a woman walking about alone to be provocative?'

'No,' I replied. I hadn't known. I could feel the horizon shrinking in upon me.

When at last I was able to log on to my email, one of the first messages I received was from a friend in Australia. She wrote that one of her friends was visiting Saudi Arabia as part of a Ministry of Education mission. 'I have given her your email address,' wrote Angela. 'It would be great if you could catch up with her and do some raging in Riyadh.' She made it sound so easy. But to get there I would have needed Geoff's written permission to travel. In Riyadh, because single women were unwelcome guests, I would have been unable to get a hotel room. As to 'raging in Riyadh'. . . I looked at the message on my screen and sighed. Not for the first time, I felt like a prisoner.

The terrain of the Eastern Province slopes almost imperceptibly down to the Gulf, evolving into tidal zones and sandy beaches that slip away under shallow azure waters. On weekends we drove south along the magnificent highway that swept down to Half Moon Bay, its broad curves snaking around the salt flats and out across the desert like a huge modern sculpture. Along its length, Saudi families came out for recreation and relaxation.

In al Khobar where our drive began, the salty tang of fried fish wafted out of popular seafood restaurants, while from the huge American fast-food outlets that occupied the prime positions – McDonald's, KFC and Wendy's – came the familiar smell of hot grease. Sedate family groups promenaded along the wide foot-paths of the corniche, carrying babies and shepherding little toddlers intently peddling their tricycles. Kids on in-line skates slid in and out around tight clusters of women strolling arm-in-arm. I did a double take at the sight of young men holding hands as they walked along. In their long white frocks, they looked as camp as could be, although Geoff assured me that hand-holding was no more than a gesture of friendship.

On the outskirts of al Khobar, by a shallow salt-water lagoon, motorists stopped at food vans for barbecued chicken *shawarmas*, or at mobile kiosks for ice-cold cans of Pepsi and 7-Up. Then they wandered into the little weekend market nearby. Although its stalls displayed nothing more than the usual mix of children's clothing, prayer rugs, wind-up toys, *abayas* and sunglasses, the shoppers thronging its dusty aisles were in a holiday mood, and didn't seem to mind.

Further down the highway, families were picnicking in the desert. Each sought out a piece of sand as far away from everyone else as possible, and there unrolled a carpet on which they settled down to share a meal, to watch a little television on a portable set, and to relax. Down on the seashore, their delighted children rode gaily harnessed ponies and camels up and down, or tooled along the beach in little rented buggies shaped like tractors.

Private companies had fenced off stretches of the coast to create exclusive beaches for their employees, with entry con-trolled by boom gates and security guards. British Aerospace and Aramco both had extensive holdings, and so did KFUPM. Our beach was a welcome refuge, a pretty bay hidden from the road by low sand dunes, with a row of cabanas along its length that offered shade and barbecue facilities. To float in the buoyant, salty water of the Gulf was an unparalleled delight that allowed us an all-too-rare sense of freedom.

A few kilometres beyond the KFUPM beach, families flocked to sample the tame amusements of the Prince Mohammad Recreation Park with its ferris wheel, carousel and slippery dip. Next door, the more adventurous practised their desert driving skills in rented Land Cruisers. They drove them up the wind-ward slopes of huge sand dunes, paused for a heart-stopping moment on the high crest, then tipped over the edge and came whooshing and wallowing down the almost vertical leeward sides.

A building boom was in progress all along Half Moon Bay, as developers carved up the coast in a rush to provide accommodation for Saudi vacationers. Everywhere resorts with names such as 'Palm Beach Village', or 'Half Moon Beach Resort' were springing up next to established private villas and princely palaces set amidst walled gardens. I peered into these resorts and saw mosques and formal townhouses. I looked at the women draped in black sitting on the seashore, at the families rigid in their isolation, and tried to imagine what a Saudi beach holiday must be like. It bore little resemblance, I was sure, to its carefree Australian counterpart, and I pitied Saudi children. But then I saw beachside kiosks delightfully shaped like giant, red-and-white-striped fish, where little ones clustered around their fathers to beg for ice cream treats, and realised that these children, too, would take away treasured memories of their holidays.

The most magnificent seaside establishment of all, immediately to the south of the KFUPM beach, was the home of Prince Mohammad ibn Fahd, son of the King, and Governor of the Eastern Province.

To the outside world the Prince's palace presented a blank front wall. Two sweeping entrances were sealed with elaborate wrought iron and opaque glass gates. In front of each gate stood an armoured all-terrain vehicle with a machine gun mounted on its roof, pointing directly at the road.

Looking into the compound from our beach, we caught glimpses of buildings sheltered amidst groves of trees, and fantasised about the luxury that they contained – I imagined white plush couches, smoked mirrors and bathtubs with gold taps.

Artificial hills covered with lush, emerald-green lawns rolled gently down to the seashore, where a military helicopter was parked on a floating landing pad, and two speed boats stood ready to challenge any intruder. Whenever we ventured too close and attempted to peer inside the compound, armed guards in sentry boxes along the perimeter fence waved us away.

I was getting used to the company of women. With our husbands away at work, we turned to each other for companionship. We rode the shopping buses together; in the hours set aside for women at the recreation centre pool, we floated and chatted and swam lazy laps up and down; together we racked our brains for schemes to counter the prevailing boredom.

Some had jobs. Employed as teachers in the British or American schools, as administrative assistants at the consulates or in expatriate firms, and as medical workers in the hospitals, they were the lucky ones. Anyone with a marketable skill – language or music teaching, aerobics or dance, counselling or chiropractic – tried to set up work for themselves. Others filled their time with study: several young women were attempting to upgrade their qualifications through correspondence courses with American or British universities.

Groups formed around various interests. Some developed a passion for craftwork: the Quilters Club, also known as Stitch 'n Bitch, was immensely popular. The members of PAWS, the animal welfare society, kept themselves busy raising money to pay the local vet for neutering stray cats, and finding homes for the many kittens born despite their efforts.

The varied population of Ferdaws seemed to offer endless opportunities for cultural exchange, and I was keen to explore them. I had heard of one group that came together regularly as a cooking club to explore recipes and to sample the cuisines of their various countries. At each meeting, one woman would play host to the others, inviting them into her apartment for a specially cooked meal. As an enthusiastic explorer of culinary delights myself, I was hoping to get involved.

I asked American Katy when the next meeting of the club would be. Of all the Western wives, she was the most determined to bridge the East–West cultural gap, and I felt sure that she would be a part of it.

'Oh, that all came to a sad end,' she said, and she explained that one of the British women had baked a pudding that everyone had enjoyed, but had later confessed that she had used just a dash of alcohol in its preparation. At the time, everyone had laughed, but one woman, a devout American convert to Islam, had gone home and told her husband about it.

'Once the word got around, none of the Muslim women could come,' she said ruefully.

This was vexing news. Making Muslim friends was clearly going to be more difficult than I had imagined.

Contact between women of different backgrounds and religions was easiest where small children were involved. Many friendships were formed through the robust play group that some Ferdaws mothers organised and took turns to supervise. Kids ranged freely through the courtyards of Ferdaws and through each other's apartments. At Katy's place, a constant stream of little boys led by her own two sons came and went, often with a mother in pursuit who would stay for a coffee and a chat.

Katy had managed to find work as a child care assistant at the university's preschool centre. She was paid far less than the Saudi women who worked there, but had been promised a real job as soon as a vacancy became available. She felt exploited. 'They love the work I do with the children,' she complained, 'but I know they're never going to give me a proper contract.' Still, her work brought her into close contact with Saudi women, and she made the most of her opportunities. Her colleagues appreciated her openness to their culture. They invited her to their tea parties and taught her to cook their favourite dishes. When they learned of her love of Middle Eastern music and dance, she found herself invited to their parties and even to the occasional wedding.

Katy and her husband, one of Geoff's English-teaching colleagues, were both talented musicians. She told me that her long-term project was to create an arts club where both Muslims and non-Muslims could come together to share their creativity.

She was pressuring the management at the recreation centre to hold a concert, open to anyone who wished to perform. Unfortunately, the project seemed unlikely to get off the ground – they were reluctant to approve of anything quite so risqué. Not daunted, Katy hosted several highly successful musical evenings in her own apartment.

Before I went to Saudi Arabia, I had rarely attended a ladies' tea party, but at Ferdaws they were a way of life, and they became the mainstay of my social calendar: a chance to get together, to chat, to exchange information, to ease the boredom. I found, somewhat to my surprise, that I was enjoying this all-female world with its gossip and its talk of children and husbands and how best to fill idle time. Depending on who was playing host, these gatherings could be more or less culturally mixed. But not everyone wanted to reach out to the locals. At one of Katy's parties, the arrival of a woman dressed in high *hijab* was the signal for an English woman to take her ostentatious leave. Later she complained that Katy's parties were 'such a bore'.

'She always has Muslim women over,' she groaned. 'You can't have a decent conversation.'

Even with the best of intentions, our cross-cultural encounters could go awry. Sometimes a husband would arrive home unexpectedly and walk in unannounced on a tea party. His arrival would send the Muslim women diving for their *abayas* in a panic.

For me, such incidents simply added to my enjoyment. In truth, I was becoming more than a little bored with tea parties. They were pleasant enough, but there had to be more to life.

On the bus, Marie was sounding off about how racist some expats were in their attitudes to the Saudis. I told her that I was having trouble meeting any of them. Although I had got to know several women from other Middle Eastern and Muslim countries, I knew no Saudis at all.

'You should come along to the Ladies Activities Committee,' she said. 'It's a great opportunity to meet some Saudi women. You'll find that they're really very nice.'

The committee, made up of the wives of academics, met in the recreation centre cafeteria. Its natural leader was a Saudi woman of immense dignity and charisma. The members included several other Saudis, as well as a Sri Lankan, a Sierra Leonian and an Egyptian. Katy, Marie and I formed the Western contingent. The women welcomed me; they seemed pleased that I had made the effort to come.

We had no agenda, and although Katy was taking the minutes, the other ladies seemed to regard this as an amusing irrelevance. The conversation ranged freely over activities that had already taken place – a bus trip to Qatif (a market town to the north of Dhahran), a magic show for children – and on to events planned for the future.

Marie had recently been to a meeting of the University Activities Committee as the representative of the Ladies group. She reported back in some excitement that the rector of the university was all in favour of family activities, and had suggested that a family night be held around the pool in the recreation centre. Katy and I were enthusiastic; the Muslim ladies sceptical.

'I predict this idea will not last for long,' said one. 'It has no future.'

'But the rector himself is proposing it,' Marie protested. 'The very highest authority.'

The women laughed. 'Men and women and entertainment together? Somewhere there is a higher authority who will not allow it.'

And they were right, of course. The family night proposal sank without a trace.

Our more conventional activities met with greater success. The Ladies Activities Committee decided to organise a beach excursion, and a group of about twenty women and children made the trip. Upon reaching the beach, we divided loosely into two groups: Arab ladies and Western women, as each group preferred to call itself. The Arab ladies, covered head-to-ankle in scarves, swimsuits, long-sleeve tops and leggings, took to the water and stayed there. The Westerners, demure enough in one-piece costumes, preferred to sit on the beach, sunbathing, talking, taking the occasional dip. The children played along the water's edge, or moved back and forth easily between the two groups.

Suddenly a frenzy of activity erupted down at Prince Mohammad's beach. Guards were piling into the helicopter. Its rotor blades started to turn. The machine lifted off and came beating up the beach towards us like a big, low-flying dragonfly. As it passed just a few metres overhead, a dozen guards craned out of the side to look at us. At the far end of the beach it swung around in a tight arc, and swept back down towards us, this time with the guards hanging out of the other side. The Western women laughed scornfully. A few indignant fingers were raised. The Arab ladies simply bent down and immersed their faces in the water.

Our first camping trip. We left on a Thursday morning, the first day of the Saudi weekend: three vehicles, four men, two women and a four-year-old boy. I took to the road with a sense of liberation, happy to be finally breaking out of the yellow school bus al Khobar shopping mall circuit. Geoff and I, both city-slickers at heart, were excited by the prospect of a desert adventure.

The highway was a six-lane ribbon that headed away from the Gulf through a curiously disturbed landscape. It was as if the entire surface of the desert had been dug up and piled into untidy mounds. Pipes and empty barrels and bales of rusty wire littered the ground, the detritus of the oil industry.

Further inland, the desert settled down to low undulations where herds of camels, goats and fat-tailed sheep grazed amongst the scrubby grey salt bush. Here in their natural environment the camels looked elegant and dignified, not at all the comic creatures 'designed by a committee' that I had always imagined them to be.

Official brown signs with graceful Arabic inscriptions appeared at regular intervals along the roadside. Our leader, Will, told us that they were there to offer praise to Allah. Every few kilometres we passed the twisted and rusting metal hulk of a car lying where it had come to rest after spinning off the highway. Powerful cars driven by sheiks in Ray Bans flashed past us, tempting a similar fate.

We stopped for petrol at a huge roadside complex complete with mosque, kebab restaurant and shops. Two camels and a sheep stood enclosed in a pen next to a butcher's shop. In a gory advertisement for the freshness of its meat, the bloody head of a recently slaughtered camel was hanging from a hook next to the door.

At Jowdah, or Judah, or Goodah, depending on which highway sign you were reading, we turned off the main road. Irrigated fields of melon and vegetable crops surrounded the village, and, off to one side, a few old houses made of sun-dried brick lay crumbling and abandoned. Sandy lanes led us between more modern houses hidden behind high walls. In the centre of town, outside an impressive new mosque, a few men and children were gathered around a car, the only people in sight. They fell silent and eyed us suspiciously as we drove past.

The road beyond the village was a corrugated track that led us into the desert. We had to wind up our windows to keep out the choking dust stirred up by our passage. But out here, away from the village, the mood changed. Now the trucks slowed down as they passed us, and old men with leathery brown faces leaned out of the windows, smiling and waving.

'Salaam alaikum!' they yelled.

When we stopped on a rise to discuss our route, an enthusiastic group of young men drove up in a Land Cruiser.

'Welcome, welcome. Please come and visit our farm,' they chanted.

I was thrilled. At last, a glimpse into the real Arabia!

But after a week of teaching young Arabs, the last thing the other members of our group wanted was to spend their leisure time with them.

'Get rid of them,' muttered Will through clenched teeth. And so we made our polite excuses and went on our way.

We made camp in a narrow *wadi* on the edge of an escarpment that had once formed the shore of an ancient sea. Centuries of rainstorms and wind had sculpted the soft sandstone cliffs into fantastic shapes, like the turrets and arches of a Gothic cathedral. Deep fissures and gullies sliced back into the plateau behind us. A huge slab of rock had fallen across the entrance to our canyon, making us invisible to the world. At the end of the day we climbed onto it, and sat breathing in the clean air as we watched the sun sink down into the empty desert. We ate around a campfire, and shared stories: of Irish wakes, of travel in wild places, of a rat that lived in a refrigerator. Our mingled laughter floated out into the stillness.

We talked of Arabia, and Will said, 'I like it here. I'm not leaving.'

Someone else said, 'Arabia has been good to me, but . . .'

The campfire threw strange, flickering shadows onto the walls of the canyon. Once or twice we heard the sound of a car speeding away into the distance, and overhead, in a brilliantly starry sky, we saw the light of a passing jet, too high to make a sound. All the tensions and frustrations of the past weeks slipped away from me as I sat there. 'Here I am in Arabia,' I thought to myself, and was suddenly flooded with happiness. I could think of no place that I would rather be; no companions that I would rather be with.

It was cold away from the campsite. A moist dew had distilled from the air, and was settling onto the desert. The night was black beyond all dreams of blackness; the silence so deep it was palpable.

Inside our little two-man nylon tent, Geoffrey of Arabia had turned his flashlight on, lighting it up like a blue Chinese lantern. As I crawled in beside him, I remembered my dream of drinking coffee in a sagging black camel-hair tent with Bedouin women. Hopelessly romantic, I told myself, and I wrapped myself up in our plush acrylic blanket with the savage leopard skin spots. It seemed somehow to capture the spirit of my Arabia

4

HARD LABOUR

Verily, We have created man into toil and struggle.
HOLY QURAN, 90:4

Wednesday evening: the start of our weekend. It was referred to with awe as *shebab* (bachelor) night, because this was the night that young men celebrated the end of the week by climbing into their powerful cars and gunning them into town. Even from a distance we could see that the traffic on the freeway was thicker, faster and more erratic than usual. Refusing to yield to the terror we felt, Geoff and I drove into al Khobar.

The quiet, half-empty city of my morning shopping trips was un-recognisable. By night al Khobar was a town of flashing neon lights, streams of honking traffic and footpaths jammed with people.

We pulled into a car park in a traffic island in the middle of the Dammam Road, near al Shula Mall. It was evening prayer time. At the far end of the paving about fifty men were down on their hands and knees praying, their backs curving into the air like eggs side by side in a carton. Nearby, taxi drivers were touting for business. 'Dammam, Dammam,' they shouted. '*Yala, yala, yala!*'

A *dhoti*-clad Bangladeshi carrying a bucket and some rags came up to us. 'Wash your car, Sah?' he asked hopefully.

Every shop, every office was closed and shuttered. Subdued

crowds of dark-skinned Subcontinental, Asian, African and Middle Eastern men loitered on the footpaths. Around the international call centres and the currency remittance offices they were packed ten-deep, waiting to phone home or to send off their earnings to their families. Waiting, waiting.

Huddled closely together, three young Filipino women in black robes made their way through the crowd. The men watched them with silent intensity, stepping aside to let them pass.

We made our way to our favourite restaurant, one of several Thai establishments, all of them staffed by Filipinos. A sign on the door read 'Closed for prayers' and heavy curtains were drawn over the windows, but as we hovered near the entrance, a waiter came out, took a quick look up and down the street, and bustled us through into the dimly lit family room.

Several customers were already seated at the tables, and were tucking into spring rolls and prawn crackers. I wondered idly where each group was from, and what had brought them to the Gulf. This was a game I'd become adept at by now. The informal demeanour of the men in jeans and T-shirts marked them as American rather than British, so they were probably professionals working at Aramco. The small groups of women, Asians and Westerners, were most likely medical workers from one of the local hospitals. If they had been domestic servants, the only other sizable group of female workers, they would have had neither the freedom nor the money to eat in a restaurant. A prosperous-looking Filipino couple with two small children was harder to place; they could have been anything from business managers to housekeepers.

At the end of prayer time, the lights were turned up and the curtains drawn back. A cassette player was switched on, and John Denver's voice pleaded with country roads to take him home. In oversized tropical aquariums, brightly coloured fish darted back and forth. Friendly waiters moved amongst the tables. Caught up in their contagious cheerfulness, we started to feel some release from the knot of tension that was a persistent part of life in the Kingdom.

Outside again, and the town was jumping. Shops and showrooms crammed with merchandise were ablaze with light that flooded out onto footpaths crowded with shoppers. The restaurants and the street stalls were open, filling the air with the smells of grilled chicken and fish. From the fruit stalls came the busy whirr of blenders whipping up a storm of crushed ice and orange, melon, grape and mango juice.

The faces in the street represented every continent, every race; the voices spoke a dozen languages. At the rear of al Shula, the grocery shops sold taro, dried fish and green coconuts: we called the area Little Manila. The streets behind the Yemeni market were thronged with Urdu-speaking men, and permeated with the tang of spices, curry and incense: we could have been somewhere in Karachi.

We ended our evening in an up-market Arabian coffee shop, tempted in by the display of delicate golden pastries in the window. In our own private booth upstairs we sat on comfortable couches at a glass-topped table, sipping from tiny cups of sweet, cloudy Turkish coffee. We ordered a selection of sweets, each one a masterpiece of the confectioner's art: layers of filo pastry stuffed with ground pistachios and walnuts, semolina cakes soaked in rosewater and honey, rice cooked in milk scented with cardamom and saffron, tarts filled with date paste, delicate cubes of quivering Turkish delight.

'What is your country?' asked the young waiter.

He was a Moroccan, he said, and glanced about to see if anyone was listening. 'Morocco is beautiful – not like Saudia,' he said. 'Here it is crazy.'

We nodded sympathetically. We had heard the same sentiments often, from all manner of expats. We had even uttered them ourselves in bad moments.

Downstairs, a few Saudi men sat drinking coffee, the smoke from their *sheeshas* filling the air with the cloying sweetness of fruit-flavoured tobacco. In the shops outside, Saudi merchants stood behind counters, and in offices, Saudi managers sipped tea with their clients and friends. Saudi families piled into shops and restaurants, and *shebabs* cruised the streets in their cars. But in the city of al Khobar, the locals were a definite minority.

Saudi society seemed as closed to outsiders as a well-guarded fortress. Most Saudis shunned all but essential contact with expats, and most expats were happy to preserve their distance. Our world was the expatriate world and, because I could not penetrate the Saudi one, this was where I directed my curiosity.

As Westerners living on campus at a prestigious university, Geoff and I enjoyed a relatively privileged position. And yet, although many of the guest workers we encountered were of far lowlier status, it was easy to feel an affinity with them. We had, after all, been drawn to the Gulf by the same hopes of a better life, and like them, we had traded home comforts, freedom, even dignity to be there. Like them, we were struggling to adjust to our new surroundings. Our day-to-day lives may have been very different, but we understood only too well the confidences of lonely waiters.

In 2000, between five and seven million expatriates were living in Saudi Arabia, or between a quarter and a third of the total population of twenty million. They made up almost 70 percent of the workforce, and an astonishing 95 percent of the private sector. Every year they sent an estimated US$18 billion out of the country in salary remittances.

Only about 100,000 of these guest workers belonged to the well-paid expatriate elite: some 45,000 Americans, about 30,000 UK nationals, and a mix of others from the world's more developed economies. The vast majority of foreigners were unskilled or semi-skilled third-world labourers. In 2000 there were approximately 1.5 million Indians, 900,000 Bangladeshis, 800,000 Pakistanis, 800,000 Egyptians, 600,000 Filipinos and 130,000 Sri Lankans in the Kingdom.

The expatriate world that I found myself in was a sub-society with its own peculiar hierarchy based on nationality and occupation. At the top of the pyramid were the professionals: the doctors, engineers, consultants and managers; and lower down, the technicians, teachers, nurses and secretaries.

Unskilled labourers were at the bottom of the heap. They took on the work that was considered too lowly, too dirty, or too unpleasant for any Saudi to consider. They were the janitors, the sanitation workers, the gardeners, the construction workers, the porters. They were almost all Subcontinentals – so much so that the very word 'Bangladeshi' had come to be synonymous with 'dog's body'. The domestic servants were their female equivalent.

In between these two extremes were all the skilled and semi-skilled workers required to keep a country running: shop assistants and managers, technicians and computer programmers, clerks and bookkeepers, waiters and chefs, mechanics and electricians, barbers and beauticians.

Modern Saudi Arabia, like all the Gulf emirates, was built on expatriate expertise and expatriate sweat. In fact, as I heard one Arabian commentator lament on Emirati TV, every inch of highway and every single brick in the oil-rich Gulf states had been laid by foreign hands.

A taxi ride.

'Where are you from?' I asked the driver.

'I am from Bangladesh, madam.'

'How long have you been in Saudi Arabia?'

'I am newly arrived,' he said. 'I am here three weeks only.'

'How are you liking it?'

His eyes regarded me mournfully in the rear view mirror.

'It is very difficult, madam. This is a very terrible place.'

'Did you work in Bangladesh?'

'Yes, madam. I am a university graduate. I am a school teacher. But I must support my parents and my sisters and brothers. In my country a school teacher's pay is very low . . . it is nothing.'

'Will you stay here?'

'What else can I do?'

KFUPM was a world in microcosm. At the very top were the Saudis: the rector, the faculty deans, the chief administrators and senior lecturers; well-connected men of considerable ability with plenty of *wasta*, or influence. All the perks of office – prestige, high salaries, luxury housing, cars, servants – were theirs.

Below them were the non-Saudi academic staff: fellow Arabs, North Africans and Westerners. Their contracts saw that their needs were taken care of, more or less, to their satisfaction. Recent arrivals might complain about their conditions, or their powerlessness in the face of an arbitrary administration. Longer-term residents had learned how to live within the system, had developed connections, even a little *wasta* of their own. Newly arrived English teachers were close to the bottom of this group.

The middle managers who took care of the day-to-day administration of the university were men who, despite their education and abilities, found themselves outside the *wasta* system. Mainly Pakistanis and Indians, this group also included some Filipinos and some local Shia Muslims. (The majority of Saudis, and all of the power elite, are Sunnis.) Some middle managers had served the university for years, and had built their positions into powerful personal fiefdoms. They had an infinite capacity to further or hinder the cause of anyone who needed official business done, and supplicants offended them at their peril. Yet their salaries tended to reflect their market value in their home countries rather than on the world market. They came at a bargain price.

At the recreation centre, the assistant manager was a Shia. At the clinic, a Filipino office staff assisted the Saudi and Pakistani doctors. At the Co-op, the staff were Keralans from southern India. The barber was a Turk. The taxi drivers who operated from a car park near the Co-op were Indians and Pakistanis. The cooks in the cafeteria up on the *jabal* were mostly Filipino, as were the mechanics who serviced the university's fleet of vehicles. The handyman plumbers and electricians were Subcontinentals.

There were a few female employees: doctors and other medical staff at the university clinic, the librarian at the recreation centre library, a lifeguard at the swimming pool, and teachers and administrative staff at the preschool and the girls school. Most were recruited from the pool of academic wives. A number of maids served in the houses of the university elite: Filipinos, Indonesians and Sri Lankans.

The very bottom of the pyramid was, of course, made up of an army of Bangladeshi labourers. They were contracted to a private maintenance company, and were trucked in daily from their labour camp. There were gangs of gardeners to plant, weed, water, and prune the campus greenery, and groundsmen to sweep the footpaths; squads of porters to move the furniture, and sanitation workers to take away the garbage; two or three assistants to every plumber and electrician; and lone pest control workers who spent their days spraying pungent toxic chemicals into cracks in the footpaths and the masonry.

The Bangladeshis were everywhere. They were always willing to drop what they were doing to help us: to carry our groceries, to wash our car, to run an errand. This was hardly surprising. By early 1999 the price of oil had fallen to below US$10 a barrel, and money was tight in the Kingdom. The Bangladeshis hadn't been paid for over four months. They were surviving on odd jobs.

Last but not least, standing guard at the entrances to the university were the security guards, Saudis to a man. The profession had some status, and was one of the very few that was made up entirely of locals.

Another taxi ride. My driver was an Indian from Kerala. He had been in the Kingdom for four years.

'How is your life here?'

'It is terrible,' he replied hotly. 'I have no life. What sort of life is this?'

'Are you married?'

'No. That is not a marriage, the wife in Kerala, the husband here. He is working, working, sending money. His children are not knowing him. I do not want this sort of marriage.'

'How long will you stay here?'

'It is enough. I want to go home.'

'What will you do there?'

'I don't know. There is no work.'

An article in the *Arab News* reported on the life of Nasir, an Indian worker who had spent twenty years in the Gulf. Nasir was based in Dubai in the United Arab Emirates, but his story is typical. He was working to support his parents, two brothers, eight sisters, a wife and two children. His children were conceived during brief visits home at the end of each of his contracts: he barely knew them. Of his wife, Nasir said, 'I think of her all the time. Every week I make a quick call, just to hear her voice. I say "I love you" and then I hang up because I can't afford to spend more.' (*Arab News*, December 12, 1999)

Consider the choices faced by a poor man from the third world. His education has been minimal. He is illiterate, unskilled, with no prospect of employment. He has a family to support. His thoughts turn to the Middle East. There, he has heard, there is work and money to be made, at least US$100 per month. He approaches a recruitment contractor, although he has heard terrible stories of double-dealing agents.

Unlike his Western counterpart, who is lured to the Kingdom with all expenses paid, the labourer must pay for the privilege of working in Saudi Arabia, and pay up front. There are placement fees, visa fees and airfares. They can amount to anything from US$300 to $1,000, and all the financial resources of his extended family are required to cover them. He may even be forced to approach a money lender and agree to usurious rates of interest to raise the funds he needs. I often heard it said that it takes most workers eighteen months to pay off the debts they incur in coming to the Kingdom.

The agent asks the worker to sign his contractual papers. He signs, even though some of them are blank, and off he flies into the unknown. With him go all the hopes of his family. He promises to send them as much of his earnings as he can spare, and to return in two years on his first vacation.

On arrival he is assigned to an employer, perhaps a large labour contractor, or perhaps an individual or a small company where he will be the sole employee. He is shown to his living quarters; typically a dormitory bed in a labour camp. The best of these camps are spartan, but adequate. The huts are air-conditioned and have satellite TV, a few trees provide shade and there is a space for a game of football or cricket.

We didn't have to travel far to see a different kind of gulag. Out along the road to Dammam there was a particularly grim example: a collection of dilapidated prefab huts surrounding a patch of bare earth with a single water tap. A sagging perimeter fence was topped with rusty coils of barbed wire. The inmates used it to hang their tattered laundry out to dry amidst the fluttering blue plastic shopping bags that had snagged there from the desert winds. Through the fence, at the end of the day, I could see the workers squatting on their haunches around a cooking pot on a campfire.

Instead of labour camps, some employers give their employees a space to sleep on a shop floor or in the corner of a factory, or cram them into rented accommodation. On December 29, 1999, the *Saudi Gazette* reported on fifty-seven men housed in a three-bedroom, one-bathroom Jeddah apartment.

Our labourer starts to work. He'll be on the job not long after dawn. His work may not be particularly taxing, and with luck he'll be headed back to his quarters by mid-afternoon. He looks forward to Fridays, his day off.

Not every one is lucky.

As summer approached and daily temperatures rose into the forties, I waited for the construction crew down the road to be laid off from their toil. The break never came. They continued to mix concrete and carry bricks all day under a pitiless sun in air almost too hot to breathe.

Contract violations were common. 'Maintenance workers at four ministry hospitals in Jeddah have not been paid for months, despite going on strike to get their employers' attention . . . the cleaners, of which there are 1,500, say that despite their work, not only have they not been paid but also they have not received their *iqamas* [internal passports], forcing them to hide from police and passport department officials.' (*Arab News*, September 27, 1999)

'The story carried in Monday's *Arab News* of 1,500 Al-Hana Company employees who went on strike for their long overdue pay is not improving . . . not only have the employees still not been paid or been given their *iqamas*, but some of them were physically abused and beaten up when they went to the company's headquarters to ask for their overdue salaries and *iqamas*.' (*Arab News*, September 28, 1999)

Occupational health and safety is a foreign concept in the Kingdom, especially where labourers are concerned. They are sent out to work on the freeways with no more protection than their orange company overalls, fall to their deaths from scaffolding, and handle dangerous chemicals without even basic precautions. The wife of a volunteer fire fighter on the Aramco compound told me about a chemical plant fire that her husband attended, just north of al Khobar. As barrels exploded into the air, filling it with black smoke and toxic fumes, and as the ground ran with rivers of flame, the fire brigade hung back at a safe distance. But a gang of Bangladeshis clad in sandals and overalls and scarves wrapped around their heads were sent in to seal off the pipes.

'As the number of Asian workers increases, so do their deaths,' reported the *Arab News* on March 1, 1999. 'The Indian Embassy reported the death of 1,360 of its workers in 1997 . . . 580 Indians died of natural causes, while 780 met unnatural deaths . . . the causes of unnatural deaths are mainly traffic accidents, industrial accidents, murder, suicide, drowning, suffocation, execution, snake bites, food poisoning, stampedes and AIDS . . . the incidence of suicide among Indian workers is rising, with 60 suicide cases reported by the Indian mission last year alone . . . Major causes . . . include frustration, depression, exploitation, economic problems back home, domestic problems, family conflicts, property disputes, and broken marriages . . .'

In November 1962 Crown Prince Faisal, effectively the ruler of the country, announced a ten-point reform plan that included the establishment of constitutional law, the reform of local government, the expansion of state welfare, and a program for the development of roads, water resources and industry. As part of the plan, slavery was to be abolished.

Slaves had been a part of Middle Eastern society since antiquity, accepted by pagans, Jews, Christians and Muslims alike. The Quran, like the Old and New Testaments before it, recognised slavery and, by proposing ways in which it should be regulated, condoned it. It urged, but did not command, kindness to slaves, and recommended, without requiring, their liberation by purchase or by allowing them to work off their debt. In all three faiths, a slave who believed and practised the religion was regarded as the equal of a free citizen in the eyes of God. The Prophet himself, by example, suggested that slaves be treated well.

I read this story in the weekly 'Guidance from the Prophet' column in the *Arab News* (July 7, 1999) 'Abu Umaamah, a companion of the Prophet, reports that the Prophet came once with two slaves. He gave one as a present to Ali and said to him: "Do not beat him. I have been forbidden to beat people who pray and I have seen this one pray ever since we arrived." He gave the other to Abu Tharr, and said to him: "I recommend you to treat him kindly."'

Islam vastly improved the lot of Arabian slaves, transforming them from mere chattels to human beings, and giving them quasi-legal rights. Under the early caliphs, who ruled the Islamic world following the death of the Prophet in 632, the laws regarding slaves were codified along humanitarian lines. For example, it became illegal to enslave free Muslims, and unlawful for a freeman to sell himself or his children into slavery. Islamic jurists established that slave-owners should provide their slaves with adequate upkeep, with medical care when necessary, and look after them in their old age. A Muslim slave-owner was entitled to the sexual enjoyment of his female slaves, but any slave woman who bore a son to her master acquired enhanced status and legal rights. Maltreatment of slaves was deplored, although the penalties were discretionary and not prescribed by law.

This was never slavery on the scale seen in the New World: the mass transportation that fed the plantation systems of the Americas. The slaves of Arabia arrived in smaller numbers – they were often poor Nigerians or Sudanese villagers tricked into making the pilgrimage to Mecca and then sold by their tour leader, or small groups brought up on trading *dhows* from Kenya and Mozambique to supplement the main cargo of timber logs.

Mostly they worked as domestic servants. They were treated

reasonably well, and were often accepted as members of their households. Slave women were employed as concubines and menials. Slave men worked as servants and assistants to their masters; often they were castrated to become the eunuchs who guarded the harem. Slave children became the playmates of the family's children, often remaining their companions for life.

Robert Lacey, in his book *The Kingdom*, describes how Prince Faisal ibn Abdul Aziz, when visiting New York in 1944, shocked the management of the Waldorf Astoria by bringing his slave Merzouk with him. 'They were still more horrified,' writes Lacey, 'when the prince insisted that his companion should eat, as he always did, at the same table as his master – for this involved admitting Merzouk to the Wedgewood Room, and no black had ever been allowed in there before.'

In 1962, following the royal decree that ended slavery, the government moved to purchase the freedom of some 4,000 slaves, paying a generous £1,000 for each of them. Amongst those most disturbed by this development were the slaves themselves, who suddenly faced an uncertain future on the open job market. (It was at exactly this time that floods of expatriate workers started to arrive in the Kingdom.) Unless their former owners were able to make special arrangements for them, the freed slaves were neither repatriated nor given citizenship. Most of them chose simply to remain with their ex-owners, working as they had always done. There was little else that they could do. They and their descendants remain in the Kingdom to this day.

In the Ferdaws laundry a small girl in a white party dress was bouncing up and down on top of the washing machines. A middle-aged woman was trying to coax her down.

'Get down now,' she said. 'Don't you want to play outside?'

The child ignored her.

'Today she is naughty,' the woman told me, shrugging. 'I am Mona, and this', she pointed to the child, 'is Johara.'

Mona was a Sri Lankan. She had been working in Saudi Arabia for five years as a maid in the home of Johara's father, a KFUPM professor. Johara was the youngest of five children she had in her care.

She took me to see her room, a dark bedroom in the professor's apartment that she shared with the family's three daughters. Four single beds were crammed closely together to make space for a small table with a sewing machine on it – Mona's way of making a little extra money.

'My husband, he ran away with another woman,' she said, 'so I come here. I must pay for my four children in Sri Lanka.'

She was happy, she said. 'My Saudi family is very nice. Very kind.'

In 1999 there were almost 400,000 female expatriate workers in the Kingdom, and three quarters of them were employed as domestic servants (*Arab News*, December 12, 1999). They came from Indonesia, the Philippines, Sri Lanka, Eritrea; wherever there were desperately poor people. They were paid as little as US$110 per month for duties that typically included cooking, cleaning, and child care. Of all the Kingdom's foreign workers, these women are the most vulnerable.

If things work out well for a maid, she finds herself living in the home of a Saudi family that treats her kindly. Her household may employ a number of other servants who will help her to adjust to her new life and ease her loneliness. Her employers will not work her too hard, will provide her with decent living conditions, and will respect her right to some privacy. They may even take her travelling, and shower her with gifts. She will have a network of friends – other maids in other houses – that she can talk to by phone, or go out to meet on her once-a-fortnight day off. Over time, she may, like Mona, develop a genuine affection for the young Saudis in her care, and they for her. All of this is not uncommon.

For an unlucky maid, things can work out very badly indeed. She may become a solitary prisoner in her employer's household, forbidden to leave for the duration of her two-year contract. With no-one to turn to and no-one who speaks her language, she will feel isolated. However, loneliness may be the least of her problems.

Her work may be onerous. She may be expected to spend all

her waking hours on duty. Her employer may neglect to pay her for months at a time and may not give her enough to eat. Her mistress may subject her to physical abuse: pinching, slapping, scratching and beatings.

'Seven Filipino maids who worked for the family of a Saudi prince in Egypt were questioned by [Egyptian] public prosecutors on December 20. The prince had accused them of stealing after they had claimed they were mistreated . . . The maids dropped a note from the window of the Ramsis Hilton Hotel on December 18 saying they had not been paid and were being mistreated . . . Two Egyptian butlers who worked for the prince tried to escape in November from the top floors of the hotel, where the prince and his family live, but fell to a lower floor. One broke his back.' (*Saudi Gazette*, December 1998)

'Jeddah. A maid has died after two women, who accused her of stealing a gold chain, tied her up and beat her . . . The Eritrean maid . . . was found lying unconscious in the Al-Aziziya district of the city . . . The servant, aged 30, later died of her injuries.' (*Arab News*, February 17, 2000)

A 1997 pamphlet prepared by the Philippines Overseas Workers Welfare Administration warns prospective maids that they may have to 'ward off advances by your master, his brother, son, and other male members of the household'. An Indonesian friend confirmed that many young maids are shipped home pregnant and in disgrace, their lives ruined. Some girls simply disappear, perhaps murdered to avoid bringing shame upon their employer's household.

It is little wonder that there are many runaways, up to 200 each month in Jeddah alone. They try to reach a safe house, or an agency that will (illegally) find them another job. Some make it as far as their embassy, where they live in limbo waiting for an arrangement that will enable them to return to their home country.

The Saudi authorities try to keep their guest workers under tight control. All new arrivals, from engineers to janitors, have to surrender their passports to their sponsors or employers. They are issued with an internal passport, an *iqama*, that they have to carry at all times and produce whenever they are asked to do so. To travel about within the Kingdom, or indeed to leave it, they need their employer's written permission. All over the country road-blocks are installed on the highways to check their papers and to monitor their movements.

To their credit, the Saudis have created laws that guarantee minimum standards for foreign workers in terms of pay, holidays and benefits, as well as courts to adjudicate disputes between employers and their employees. However, queries to 'The Law and You', a question-and-answer column in the *Arab News*, reveal a persistent pattern of chiselling in regard to salaries and conditions, while it is not at all clear that the courts effectively protect workers' rights. Critics claim that the legal system is heavily biased in favour of employers.

Take the example of J.B., who wrote to 'The Law and You' to ask about his entitlements after nine years of service. 'What shall I do if they refuse to pay?' he asked. 'If I sought help from the Saudi Labor Office, will I have full assurance or assistance to let our company pay all the amount due for me . . . and how long will it take for any legal hearing?'

'If they refuse to pay you,' came the reply, 'you can seek the help of the Labor Office. Rest sure the Labor Office will help you to settle your claim. Hearings depend on how you present your case and on session schedules set by the Labor Office. It may take months, a year or even more.' (*Arab News*, April 10, 1999)

This letter writer was an educated man who might be expected to understand the workings of the law. The ability of an illiterate labourer or an imprisoned domestic servant to seek redress through the Labor Office must be slight indeed.

If a worker does take his case to the Labor Office, he will probably lose his job. He then has to survive without pay while he waits for a ruling, as many contracts make it illegal for an employee to seek other employment. As his employer holds his passport and must grant permission for him to leave the country, the worker can, in effect, be starved into giving up all his claims just to get out. He and his fellow workers should be wary of acting together to enforce their rights. Strikes and collective actions may result in harsh punishment.

'Ten limousine drivers from Al-Wifaq Limousine Co., working at the airport, refused to go to work last weekend, objecting to their alleged mistreatment at the hands of the company owners . . . the company asked the police to arrest them, claiming that they owed the company some unpaid loans. The [sic] were later released . . . "It is amazing what these drivers are doing now," said [owner] Al-Khameesy, "though we have proof against them which could throw them in to prison for years for stealing . . ."' (*Arab News*, March 1, 1999)

Expats and human rights groups agreed that the labour courts were subject to manipulation by influential employers. There have been cases where workers in dispute with their employer (as well as the foreign partners of Saudi businessmen) have been arrested on spurious criminal charges. A detained worker can be held without trial, tortured to obtain a confession, and even executed. International human rights groups have documented evidence of such cases.

Even if there is a decision in favour of an employee, there is no guarantee that the employer will comply with the ruling. The courts can do nothing if the Saudi boss is simply an incompetent businessman who has run out of funds.

So serious are the flaws in the legal system that in 1995 the Egyptian Organisation for Human Rights labelled the Saudi sponsorship system 'a fraudulent way of avoiding the provisions' of the Convention on the Abolition of Slavery.

Mahmud, a Madras Indian, became my regular driver, or rather, by a process in which the Co-op drivers divided up the Ferdaws customers, I became his passenger. I had no choice in the matter.

'Do you speak English?' I asked him on our first ride together.

'Madam, I am speaking very good English. I am English very good. Same same Arabic. Same same Urdu. All very good, EX-cellent speaking.'

He was a small, dapper man with nut-brown skin and hair streaked with silver. He drove his taxi like a fiend.

'Please slow down!'

'Madam, I am driving taxi twelve years Saudia. I am very good driver, very safe. Twelve years no accident, no trouble. You NO WORRY.'

'Twelve years!' I said. 'Do you like Saudi Arabia?'

'Saudia very good place. Very good. I am very good Muslim man. I am five times going Mecca. Now my wife, she is coming here.'

'You must be a very rich man,' I said, 'to bring your wife here.'

'I'm working twelve years very hard, working, working. Now children study – finish. University – finish. Daughter, I am giving dowry, she marry. My wife, she is coming Saudia, Mecca going. Soon I am retire. *Khelas!* Finish!'

'Retire to Madras? Do you have a house in Madras?'

'Ve–ry big house.'

It has been said that Saudi Arabia is a first-world economy grafted on to a third-world base. At the top, wealth flows from the Kingdom's oil revenues into glittering shopping malls, designer boutiques, expensive cars and luxury villas; but beneath this veneer there are masses of workers from the world's emerging economies providing goods and services at bargain rates.

Because their wages are low and their family responsibilities are enormous, and because they can, many workers try to supplement their incomes by moonlighting. The black market that they have created is a boon for anyone with a little ready cash, well-paid expatriates included.

I was uncomfortable with the notion of having a servant: it's not really the Australian way. After all, I was not exactly overworked, and the suggestion that I hire a houseboy – well, the very word made me cringe. That was until I met the delightful Sonny, a Filipino who worked on the *jabal* and moonlighted by cleaning apartments.

On Fridays, his morning off, a smiling Sonny would appear at our door. For two hours he dusted, swept, washed floors, scrubbed the bath, washed the windows, and cleaned the stove, all the while radiating brightness and good humour. He demanded music, and when he had exhausted my small collection of CDs, he provided it himself by singing jazzy riffs to accompany his labours. He left the apartment sparkling.

Sonny had been in the Gulf for fifteen years and, although his pay wasn't great, he had worked hard, taking on as much extra work as he could find. He had a wife and several children in the Philippines, and when his youngest finished university in a year or so, he intended to retire and go home. I paid him 70 riyals (US$19) for his morning's work, and felt happy to be contributing to his retirement fund.

It was forbidden at the cost of fines, imprisonment, or deportation for guest workers on restricted visas to take on extra work on the side or to set up a private business. They could not change jobs at will: to break a contract was a complex process that required the cooperation of the employer and the payment of a substantial fee. And yet the labour black market was thriving. Almost every expat was trying to earn a little extra, from the academic who was ghost writing a PhD, to the Bangladeshi offering to carry your groceries.

Causing even more anxiety to the Saudi authorities than moonlighting workers were the Kingdom's many illegal residents. These were workers who had gone AWOL at the end of their contracts, or pilgrims who had stayed on after their *haj* or *umrah* visas had expired. In 1997 the Passport Department started a drive to round up these overstayers, inviting the public to dial the 992 hotline to turn in illegal residents. Fines were imposed on anyone employing, harbouring or aiding an illegal. By September 1999 the Passport Department claimed to have deported more than 1.5 million illegals. Director Lt. Gen. Asaad Abdul Kareem Al-Fareeh promised that the campaign would continue 'until the day arrives when the last overstayer has been deported from this land. The hunt will cover every town, village and every neighbourhood and street. Such a day is not far away.' (*Arab News*, September 12, 1999)

Strong words, but it seemed unlikely that the Saudis would

ever succeed in their efforts to control their messy black labour market. It was far too entrenched, and too many people, Saudi and foreigner alike, benefited from it.

The relationship between the Saudis and their foreign workers is fraught with contradictions. How, for example, can a respectable woman be chauffeured about by her private male driver, when custom dictates that she should never be alone with an unrelated man? Is it not ironic that this most private of people have taken into their homes such an army of outsiders? How should they respond to evidence of exploitation and abuse when their religion places such a high value on compassion? And at what cost does a people become accustomed to luxury and to dependence on foreign servants?

Commentator Rashed Al-Hamdan voiced the ambivalence that many Saudis must feel. 'Ours is a developing society,' he wrote, 'and many changes have taken place over the years. Over the years our family has become extended, and our women have become lazier, and most of all there is no cooperation and unity in our houses. These reasons have forced us to look for house-keepers and drivers. And these recruited members of course brought their traditions and cultures which differ from our traditions and our religion sometimes, but still we had to accept it, for the sake of the lady of the house.' (*Arab News*, December 28, 1999)

In recent years, the Saudis have been facing a new problem. A booming population has led to massive unemployment and mounting poverty. Everyone knows that there is a rough parity between the number of Saudis without jobs and the number of expatriate workers in the Kingdom. The resentment that this gives rise to finds expression in another entrenched social attitude: blaming the expats.

There is a tendency to scapegoat foreign residents for the social ills of the Kingdom. Saudis can't find work because expatriate workers take all the jobs, despite evidence that Saudis are either unwilling or unable to take on the work that expatriates do.

There is a heroin problem because of Pakistani smugglers, and a drinking problem because of British bootleggers. The beggars on the footpaths of Riyadh and Jeddah are overstayers who are exploiting Saudi charity. The carnage on the roads is caused by expatriate drivers.

Foreigners are blamed for most of the Kingdom's crime. The small but persistent headlines in the *Arab News* tell the story: 'Three Pakistanis executed for murder' (October 28, 1999), 'Seven Nigerians executed for bank hold-up' (May 14, 2000), 'Indian beheaded for murder' (May 24, 2000), 'Two Eritreans beheaded' (May 24, 2000). Meanwhile there is evidence that some of the foreigners imprisoned and executed for criminal activity are innocent: they are convenient scapegoats who were simply in the wrong place at the wrong time.

Saudis worry that they are being taken for a ride by smart foreigners. A cartoon from the *Arab News* shows a foreign technician seated at a work bench in front of some electrical appliances. He is holding up a booklet entitled 'How to fix home devices'. 'I made this booklet as a gift to our customers,' he says. 'Are you out of your mind?' screams his shocked colleague. 'How are we supposed to fool Saudis then?' (*Arab News*, May 10, 2000)

'Most claims that arise from domestic-help abuse are false,' wrote one correspondent to the *Arab News*. 'That's right! The truth behind this is clear: there is more money for these workers outside than inside. Making false claims is just a way of justifying their way of exit from their sponsors.' (December 8, 1998)

Some are sensitive to the plight of their guest workers, and to criticism of their treatment of them. In July 1999, *Arab News* columnist Tariq Al-Maeena reported on a conversation that took place at his weekly card game regarding a case of maid abuse.

'We all felt that [the abusive madam and her children] were an aberration of society, and not a true reflection of what we are. We are generally a humane lot, and when those amongst us commit such dastardly deeds, it is not something we condone or ignore.' (*Arab News*, July 16, 1999)

I felt sure that he was right. And yet the stories of abuse continue, too few voices are raised in protest, and little is done to address the problem. As long as they allow their most vulnerable workers to be exposed to such peril, the reputation of every Saudi is tainted.

Despite the hardship and the dangers, unskilled and semi-skilled workers continue to flood into the Gulf. Their courage and self-sacrifice goes largely unsung, although they are responsible for the well-being of whole families, villages, and even nations. Some fall by the wayside with calamitous results for themselves and their dependants. For most the gamble will pay off, but at a price.

They put up with hard work, low pay, miserable conditions, sexual frustration and loneliness, all to support families they barely know. Their earnings pay for their sisters' dowries and for their parents' medical care, for their children's education, and finally perhaps for a home for themselves. On rare trips home they are expected to shower their loved ones with gifts of jewellery, household appliances and cash, although they have come to feel somehow separate, detached from them.

They have built lives for themselves in the Gulf. Their work mates are now closer to them than their own family and the people of their village. With them they share an experience that is hard for outsiders to comprehend.

Are there any monuments built to honour their sacrifice? A tomb of the unknown Bangladeshi in Dacca? A tribute to lost maids in Jakarta? Perhaps grateful Saudis could dedicate a fountain in Riyadh. Until they can offer systematic protection and justice to their foreign workers, it is the least they could do.

Down at the KFUPM beach, a Saudi security guard checked our *iqamas* and raised the boom gate to allow us in. Halfway along the 200-metre road that ran across the desert to the car park, we passed a lone Bangladeshi engaged, as always, in work of the utmost futility. Armed with a large broom he was sweeping sand from the bitumen. He stared at me as we drove slowly past, his eyes bottomless black wells in an expressionless face. What did he see? I wondered. Wealth? Privilege? Incredible blind luck?

To assuage the guilt I felt, I reminded myself that the life he had left behind was probably even more desperate than his life in the Gulf, that his journey here was probably the most positive choice he could have made in his circumstances. I told myself that I had tasted oppression as a woman amongst the Saudis, and remembered that Geoff had spoken of being made to feel like a slave. I shrugged helplessly, still feeling guilty.

Sunset down at the seashore, music and laughter were spilling out from one of the cabanas, and fishy smoke was rising from a barbecue. A group of irrepressible Filipinos in Hawaiian shirts were playing guitars, singing love songs.

5

OASIS DREAMING

For in the wilderness shall waters break out,
and streams in the desert.
ISAIAH, 35:6

F or eons, rain that has fallen on western and central Arabia
has filtered down through layers of limestone to collect in
underground aquifers. Following the tilt of the land, these waters
drain away to the east, rising to the surface wherever there are
faults in the rock. At various points along the coast of the Eastern
Province, the miracle of fresh water occurs.

On a Friday morning, we set out to visit one of these places:
the legendary oasis of Qatif, situated only thirty kilometres
to the north of Dhahran. Geoff did the driving. His friend and
colleague, Doug, armed with a road atlas and his trusty *Lonely
Planet* guidebook, was our navigator. I was content to sit in
the back seat, gazing out at the passing display of villas, compounds, showrooms and desert; but my thoughts were elsewhere,
wandering around in an oasis of my imagination. I saw a small
pool of water, a palm tree and a camel. I added a tattered man
with his tongue hanging out, crawling on hands and knees across
the blazing sands towards the pool.

I had, by now, spent enough time in the recreation centre
library reading about the Saudis and their country to be able to

replace this comic-book vision with one that was both closer to
reality and infinitely more entrancing. Far from mere puddles in
the desert, the oases of the Eastern Province were sites of
abundant water flow and fecund life, and of human settlement
dating back more than 5,000 years. Now in my mind's eye, I
joined a Neolithic band of hunters and gatherers as they
wandered through the green shade of a palm grove. I imagined
bare feet sinking into soft grasses, the splash and trickle of water,
the echoing call of the bulbul, and the soft rustle of small animals
scurrying through the undergrowth.

Eventually the people who roamed the oases learned to
domesticate animals, to grow cereal crops, and to live in settlements. Archaeologists tell us that they built dwellings of mud and
palm fronds, that they made pottery and fine flaked-stone tools,
and that they kept cattle. In small boats made of reeds or palm
fronds lashed together, they fished and collected shellfish along
the coast. Somewhere in the vicinity, although precisely where it
happened no-one knows, humans learned to irrigate their fields,
and thus set in motion the process that gave rise to the great civilisations of the Fertile Crescent.

The first great city state, the Sumerian city of Ur, was
situated at the northern end of the Gulf in modern-day Iraq. By
the third millennium BC, in settlements along the coast and in
the large oases of Tarut Island, Qatif, al Hasa and northern
Bahrain, eastern Arabia was home to its own civilisation.
Known as Dilmun, it was linked by both culture and trade to
the Sumerians, who are thought to have looked to eastern
Arabia for their origins.

The chief god of the Sumerians, the god of the intellect and
of wisdom, was Enki. Enki made the grain grow, gave people the
plough, and was credited with the invention of civilisation. He
was also known as the dweller in the abyss, and the god of
the sweet waters under the earth – a reference, perhaps, to the
great oases.

Was it possible, I mused, that our civilisation began not to the
north near the rivers of Mesopotamia, but here on the eastern
coast of Arabia. Could this be what the story of Enki was telling
us? Was I, even now, drawing near to the Garden of Eden?

I woke from my reverie to the sounds of gentle bickering over which road we should take. In the front seat, navigation was proving more difficult than expected. A wrong turn led us down to the seashore, where the still waters of the Gulf were liquid mercury under a sultry, overcast sky. The only sign of life was a group of fishermen out on a breakwater, at work mending their chicken-wire lobster pots. We wandered over to have a look at what they were doing, and to ask directions.

They regarded us warily, without smiling. Or perhaps it was just me: I had the distinct impression that they might have been a lot more friendly if I hadn't been there. Doug and Geoff did their best to communicate, mainly by pointing quizzically about and repeating 'Qatif?', 'Qatif?' The fishermen replied with waves of the hand and pointing of their own. We headed back to the highway not much the wiser.

I returned to my thoughts.

Five thousand years ago, Qatif sat astride trading routes that ran from the Indus valley and Yemen to Mesopotamia. From 3,000 years ago, following the domestication of the camel, caravans set out from Qatif to cross the desert, bound for markets to the north and west, loaded with incense from Yemen and spices from India. Qatif's merchants grew rich on trade, and on their own exports of agricultural products, horses and pearls. For most of recorded history, Qatif and nearby Tarut Island were the centre of maritime trade on the Gulf. Sinbad would almost certainly have called in at the port on his voyages to the south. The great Moroccan traveller, Ibn Battuta, visiting the oasis in the fourteenth century, described Qatif as 'a large, beautiful and prosperous city'.

Over the centuries, the oasis was coveted, fought over and occupied by the Persians and Byzantines, by early Muslim dynasties, by Ottoman Turks and Egyptians, and by local Arab tribesmen. Europeans, too, sought to control Qatif – the Portuguese by conquest in 1520, and later the Dutch and the British through alliances with local rulers.

In time the town's glory diminished as trade routes shifted away from the Gulf, although it remained a significant centre of population and prosperity. Somewhere I had seen a series of evocative black and white photographs taken in the late 1940s and early 1950s that capture Qatif as it was then, before the impact of modernity. In these images, groves of tall date palms border irrigated fields, dark-skinned men in turbans and voluminous white robes linger under the shady arches and palm-frond ceilings of the old *souk*, and the whitewashed, mud-brick houses of the merchant quarter are substantial and imposing. This was the Qatif I hoped to discover.

Doug was still having trouble pinpointing our location on the map, not surprising given that the maps in our street directory were years out of date and that all the street signs were scripted in Arabic. Still, we seemed inevitably to be drawing near to central Qatif.

A succession of wholesale and commercial plant nurseries full of neat green rows of shrubs and young trees bordered the highway that led us into the oasis. Sadly, there was little to be seen of the old date groves: they were being swallowed up by an ugly suburban sprawl. On the edges of town, ruined stands of dead and dying palms stood forlornly to attention in fields that were being cleared to make way for commercial centres and small factories.

Despite the rash of construction, Qatif did not look prosperous. In the age of petroleum it has been entirely eclipsed by oil towns like al Khobar and industrial cities like Jubail up the coast. Her residents, like many of the traditional residents of eastern Arabia, are minority Shia Muslims, and so are cut off from the lines of power and influence of the majority Sunni state. We surmised that most of the money set aside for development and infrastructure was passing them by, and that government handouts were going elsewhere.

Qatif's dusty commercial hub was rundown, her houses in need of maintenance. In the centre of town, marooned on a roundabout, sat an old *dhow*, one of the Gulf's traditional wooden ships, looking more like a shipwreck than a monument to the area's proud maritime past. A drive-in petrol station showed the new spirit of the times: the pumps were shaded by larger-than-life model cars sitting on top of tall poles.

We parked near the roundabout. From all sides, men carrying

rolled up prayer mats were converging on a large mosque at the far side of a barren, dusty field, drawn by the Friday sermon that was being broadcast from its minarets. Judging by the sound of the imam's amplified voice, they were being treated to an angry harangue.

'He's probably telling them to rise up and rid themselves of the foreign devils who have just wandered in,' quipped Doug, and we laughed hollowly.

And yet the town was more friendly than it first appeared. As we walked through narrow alleyways between modest dwellings, young men smiled at us. 'Hello! How is Qatif?' they yelled, and to their delight, Geoff called back *'Qatif zain!'* – Qatif is good – although really there was little to see.

Our guidebook directed us to a small group of derelict buildings behind the taxi station; amongst them, the half-destroyed shell of a traditional house. On its exposed upper level stood the remains of a hall with an arched doorway framed in graceful plaster arabesques. It was all that remained of the old merchant quarter that had once covered all of the razed field next to the mosque.

We piled back into the car and set off in search of Tarut Island. Tarut, with its excellent harbour, was Qatif's trading partner and link to the sea. The black and white 1950s photograph of the island is an aerial shot of spreading palm groves. In the centre are the ruins of a sixteenth-century fort, believed to have been built by the Portuguese. Close up against the fort are the flat, square roofs of a traditional village, its thick mud walls looking for all the world like the cells of a giant wasp's nest.

We were lost again. Doug held the map first this way and then that, squinting at it in puzzlement. An increasingly testy Geoff drove grimly on, trying to read the Arabic street signs with all the skill of a dyslexic first-grader. I had lost all sense of direction.

We came upon the island almost by chance. It lay across a short causeway, and we were not sure that we were actually there until we saw the crumbling red towers of the old fort looming up ahead of us above a roundabout. It looked smaller and more vulnerable than we had expected, as if a decent rainstorm would wash it away.

'Forget the cannons,' Captain Geoff said. 'Issue the men with spoons, and we'll take it from the front.'

The village was still there, nestled amongst the palms to the rear of the fort. We wandered through the empty labyrinth of its narrow alleys, following their twists and turns between walls that rose two and three storeys over our heads. Heavy wooden doors patterned with metal studs marked the entrances to the dwellings, and high up, lattice screens shielded recessed windows. There were signs of habitation – the movement of a curtain as we passed, the muffled sound of a radio, footprints in the sand – but a sense of abandonment hung over many of the houses. I ran my hands over the grainy surfaces of the mud-brown walls, imagining the hands that had patted and smoothed them into being long ago. In places the render had peeled away, exposing bricks of bleached coral.

The fort was surrounded by a high metal fence, and there was a sign that warned us to keep out. But there was a large hole in the fence where the mesh had been curled back, and no-one about to see or hinder us, so we slipped through.

Inside the fort at its lowest point, stone stairs led down into a well, where the still waters of the oasis reflected the sky. The steps were 5,000 years old, a relic of the Dilmun era. Until quite recently, the women of the surrounding villages had climbed down them to bathe.

A well-worn track led up the hill inside the fence. From the summit, we gazed down upon a trio of bulldozers parked next to a pile of mud-coloured rubble that lay at the edge of a tract of recently levelled ground. Apparently the locals prefer houses with plumbing and air-conditioning these days, and who can blame them?

We bought ice creams in a small shop near the roundabout, observed by a small group of children from the other side of the road.

'Hello!' they called.

'Hello!' we called back, and waved.

They dissolved into laughter. 'What iss your name?' called the oldest girl, to the admiration of her fellows, and they all took up the cry, 'What iss your name?' The friendliest kids we ever saw in Arabia.

Along the road leading down to the port, the massive hulks of old *dhows* lay high and dry, disintegrating. These wooden boats are not peculiar to Tarut Island. While massive oil tankers dock not far away at Ras Tanurah, one of the world's largest loading docks, much of the Gulf's local trade is still carried on *dhows*. They form the backbone of local fishing fleets. They ferry appliances and furniture and pots and pans up and down the coast in lots too small to fill a container, landing them at ports too small to receive a container ship. Larger *dhows* bring grain from Pakistan, and logs from Kenya.

In the harbour, formed by an extensive stone breakwater, a fleet of these wooden ships was moored. Still more of them lay beached in the tidal shallows, and from them came the sounds of hammering and sawing as their crews worked to prepare them for their next voyages.

It would have been fascinating to stroll out along the breakwater to look at the ships and the work of their carpenters more closely, but the guard at the entrance saw us as a risk to security, and barred our way.

Up on a grassy knoll overlooking the harbour, the bulldozers had been busy again. In what seemed to be an act of wanton destruction, Qasr Darin, the imposing nineteenth-century fort built by the Ottomans to protect their lucrative trade in pearls, had recently been levelled. In place of her walls, shattered mud bricks lay about in piles.

Close by the ruins stood a small café. We pushed aside the strips of flapping plastic that covered the door and wandered in. The café was empty. No-one sat at the white formica tables, and no food or drink graced the shelves behind the counters. The owner emerged from a back room in a crumpled white shirt and loose trousers, sleepily scratching his head.

We ordered coffee.

'*La!*' said the owner, clicking his tongue and jerking his chin up. 'No coffee.'

'*Fi* Pepsi?'

'*La*, No Pepsi.'

'What do you have?'

'Chicken and rice,' he replied, and I still don't know why that seemed so funny.

From the top of Jabal Qarah, a hill in the al Hasa oasis, the view is breathtaking. Stretching away to the horizon in every direction is a dark green ocean: the crowns of millions of date palms. Here and there other bare hills emerge from the plain, a minaret marks the presence of a village, or an accretion of modern buildings reveals a larger town. They create scarcely a ripple in the never-ending green.

Al Hasa is one of the largest naturally formed oases in the world. Its history is, if anything, even more fabulous than that of Qatif. Where Qatif ruled the sea routes of the Gulf, al Hasa sat at the hub of inland trade. It was an important stop for the great camel caravans that carried incense from Yemen in the south up to Mesopotamia in the north, and later westwards into central Arabia and on to Rome and Byzantium. Throughout the centuries, until the advent of the petroleum age, al Hasa maintained its dominance of trade and its status as the centre of economic and political power in the Gulf of Arabia. It is still the agricultural heartland of the Eastern Province.

We came by train on our first visit, arriving in the late afternoon. As we slipped through mile after mile of verdant green, I tried to imagine how the oasis must have appeared to earlier travellers swaying in from the barren wastes on the backs of their camels. I saw them exhausted by the long journey, their throats parched with thirst, their skin cracked and raw from the sun. Their arrival sets the dogs to barking, and voices call out asking what news they bring. After the glare of the desert, the cool shade is soothing to their eyes, and the gurgle of running water in the irrigation canals a delight to their ears. They plod down dusty roads to the centre of the oasis, passing shepherd boys tending flocks of goats and sheep, and men driving donkey carts piled   high with cattle fodder. Small children rush from their houses to watch their progress. As evening settles, the soft light of lanterns and smoky aromas from cooking fires accompany them on the way to the *caravanserai* where they will pass the night.

We emerged from the station into Hofuf, the largest town in the oasis, just before sunset. Because it was Ramadan, the citizens were engaged in a mad scramble to get home in time to break the fast with their families. It was difficult to find a taxi driver who would agree to take us to our hotel, but eventually one of them said that he would, as long as we didn't mind him delivering one of his friends home at the same time. In the ensuing ride, we became completely disoriented.

The town we drove through was thriving. A long street of auto spare parts shops displayed an endless selection of hub caps, mufflers, radiators and fan belts, evidence that Hofuf was still the setting off point for long desert journeys. Around the taxi stand, tea houses were preparing to open, and kebabs and chickens were already turning on charcoal spits in brightly lit restaurants.

At the Hofuf Hotel we were welcomed into a pleasant café overlooking a shady grove of palms. Our waiter brought us cloudy black coffee and dates flavoured with honey and cardamom to break the fast.

The next morning the streets were full of people, and the area surrounding the market had come to life. In the middle of a traffic island an old man sat selling brown tubers that at first I took to be potatoes. To my astonishment, a closer inspection revealed them to be large truffles, their growth sparked by recent rains in the area. At SR200 (US$53) a box they were expensive, but if I had had access to a kitchen, I would surely have bought some.

In the kitchenware street, shining aluminium cooking pots were stacked one on top of the other in descending order of size. The ones at the bottom were large enough to be used in the preparation of *kabbzah*, the most popular dish in all Arabia.

The preparation of *kabbzah*, as far as I can determine, is as follows:

1. Into a large pot place the entire carcass of a sheep, a goat or a small camel.
2. Add some seasonings – onions, allspice, cinnamon, and another spice that looks exactly like lichen chipped from a rock.
3. Cover with water and bring to the boil; then simmer until tender
4. Now add rice – a lot of rice – and turmeric or saffron to make it a rich yellow. Stir, then cover the pot and cook until the rice has absorbed the liquid. Add a few generous dollops of butter and stir them in.
5. Turn the *kabbzah* out onto an enormous brass platter, and have your servants carry it in to your guests as they sit cross-legged on a carpet. Eat *kabbzah* with your fingers. Make sure that the choicest morsels go to your guests.

Closer to the *souk* we picked our way through makeshift stalls partitioned with lengths of black cloth and bright blue plastic tarpaulins propped up on sticks. Veiled women sat cross-legged amongst cloth-wrapped bundles, silently holding out tea towels, tablecloths and embroidered pillowcases for us to inspect, waving us closer with their hands.

The way into the *souk* proper was through a series of arched entrances in a low wall shaded by tattered and faded canvas awnings. From the moment I stepped inside, I was captivated. We found ourselves in a dark, narrow alley, where the only illumination was that spilling out from the stalls ranged along its sides, each one lit by bare, low-watt light bulbs. As the alley receded into the distance it was criss-crossed by other alleys, so that the market felt like a giant all-enveloping, rabbit warren. Women padded by us in their black gowns, almost disappearing in the near dark. The white *thobes* of the men glowed softly in the gloom.

A rush of fragrances assailed me: spicy cinnamon and cumin, sweet jasmine and orange blossom essence, musty saffron, henna and musk, sharp camphor and cedar, rich sandalwood, musk and vanilla, tea leaves and coffee beans, orris root, frankincense and beeswax. The odours curled about me and went straight to my head.

At an incense shop stacked from floor to ceiling with bags and barrels and bottles and boxes we paused. Beside me a woman reached a hand out from under her black cloak to pick up a small ball of clay and sawdust infused with oil. She held it up to her veiled nose and inhaled deeply, then held it out to me.

'This very beautiful,' she said.

'What do you do with it?' I asked, taking a hearty sniff. It smelled of roses. She tried to explain, but gave up.

'Very lovely, very beautiful,' she repeated.

At last, spontaneous contact. As she wandered away, I felt a rush of gratitude, but I didn't buy the rose balls.

Instead I bought SR40 (US$11) worth of Persian saffron. The shopkeeper scooped it out of a large glass jar into a horn of paper and twisted it closed, more saffron than I had ever thought to possess. For the rest of that journey I would swoon to its heady aroma every time I opened my suitcase.

On a later visit we drove down to al Hasa, and this time we were able to explore the oasis beyond Hofuf. The roads followed the course of wide concrete channels filled with rapidly flowing water out to where lush crops of lucerne, lettuce, rocket, coriander and onions flourished in the dappled shade of date palms; where melon and grape vines tumbled over trellises in orchards of apricot, pomegranate, quince, fig and lemon; and where black and brown goats and squads of chickens foraged in fallow fields. The water that surges through al Hasa's aqueducts (in 1950, the output from one well alone was measured at 90,000 litres per minute), and that sustains all of this life is thought to have fallen to earth as rain more than 25,000 years ago.

Eight or so kilometres east of Hofuf we came to Jabal Qarah, a large outcrop of pale sandstone topped by a layer of darker, harder rock. The forces of erosion had been at work on the *jabal*, rounding its hard cap, and washing away the softer rock underneath. The slabs that had calved off from the *jabal* looked like thatched African huts rising up amongst the square houses of the village at the foot of the hill.

We had come to see Jabal Qarah's famous caves, although I confess that I'm not much of a cave person. I feel that I've seen my share of dank holes smelling of bat urine, and of rock formations with names like 'the Seven Dwarves' or 'the Bridal Veil'. The approaches to the caves at Jabal Qarah did nothing to cheer me: a narrow concrete path winding into a small canyon, a dilapidated public amenities block, a scattering of litter that hadn't quite made it into the overflowing bins, a single electric wire strung between poles leading into the cave. Just before the entrance, the wire had been severed. Terrific! I thought. We'll be stumbling around in the dark.

And soon we were doing just that. But the caves were like nothing I had imagined. A network of vertical fissures ran back deep into the *jabal*, so narrow in places that just one person could pass through at a time. We groped our way through the inky blackness, our footsteps muffled in a carpet of soft, dry sand. The air in the caves was still and warm, the silence profound. Occasional rays of sunlight filtered down from cracks high above us, lighting up airborne motes and flooding into chambers hollowed from the rock. I felt that if I listened closely enough, I might hear the whispers of lost generations; that this impossibly ancient place was at once cathedral and womb.

Seen from the air, Arabia is a brown and barren land; a mineral landscape sculpted by lava flows and erosion. In some places, however, a pattern of perfect, bright green circles interrupts the desert waste. Each one is a field of wheat or alfalfa irrigated by a line of sprinklers pivoting slowly about a fixed point.

In the 1980s, as a matter of national pride, the Kingdom embarked on a program to make itself not only self-sufficient in, but an exporter of wheat. Soon the crop circles were turning out up to five million tons of grain each year, five times the nation's needs. But this success came at a price. For the money that was paid in subsidies to farmers to produce each ton of wheat, the Saudis could have imported four times that amount from Australian or American suppliers. In the absence of an established market, much of the crop was given away or simply left to rot.

The true cost of the wheat program, however, is measured not in financial terms, but in the squandering of water resources. Spray irrigation is hardly efficient: much of the fine mist that sustains the wheat crop is lost to evaporation in the parched air and harsh sunlight. Although the agriculture program has now been cut back and farmers are being encouraged to use more efficient forms of irrigation, water levels in the aquifers are falling, and irrigators are forced to drill ever deeper to reach the water that remains in them.

We followed an irrigation channel out of the town of al Kharj, about 100 kilometres south-east of Riyadh, to get to the wells of Ayn Dhil. There, at the head of the channel, water was gushing from pipes feeding into a holding tank beside an old pump house. Behind the pump house, a hole in the ground roughly ten metres in diameter marked the site of one of the wells. It was surrounded by a high mesh fence.

We watched as a pick-up truck drove up in a billow of dust and crunched to a halt, disgorging a small crowd of youths. They strolled up to the fence, eased themselves through a gap where the mesh had been curled back, and made their way with a show of bravado to the edge of the hole, where they stood gazing into the depths. The spectacle didn't hold their attention for long. Soon they had piled back into the truck and were speeding away.

After they left, I too squeezed through the fence and edged towards the crumbling rim. Once the waters appeared at ground level in this aquifer. By the late 1970s the level had dropped by about fifteen metres, and men and boys who wished to swim there had to climb down a ladder to dive into the water.

I stood as close as I dared to the edge, and, fighting a wave of vertigo, craned to look down. Below me I could see swifts flitting back and forth and perching briefly on the craggy walls, but there was no sign of water. Today, it lies more than seventy-five metres below the surface.

In their love affair with water, the Saudis have installed avenues of thirsty trees, and green parks with public fountains in their cities. They have surrounded their villas with lush gardens, lawns and swimming pools, and fitted out their bathrooms with showers, spas and flushing toilets. Each year, their cities use up over 2,000 billion litres of water. Half of this is desalinated sea water; the rest is fossil water pumped from underground sources. Once used, it cannot be replaced. Public awareness campaigns urging citizens to conserve water have so far had little impact.

Compounding the problem, two thirds of Saudi households are not hooked up to sewage treatment plants. Their waste water is simply pumped out into the desert and left to evaporate, or to filter down and pollute the underground reserves.

Saudi Arabia is not the only nation faced with looming water shortages, and the Saudis are not the only people who are mindlessly squandering this most precious resource. But their lands are amongst the driest and most marginal in the world. How long, I wondered, will the fountains continue to gush and the sprinklers continue to drench the gardens and the trucks continue to deliver tanker loads of fresh water to thirsty villas in sprawling cities? What will these cities look like in another hundred years? And if the waters fail, will modern Saudis be as resilient as their desert-dwelling forebears?

6

BLACK BAGS AND
PRECIOUS PEARLS

And women shall have rights similar to the rights against them, according to what is equitable; but men have a degree of advantage over them.
HOLY QURAN, 2:28

I n the centre of the room, young dancers were crowded onto a raised floor. As they jigged about to the loud thump of a reggae beat, spotlights bathed them in colour: now blue, now green, now red. A mirror ball suspended from the ceiling revolved slowly, emitting tiny shafts of light that twirled across the far walls and slid over us as we sat lounging at the tables. As the song ended, the dancers applauded wildly.

Next the DJ put on a popular Arabic song, filling the room with the sinuous rhythms of a stringed orchestra and hand-beaten drums. The young dancers groaned in disgust, but now older ones arose from their seats. Dark-eyed women in chic Italian dresses tied chiffon scarves low on their hips and began an undulating belly dance. In a room filled with dancers aged from eight to eighty, there wasn't a male in sight. Even the DJ was operating by remote control from a room somewhere else in the building.

Yes, it was the all-female disco, courtesy of the Ladies Activities Committee. When it had first been suggested at one of our meetings, I had been puzzled. 'A disco?' I exclaimed, not quite able to get my head around the concept.

The ladies were enthusiastic. 'We can hold it in the recreation centre cafeteria,' they said. 'We'll hire a DJ. We'll get a caterer to prepare some finger food. It will be such fun, you'll see.'

And it was fun. For one night our cafeteria was transformed into a cavernous nightclub full of excited young girls and happy, relaxed, sexy women. The caterers had done us proud: the banquet table sagged under piles of kebabs and stuffed vegetables; trays of curry, barbecued chicken and steaming rice; mountains of fresh fruit and cans of icy soft drink. So much for finger food! Between dances we threw back glasses of Saudi champagne: apple juice mixed with fizzy lemonade.

But the night would not have been complete without a touch of drama. The rotating coloured filter on one of the spotlights became stuck; a member of the committee took the microphone to warn us that the DJ was coming in to fix it. In a flash the room faded to black as all but the youngest girls took refuge in their *abayas* and veils, leaving only the heady smell of their perfume in the air. As the brave young man made his way through the tables and climbed onto the stage, the teenagers erupted into giggles and screams, and then a chant in favour of Western music. 'ING-LISH! ING-LISH! ING-LISH!' they yelled, stamping their feet in time. His work done, the DJ bolted from the room, blushing furiously. In a flutter of black, the women re-emerged, laughing.

Outside in the car park, small groups of men stood about waiting to drive their womenfolk home . . . and waited . . . and waited. The party went on until well after three in the morning, proving – this time at least – the local saying that, while men may have all the power, it is the women who have all the fun.

Sadly, diversions like the disco were proving to be all too rare. After several months in the Kingdom, I was starting to find that the experience of being an expat wife was wearing thin.

I was not without resources. I had, in fact, come prepared for just this situation with a list of 'self-improving' activities. I had already started to explore Middle Eastern cuisine, and was able to serve up endless variations on eggplant, tomatoes and greens. Geoff, however, was in the habit of eating a large lunch at work with his colleagues, and wasn't all that interested in my efforts. He tried, but I had the impression that I was force feeding him. I tried yoga, but without a teacher found it hard to stay motivated. I sat down with my *Teach Yourself Arabic* book and cassettes, but after I had learned to count to ten and to greet people my enthusiasm wavered. There was little opportunity to practise the language: the local lingua franca was more English than Arabic. I spent hours watching the ghostly images on our sad old television, the endlessly recycled programs of the BBC World Service. The days melted into each other in a vapid blur. I was stymied, overwhelmed with a sense of futility. In short, I was bored.

Some of the less attractive aspects of my personality were riding dangerously close to the surface. Although I was still conscientious in my determination not to be a whinger, I had become more demanding. I desperately needed to escape from the apartment, and if that meant leaning on Geoff to drive me somewhere at the end of his working day, so be it. It didn't help that we had so few places to go to, apart from the local restaurants and shopping malls. How I longed for a cinema.

Like many of the wives, I turned to retail therapy, as if this was the price we extracted from our husbands to compensate us for our sacrifice in joining them in the Kingdom. I developed a desire for oriental carpets and elaborate gold jewellery. A good investment, I told a horrified Geoff. He reminded me that we were there to save money. I realised that he was right, and restrained my impulse to shop, but secretly I fumed. Used to having my own income, I resented not being able to spend as I liked, resented having to ask for an allowance.

Worst of all, I was settling into a kind of dull passivity. At times I withdrew into exasperated silence: what, I asked myself peevishly, could I possibly talk about when I was so deprived of stimulation? The shopping trips had ceased to amuse me. The endless round of tea parties had become tedious. There was still the library and the swimming pool at the recreation centre to draw me out of my apartment, but they did not fill the void left by a lack of meaningful employment. I felt as if I was frittering my life away.

It came as a relief, and not just for me, when Linda called. Would I, she asked, be interested in taking over her English class at the British Council in Dammam?

Would I? I jumped at the chance

'There's just one thing,' she said. 'You'll have to wear an *abaya*.'

Oh dear. At this stage I still could not look upon Arabia's cloaked and veiled women without thinking of bats or spooks or vampires. I immediately thought of our Aramco friend Gail's story. She had gone back to Ireland for her father's seventy-fifth birthday. She didn't tell him she was coming; she wanted to surprise him, and in this she succeeded beyond her wildest expectations. When everyone was assembled at the party, she entered the room covered from head to toe in her Arabian black, bearing a cake ablaze with seventy-five candles. Before she could whip off her disguise, an expression of horror spread over her poor old father's face. He thought that the grim reaper had come for him armed with a foretaste of the fires of damnation.

Geoff took me in to al Shula Mall to a shop that sold *abayas* and *ghutras*. The shopkeeper, a genial old Arab with a neatly trimmed grey beard, took one look at us and brought out his cheapest number: SR60 (US$16) for a shiny polyester *abaya* with studs down the front and coloured brocade trim. It was about as attractive as a decorated garbage bag and, come summer, would have been as comfortable. I settled on a more expensive version in a light polyester-crepe fabric, its wide sleeves trimmed with bands of black velvet. In any other circumstances, it would have been elegant. The shopkeeper brought out a long black scarf that matched the velvet on the sleeves. I wrapped it twice around my head so that it circled my face and tucked it tightly in at the temples as I had seen the Arab ladies do, then checked the effect in the mirror. I looked like one of Macbeth's witches.

My disappearance delighted the shopkeeper, who chuckled wickedly as he handed me the finishing touch: a black veil. It was a strange little garment constructed of layers of gauze attached to a band that passed over the nose and above the ears to tie at the back of my head. Two thicknesses of cloth hung down over my lower face, and two thicknesses, attached to the band at the sides, flipped back over the top of my head. My eyes looked out through the narrow slit between them. If I wished, I could lower the top layer to achieve total blackout. The effect was suffocating.

I decided to pass on the scarf. Black was never my colour, and I already had one in a more flattering shade of blue and gold. As for the veil, I gladly left it in the shop. I knew that my pale eyes would never look as alluring as the dark ones of the Arab ladies gazing out from behind their veils. Besides, it was unlikely that I would ever be called upon to wear one.

An information sheet issued by the Australian Embassy in Riyadh states: 'As the Embassy understands it, the Saudi Government does not require non-Muslim women to wear the *abaya* or head scarves.' The same sheet advised us to dress conservatively, to avoid tight-fitting clothing, and to cover our arms and legs. In Dhahran and al Khobar this was sufficient, although in more conservative places we knew that Western women were forced to cover up, even to veil. Almost all of the Eastern Province's Western women hated *abayas*, and took pride in resisting the pressure to wear one. 'After all,' one American told me, quite unconscious of how patronising she sounded, 'we have to set an example for the Arabs.'

To expats, Saudi women in their *abayas* were 'black bags'. I, too, found the sight of them confronting, even after I had become accustomed to seeing them about me. I was appalled that women should seek to eliminate themselves from the landscape, or worse, that they should be forced to do so. Like most Westerners, I regarded the *abaya* as a form of oppression.

Now I wondered if my ideas were overly simplistic; if somehow I was confusing symbol and reality. I noticed that some of the Arabian women wore their robes with elegance and pride, and others with an air so everyday ordinary that it was as if they had put on a raincoat to go outside. I started to realise that the *abaya* might be seen in many different ways: not just as an imposition, but also as a liberator that allowed women freedom of movement. Even the veil, I thought, might give freedom of a sort. Might Saudi women be poking their tongues out at the world under all that black?

I couldn't wait to meet my Arabian students: there were so many questions I wanted to ask.

It was raining on my first day of teaching, a downpour that had started the day before and would go on without pause for days to come. The freeway to Dammam, built without drainage channels as befits a facility in the desert, was awash with lakes and troughs of water. Visibility was down to only a few metres. Even the redoubtable Mahmud was daunted as we wallowed along the road, wipers batting furiously across the windscreen, our sleeves wiping small peepholes in the fogged-up windows. Other drivers seemed not to have noticed the weather, and roared past us at their usual breakneck speed.

'Shhhh . . . *aitan!*' gasped Mahmud, visibly paling as a car loomed out of the rain and missed us by inches. Further along, emergency vehicles with flashing lights were attending a multi-car pile-up. At the clover-leaf interchange two highway patrol officers were peering down into the desert some fifteen metres below at a crumpled vehicle that, before it had become airborne, had bitten a neat, car-shaped hole in the safety rail. Near the Dammam turn off, a large, green American car was balanced on its nose and wrapped vertically around a light pole like a slice of bread around a sausage at a barbecue.

Our destination on the outskirts of Dammam was a cream-coloured, three-storey building with a billboard on the roof that proclaimed it to be the Women's Charity Center. Its windows were hidden behind brass filigree screens, and a high concrete wall surrounded it. A short dash through the pelting rain brought me into a world that was entirely female.

The first floor of the south wing housed a school for mentally disabled children, who could sometimes be seen playing happily with their carers in the central indoor playground. The rest of the building, apart from a small cafeteria and some offices, was devoted to classrooms. The centre had the dual aims of giving young women vocational training as well as somewhere to go outside their homes. It offered classes in sewing, hairdressing, child care, computers and languages: French and English. The British Council had been given two classrooms and an office at the rear of the north wing.

The five earnest young women waiting for me in my classroom had removed their *abayas* to reveal fashionable fitted blouses and long skirts. (Trousers were not permitted in the centre.) They regarded me with guarded expressions, sizing me up.

They had given Linda, their previous teacher, a hard time. One look at her straight black hair and dark eyes had convinced them that she was not English, but Japanese. This time they wanted to be sure they were getting the genuine article. My blonde hair reassured them. How could they have known that they had traded an upper-class British accent for an Australian one?

I had been warned that they did not take well to Western teaching methods; that they would be uncooperative, difficult and demanding. In fact, they settled down to work determinedly. Everything I asked them to do they did diligently, even asking for homework when I failed to set it for them. Geoff, still grappling with classes full of unmotivated young men, could not believe my luck.

My students were serious, but with a quick and ready wit. They knew nothing of the world, and very little even of their own country, having never travelled beyond their own region. They were deeply pious. At the mid-morning break they donned their *abayas*, covered their hair, and knelt down in a corner of the class-room to pray.

Their one concern was that we finish the prescribed textbook in our six-week course. They had paid to do so, and they intended to get their money's worth. Any modification of the exercises in the book made them uneasy.

There was, however, a problem. In classic British style, the book never missed an opportunity to drop in a reference to bacon, or to make a little joke about alcohol. 'I like ice cream,' it read. 'I like whisky.' 'Would you like a ham sandwich?' I tried to skip over the offending words.

'Teacher, what is "whisky"?'

'It's a drink; it is alcohol,' I explained. There was a short conference in Arabic.

'Teacher, it is *haram*, yes?'

'Yes, *haram*.'

They nodded wisely, and conferred again. 'It is not a problem,' they assured me.

But it was a problem, because the director of the centre kept a close eye on our lessons to ensure that there was nothing un-Islamic taking place in them. I had to keep looking over my shoulder to make sure that my class was not being monitored.

When classes finished at midday, the women from the centre put on their *abayas* and veils and spilled out onto the street, where their husbands, brothers, fathers and drivers were waiting to take them home. Mahmud was usually there too, but sometimes when another customer kept him busy, he arrived late.

One day he was particularly late. I watched as the students piled into their cars. I watched the car park gradually empty. Finally only one woman was left there beside me. She was covered in black from head to toe, with only her eyes visible through the slit in her veil. I recognised the mature shape and imposing posture of the director of the centre. I smiled.

'Has anyone talked to you,' she asked me, 'about covering your head?'

'No, they haven't,' I replied, somewhat disingenuously. Linda had warned me that I would come under pressure to wear a headscarf.

'Please,' she said, 'it would be a good idea if you put on your scarf. Here there are many spies from the government who are watching everything we do. Always they are coming here, waiting to see some bad behaviours, and if they see them, they will go back to the authorities and tell them they must close us down.'

The spies were the local *muttaween*. Although I hadn't seen them there yet, I knew that they were often to be found hovering around like angry hornets, a scourge to the girls and an ever present threat to the centre itself. They disapproved of education for women and believed that the proper place for our students was at home with their families. At the merest sign of immorality – an unveiled face or an *abaya* fastened too loosely – they would pounce.

I was not too concerned about a confrontation with the

muttaween. I had my *abaya* on and a scarf laying loosely about my shoulders, ready for just such a situation. But forced to weigh my desire for freedom of expression against the rights of the young women of Dammam to an education, I felt I had only one choice.

I took my scarf and tied it over my hair. It seemed the least I could do.

When Princess Effat, widow of King Faisal, died in January 2000, her son Prince Turki penned a moving tribute to his mother. 'When you decided, you and your husband, that your sons and daughters deserved an education, you did not bring home teachers for them; you built learning centers that are still there benefiting all,' he wrote. 'When the drive to educate boys in the Kingdom was launched, you campaigned to make the education of girls equal to that of boys. It was a defining moment in King Faisal's history when a group of prominent citizens came to him protesting the establishment of girls schools in their region. He told them: "If you don't want to educate your girls, it is up to you. Don't send them to schools. But, for those who wish to educate their daughters I will open schools, even if they be in the middle of deserts".' (*Arab News*, February 29, 2000)

Education for girls was widely regarded as a challenge to traditional values, one that would undermine a woman's time-honoured roles as wife and mother, and her husband's role as master of his family. As late as 1963 the National Guard had to be called out to control protesters who were threatening to assault a building in Buraydah that they suspected was to be used as a school for girls.

Traditional education in the Kingdom came in the form of *madrassa* schools, where boys learned to recite the Quran. The first modern boys school did not open until the 1940s. The first girls school was opened in Jeddah in 1956 under the sponsorship of Princess Effat. Because she knew that education for girls would be controversial, the Dar al Hanan, or House of Affection, started life disguised as an orphanage.

Despite royal attempts at persuasion, Saudi families were at first reluctant to send their daughters to the Dar al Hanan, but by 1957 the school had enough students enrolled to go public with its aims. Princess Effat was careful to argue that girls should be educated so that they could become better mothers, better homemakers, and better Muslims. Her own aims were broader. 'A girl can carry out any job properly and can do anything,' Madam Rouchdy, the general manager of school, recalls her saying, 'as long as she behaves and dresses according to Islamic rules. She has no limitation as long as she is not exposed to any physical danger.' (*Arab News*, March 9, 2000)

Girls schools were soon established throughout the Kingdom. When a group of renegade zealots seized the Grand Mosque in Mecca in 1979 and included in their list of demands that higher education for girls be banned, the battle had already been lost. Today, all girls go to school and more girls than boys go on to university.

Education is strictly segregated: girls schools, boys schools; women's universities, men's universities. Male teachers at women's universities deliver their lectures to empty auditoriums; their female students watch the proceedings on closed-circuit television in another lecture theatre. Questions are passed to the lecturer by way of written notes placed in a tray. When the teacher needs some feedback from his students, he asks 'Do you understand?' and the girls press a buzzer in reply.

Separate, but far from equal. Everything I read and everything I learned from my students convinced me that, compared to their brothers, girls in the state system face inferior facilities, teachers who are less qualified, and limited access to resources such as libraries and gymnasiums. Studies for women are restricted to fields that are deemed to be appropriate for them. They may study nursing, but not medicine; interior decorating, but not architecture. Most women are enrolled in teacher training, Islamic studies, nursing and social science courses, because these fields offer the greatest chance of employment. Little wonder that many of the elite sidestep the state system, preferring to send their daughters (and their sons, for that matter) to American or European schools and universities both within the Kingdom and abroad.

Despite the limitations of the state system, demand for tertiary study places far exceeds supply, and many young women end their high school days having failed to secure a place, with marriage as their only option. Private colleges are being established to ease some of the pressure. Offering courses in computers, business, translation, pharmacology, fine arts and even engineering, they hold the promise of wider career choices for women in the future.

As students, young women tend to be more motivated than young men, and to perform better on comparative tests. Many claim that this is because they have so few diversions, and little else to do but study. My encounters suggested a different explanation: that young women are feeling the winds of change. They hope that they will be called upon to play a part in their nation's development, one that will see a redefinition of their traditional roles. They are ready to rise to the challenge, although the obstacles they face are enormous.

I had been in the Kingdom long enough to realise that any change in their status would be neither rapid nor dramatic. But through education, Saudi women were preparing themselves. I was glad to become a part, however small, of the process.

At the Women's Center, I had graduated to teaching an evening class of fifteen women. The students' English language skills were at intermediate level, so I was looking forward to some genuine exchanges that might give me insight into their lives.

They were a mixed group. Some were teenagers, others were in their twenties and thirties. Some came to class after a day spent at university or at work, others were full-time mothers. Some were from privileged backgrounds; they came to class accompanied by their maids, who then sat outside in the hallway for the duration. Most were not so privileged.

'Why do you want to learn English?' I asked in that first lesson. A few said that it was purely for their own enjoyment. 'I need English to shop', they told me, or 'I like to watch English videos', or 'I need it when I travel', or 'I like to study English, it is my hobby'. Most of the group, however, had more serious intentions:

'My children study English at school, and I want to help them.'

'I must learn English to get a place in the university.'

'I go to university and my classes are in English.'

'I want to be an English teacher.'

'I want to get a job. English will give me a better chance.'

The group included a Quranic studies teacher, a teacher of Arabic, a preschool teacher, and the headmistress of a girls school. However, the university students, most of them aspiring teachers, were gloomy about their future career prospects. They told me that it was difficult to find work, that without connections it was almost impossible. In the hope of securing paid employment, one young social work graduate had worked as a full-time volunteer in a local hospital for more than a year, but when I asked her about her chances, she shrugged hopelessly.

'I love my work,' she told me. 'I love to help people, and I work very hard. But I think never I will get the job.'

These women reminded me of students I had taught in Australia: newly arrived immigrants full of hope and resolve, anxious to begin a new life, but essentially social outsiders wondering if they would ever be able to break in.

In an *Arab News* article, journalist Molouk Y. Ba-Isa took issue with a Western report that claimed Saudi women only 'hold jobs in professional fields where men are inappropriate, as doctors, nurses, teachers and bankers who cater to women . . . I didn't know whether to laugh or cry,' she wrote. 'In one split second all the ladies who worked as interior designers, dressmakers, clerks, and computer programmers were written off. What happened to the businesswomen, the artists and the laboratory researchers? . . . According to [the report], as a journalist, I didn't exist either . . . Why is it that just because we Saudi women are not readily visible, the West diminishes the value of our contributions?' (*Arab News*, May 28, 1999)

She has a point. More and more Saudi women are entering the

workforce, and the range of work available to them is opening up. Increasingly, social commentators insist that women must be allowed to participate in the nation's economy, whether as employees, businesswomen or investors.

There is nothing in Islam which forbids a woman from working. Indeed, the Prophet's first wife, Khadija, was both a successful merchant and his employer. Local tradition, however, puts many obstacles in the way of women who want to work.

Chief amongst these is the Saudi notion of family honour, which gives rise to an almost total public segregation of the sexes. To preserve themselves from even the suspicion of moral or physical danger, women cannot work in any situation that involves face-to-face contact with men. They must look for positions that enable them to remain cloistered, or in which they will deal with an exclusively female or juvenile clientele.

Even if a woman is lucky enough to find such a position, she faces countless other difficulties, from her family's possible reluctance to allow her to work, to the more practical issue of just how she is to get to her job, given that she is forbidden to drive and that there is a lack of public transport for women in most towns in the Kingdom.

Some 50 percent of women who graduate from Saudi universities are unable to find work. Of the 600,000 women who do hold jobs, 400,000 are expatriates. The vast majority of Saudi working women are still employed in the caring professions.

By far the most popular choice of career for girls is teaching, but an oversupply of female teachers in the girls schools of the larger population centres means that new graduates can find positions only in rural or remote areas. To accept one of these positions, a woman must solve the problem of transport (by persuading a family member to drive her, or by hiring a driver for a long, expensive and possibly dangerous daily commute) or agree to live separately from her family – an unthinkable proposition for most.

Nursing would seem, on the face of it, to be an obvious career choice. After all, Saudi hospitals are full of female patients who can only be cared for by female medical staff, and state officials publicly proclaim their desire to replace the legions of expatriate nurses with locals. Yet despite campaigns to promote nursing as a respectable career, most Saudis think that a nurse is little better than a maid, and it has proven difficult to attract young women to the profession. It is even harder to retain them. Husbands and fathers disapprove of the long hours and the night shifts required, and when the demands of job and family conflict, a Saudi woman must place her family first. In 1999, Saudis made up only 14 percent of nurses in government hospitals, and only 1 percent of those in private hospitals (*Arab News*, May 21, 1999).

There are openings for women in areas such as the media, banking, design, technology and market research, and in specialised health and education fields, but these jobs are still the privilege of a lucky, Western-educated elite.

In the absence of opportunities for formal employment, many women take matters into their own hands and set themselves up in business. Often they are driven by need: they may have an unemployed husband, or be widowed or abandoned with a family to support. Many are involved in small-scale enterprises, working from home as dressmakers or beauticians. Others work at the very highest level as executives in large-scale businesses. The Olayan Financing Company, which manages the Saudi and Middle Eastern affairs of the giant Olayan Group, one of the Kingdom's leading business conglomerates, is headed in all but name by a woman, Lubna Olayan. In typically Saudi fashion, she receives barely a mention in the local press.

For working women the day-to-day frustrations caused by the gender divide are legion. Even a simple matter such as bringing in a repairman to fix a computer or photocopier is fraught with difficulty. At the Women's Center, we had to wait until the last classes of the evening were done and the students and staff had gone home before technicians could come in to fix our machines. The patience of the centre management in dealing with these annoyances never ceased to astonish me.

In 1998, according to an article in the *Arab News*, the Dhahran Palace Hotel Ramada took the unprecedented step of hiring seven Saudi women to staff its reservations office, having found that their attempts to hire and retain Saudi men for these positions were unsuccessful. The work, which included secretarial duties, handling the telephone switchboard and logging room reservations, involved no face-to-face contact with men. The hotel took care to ensure that the women's honour was preserved: they worked in isolation, always in groups of at least two, and always in their *abayas*. Their food was supplied so that they would have no need to go out, and they were driven, always in groups, to and from work. Despite these precautions, the hotel manager reported problems. The women had to put up with obnoxious phone calls and heckling. Some men refused to deal with them over the telephone, and insisted that a male member of staff take their call. The hotel was visited by the *muttaween*, who asked to inspect the premises and to speak to the women so as to bully them into resigning. The women themselves were delighted with their jobs. 'It was so boring sitting at home,' said one. 'I don't need to work for the money,' said another, 'but I need to work for my mind.' The hotel management announced that they were pleased with the experiment, and would continue to employ the women (*Arab News*, January 17, 1999).

'Tell me about *thobes*,' I said to my class one day. 'How do your men stay so clean?'

I was intrigued by the long white shirts, worn almost as a uniform by Saudi males. The *thobe* industry was enormous. Al Khobar had hundreds of tailor shops, some of them of surpassing luxury, where men could be seen submitting to the tape measure and pondering their selection from rack upon rack of white broadcloth. In the display windows, the *thobes* worn by headless mannequins were almost Victorian in their primness, with their high, parchment-hard collars and starched white cuffs.

The men always looked impeccably fresh and crisp in their whites, and even small boys dressed Wee Willie Winkie-style stayed spotlessly clean. I suspected that businessmen kept a supply of freshly laundered *thobes* in their briefcases to cope with the inevitable grime and spills of a working day.

'I will tell you the truth,' said one woman. 'In my house I have many servants, but my husband asks me to wash his *thobes* and to iron them too!'

'My husband too,' another chimed in.

'And my father.'

'My brother is the same.'

'But why?' I asked. 'Can't you send them to the drycleaners?'

'No,' said the first woman. 'He wants me to wash them with my own hands. He says that this is the wife's job. When she washes his *thobes*, she is showing her love for him.'

'How many *thobes* does your husband own?'

'I don't know . . . He has maybe fifty or sixty, maybe more.'

Later I asked the women to tell me about their *abayas*.

'When I was small I was hating the *abaya*,' said Amal, a confident eighteen-year-old, 'but now I like it very much.'

At KFUPM I had seen young girls in their first *abayas* looking like young fillies, all legs and arms as they struggled to control their billowing robes. In al Rashid Mall I saw small groups of teenage girls strolling languidly past groups of boys, pointedly ignoring them. Now and then one would casually allow her *abaya* to slip from a shoulder and to trail across the floor behind her. But by age eighteen or so, all had settled into demure woman-hood, and had their *abayas* firmly under control.

For young girls, the donning of their first *abaya* is a rite of passage, and they approach it in much the same spirit as young Western girls do the purchase of their first bra. The most pious student in the class, nineteen-year-old Nuria, told us how she had insisted on having her first *abaya* at the age of eleven, although her parents pleaded with her to delay, and how proud and grown up she had felt when she wore it. Now she and her classmates looked back upon their childhood with intense nostalgia. 'When I put on my *abaya* for the first time, I put on all the cares and responsibilities of an adult,' she said, and the rest of them nodded ruefully.

'With my *abaya* I can go shopping wearing my usual clothes,' said Waleda, 'or even my pajamas, without being embarrassed.' I found it difficult to imagine the elegant nineteen-year-old in any but the most fashionable of clothing, but I could see her point. The *abaya* was convenient, if nothing else – it could be thrown on over whatever we were wearing at home before an excursion to the world outside, and the headscarf eliminated bad-hair days. Some of my Western friends had discovered that an *abaya* enabled them to forgo the expat uniform of baggy, form-concealing clothing and to wear something more fashionable.

'I think black is the most splendid colour,' Waleda continued. 'and I can't imagine an *abaya* with other colours like yellow, red, green and blue. That is disgusting! The *abaya* imposes on the woman a special way of talking, walking and moving.'

At first all *abayas* seemed alike to me: black bags; nothing more. But as I started to notice what my students were wearing, I realised that they saw their cloaks as a fashion statement. This one appeared in a fine georgette number embroidered with swirls of black; that one in a robe of silk crepe with tassels at the throat and sleeves; another in a slim silk sheath lined in the palest peach chiffon. In the shops hundreds of styles were available – *abayas* in cotton, rayon, silk, wool or polyester; *abayas* voluminous or sleek, lined and unlined; *abayas* trimmed with velvet or satin or brocade, or quite plain. Some of them were beautiful, and some women wore them with elegance and grace.

It was a grace that eluded me. My *abaya* tripped me as I climbed the stairs, and choked me as I stood up from my chair with my foot on the hem. I caught its loose sleeves on doorknobs, and caught its skirts in doors. Once I even wore it inside out, unable to tell the difference in the dim light of my apartment. When I realised my mistake I was out in public, and it would have been scandalous to whip it off and turn it right side out.

'I don't like the *abaya*,' announced Salma, a feisty sixteen-year-old, 'but I like the *hijab* because this is what Islam wants the woman to wear.'

Hijab is a general term for the modesty in dress prescribed by Islam, and is variously interpreted in different Muslim cultures. In Turkey it is a scarf covering the hair; in Afghanistan it is the *burka*. In the Gulf, it is the *abaya* and the veil. The quality of *hala*, or modesty, is one of the key virtues of Islam, and is much prized in both men and women. A story I once heard that dates from the early days of Islam illustrates its importance. According to this tale, a woman hears that her only son has been killed in a battle. In a panic she runs out into the street to find out what has happened, but before she does, she takes the time to cover up.

When asked how she had the presence of mind to do this, she replies: 'I may have lost my son, but I have not lost my *hala*.'

The Quran says that women should cover themselves. 'And say to the believing women that they should lower their gaze and guard their modesty, that they should not display their beauty and ornaments except what must ordinarily appear thereof; that they should draw their veils over their bosoms.' (Holy Quran 24:31) This text is somewhat ambiguous as to whether women should or should not cover their faces. However, my students assured me that the Prophet Mohammad considered that the veil was a sign of reverence and modesty in women, and that his own wives covered their faces.

All over the Islamic world, in places such as Algeria, Egypt, Turkey, Iran, Malaysia and Indonesia, women have adopted *hijab* as a statement of their Muslim identity, an assertion of Islamic values that has political as well as religious dimensions. Thirty years ago, their mothers may well have rejected *hijab* for Western dress and liberal, socialist or nationalist values; now the daughters are reversing the process.

It was my impression that for Saudi women the wearing of the veil was not a reassertion of Islamic values. Because they had never departed from tradition, their dress expressed its continuity.

Not every woman was an enthusiastic adherent of the veil and the *abaya*. The students in Marie's French language class professed shock when she arrived in black. 'Why do you wear it?' they demanded. 'We have to, but you don't.'

I asked Hibba, one of the Saudi ladies on the Activities Committee how she liked living back in Arabia after her years in the US. 'It's fine,' she said, and she fiercely pinched a fold of her *abaya*. 'Except for this!'

Back in the class, Salma was continuing her defence of *hijab*. 'The woman has to wear something to protect her and save her from bad eyes,' she said.

The literal translation of *hijab* is 'shield', and here we get to the heart of the matter. A woman can shield herself from harm and corruption by wearing her *hijab*. Women need to cover up, because the very sight of them is enough to arouse feelings of lust in a man. Westerners are apt to scoff at this. That's the man's problem, we protest. Why should women be forced to wear the burden? In Saudi Arabia, there is a crazy logic to the idea: women do need protection from men. The question is, which came first – the male obsession, or the disappearance of women behind the veil? I felt sure that if men and women had been allowed to mingle more freely there would have been far less sexual tension between them.

Maryam was one of the older students, a mother in her thirties. 'Some bad women use an *abaya* to cover their bad behaviour,' she said.

This is the other side of the coin. My students told me that even Saudi girls could behave badly, conducting affairs or keeping trysts with lovers under the anonymity of the veil. And it's not just women who use the *abaya* as a disguise. In the year before my arrival, a group of teenage boys in veils and *abayas* had attempted to gate crash a fashion show organised by the Ladies Activities Committee. In 1999 a group of Pakistani illegal immigrants attempted to evade police by passing themselves off as women, only to be exposed when an informer turned them in (*Arab News*, September 12, 1999).

But is was Nuria who had the final word. 'The *abaya* is one of the pillars of woman's dignity and respect,' she said firmly, 'because she is not a piece of cake, that many flies can taste or spit on . . . but she is a pearl in its shell. Nobody can see her beauty except her husband or her father, her brother, her uncle and her nephew.'

I listened with the feeling that I was learning far more from my students than they were learning from me. When I first went to Arabia, I had known what to think about the *abaya*: it was nothing more than a manifestation of patriarchal oppression, and given a choice women would cast off their veils. I had in mind the example of the misogynist Taliban in Afghanistan, who had decreed that women must cover themselves even to the extent of wearing soft shoes so that men would not be distracted by the sound of their tapping feet. I was aware that the Taliban drew much of their inspiration from the strict Saudi version of Islam, and that in Arabia the *muttaween* represented a similar attitude towards women. Now I had to modify my views; to acknowledge that Saudi women themselves took enormous pride in their dress.

Some of my students did complain that it was their brothers and their fathers who decreed how much they should cover themselves. More often though, like women everywhere, they dressed with the censure or approval of other women in mind. In conservative areas or in conservative company, they would cover up completely in *abaya*, veil, and even gloves and black stockings. In more liberated company, they might dispense with the veil and allow their faces to show.

Neither the white *thobes* of Saudi men nor the black robes of the women are practical garments. It is hard to imagine someone doing a hard day's manual labour in either. As well as representing the modesty of the wearer and his or her allegiance to Islam, these clothes speak of respectability and of social status. After all, only a very well-heeled society can afford to have its men dressed in spotless white, and its women completely cloistered. The veil and *abaya* have everything to do with self-esteem.

Again and again the women spoke of pride in their dress. They were proud of their exclusivity, proud to be Muslim, proud of their modesty. It occurred to me that the pearl in its shell was the oriental version of our own princess on a pedestal – a seductive idea, to be set up above the crowd and worshipped. But at what price?

For a short while I taught a class at the richly endowed Dhahran Arts Center, a recreation club frequented by the women of the area's elite families. The teenage girls who came to my class there were bright and articulate, and confident about the future.

'I want to be a dentist,' said one, 'because this country needs women dentists.'

'That's very true,' I said, and wished her well.

'I want to manage a five-star hotel,' said another with a determined, almost defiant expression on her face.

'That's great,' I said, full of admiration, and I wished her luck too. I didn't dare to add, 'You'll need it.'

Perhaps she was right to be optimistic. She had the talent and the resources and the connections to be whatever she wanted to be, even in Saudi Arabia.

The Arts Center was set up in the early 1980s under the sponsorship of Princess Mashael bint Faisal. It was housed in a large villa in an exclusive Dhahran neighbourhood, and no expense had been spared in fitting it out. A fabulous modern kitchen had recently been installed for the Italian cooking classes; the gym had a new sprung wooden floor for aerobics; the art studios were light and airy; the computer classroom was state of the art. The halls and common rooms were furnished with plush wall-to-wall carpets, generous drapery and soft couches, and were decorated with local artefacts and antiques – studded wooden chests, beautiful rugs, old brass and silverware, textiles and pottery – as well as with paintings by students in the art classes.

Like the Women's Charity building in Dammam, the Arts Center had been established to give women a place to go outside their homes. Unlike the Charity building, it catered to the wives and daughters of elite families. The women who frequented the Arts Center were sophisticated and self-assured. Many of them were Western-educated; most had travelled extensively, and some maintained apartments in Paris or London or New York. Their wealth eased the restrictions imposed upon their sex by society. Like the women at the KFUPM disco, they were having fun.

My time at the Arts Center was brief. The women there could be gracious and charming, and I was fascinated by my glimpse into the exalted circles in which they moved. Ultimately, however, I found the more modest circumstances and the real-life challenges of my students at the Women's Charity Center to be far more interesting.

The young women in Dammam were not unhappy. They enjoyed their classes. They had their hobbies. They loved to go shopping. They talked to their friends on their mobile phones. They treasured their families, and spoke of them with great affection. Every week they attended the endless tea parties that revolved through the houses of each of their aunties and sisters and female cousins in turn. And yet when they asked me how

I spent my spare time, and I told them about a party, or a trip to the beach, or a camping trip, or even a walk about the university campus, they looked at me wistfully.

They told me about the long hours they spent in their bedrooms studying, listening to music, passing the time. Of the envy they felt for the freedom that their brothers enjoyed, although in truth, there was little for young men to do besides hang out with their friends in coffee lounges, or drive their cars about. Their sisters, denied even these pleasures, were in the grip of an epidemic of boredom.

Of all the restrictions that I faced as a woman, the ban on driving was the most vexing. How I longed for the freedom to drive myself into town, or down to the beach, or out into the desert whenever I felt like a change of scene. How like a prisoner I felt without that simple freedom.

The ban created a heavy load for Saudi families too, whether they opted for the expense of hiring a driver, or whether the men chose to chauffeur their women and children about. Men complained that they had trouble observing normal working hours because they had to deliver their sisters or their children to school and pick them up afterwards, or that when they came home ready to relax at the end of a working day, their wives were desperate to be taken out. As for the families that could afford neither car nor driver, the options for women were limited indeed.

Even the authorities want to see the ban lifted, given that billions of riyals are sent out of the country in salary remittances to foreign drivers every year. Articles, no doubt officially sanctioned, appeared frequently in the press exploring the issue. Perhaps, it was suggested, licences could be issued to women over the age of thirty-five. Or perhaps women should be banned from driving alone, but might be permitted to drive their children to school. This proposal was abandoned when someone questioned how the mothers would manage to get themselves back home again once they had dropped their children off.

I expected that my students would be enthusiastic supporters of the right to drive. To my surprise, they were ambivalent about the issue.

'It is dangerous for a woman to drive alone,' said Maryam. 'The men and boys will be crazy when they see her.'

'What will happen if the car breaks downs? Maybe the woman will be raped,' said Waleda.

All over the Gulf, women are moving into areas previously closed to them. In Dubai, there are female taxi drivers (*Arab News*, May 5, 2000). In Kuwait, there was talk of women being recruited into the armed forces (*Arab News*, July 7, 1999). In Oman, women are taking their place in their nation's legislature. Saudi women have some way to go to catch up.

Things move very slowly in the Kingdom, and change must always be balanced against tradition. 'We'll open all doors for Saudi women to enable them to make their contributions,' said Crown Prince Abdullah in a 1999 address to a function in the Eastern Province (*Arab News*, April 21, 1999), but even crown princes are subject to censure if they suggest too radical a reform. The papers soon carried a clarification, issued by a source in the Prince's office, that his message 'should not be interpreted as a call for women's liberation' (*Arab News*, May 6, 1999).

Acts of rebellion are rare, although my students did tell me, with delight, about one Western-educated local doctor who was arrested for driving her car around the streets of Doha, and for failing to wear proper *hijab*. When she was subsequently fired from her job at a local hospital, her father came to her rescue and bought her a hospital of her own to work in.

Many of the women I met were convinced that change was on its way, although they expressed impatience with its slowness. 'We all know that Islam does not require this. It is only a Saudi custom,' they would announce in a tone of immense resignation whenever they spoke of the limitations they faced.

But, after all, it is not clear that every woman wants change.

At our Ladies Activity Committee meeting we were counting

the proceeds of our fete – some SR4,000. One of the Saudi ladies volunteered to send her son into al Khobar to deposit the amount into the committee's account at the Bank of Riyadh.

'Oh, but there's a women's branch in Pepsi Street now,' someone suggested brightly. 'You can go in and deposit it yourself.'

'Why should I do that when I can have my son do it for me?' she replied.

7

ROYAL FLUSH

I realised that the Bedu...were doomed. Some people maintain that
they will be better off when they have exchanged the hardship and
poverty of the desert for the security of a materialistic world.
This I do not believe.
WILFRED THESIGER, Arabian Sands

The posters first appeared late in 1998, pasted up in shop
windows all over al Khobar. They featured a stylised date
palm, its trunk formed by a vertically held drawn sword, super-
imposed upon the outline of a sandcastle fortress. Underneath
was an inscription in Arabic, then a caption in English that read
'K.S.A. 100 YEARS'.

I was perplexed. Try as I might, I could think of nothing that
had happened in 1898 or 1899 that could be regarded as a foundation event for the Kingdom. At that time the al Sauds had been
at the very nadir of their fortunes. Ousted in 1891 from their traditional seat of power in Riyadh by the rival al Rashid clan, they
were living in exile in what is now Kuwait. And then it dawned
upon me. Reckoning by the Islamic calendar, we were about to
celebrate 100 lunar, not solar, years of Saudi rule.

By our calendar, the Kingdom had its inception in 1902. At
that time, the western region, with its key cities of Jeddah,
Medina and Mecca, was ruled by the Hashemites (later to
become the wartime allies of Lawrence of Arabia) and their
Ottoman overlords. In the east and the north, too, the Ottomans

were the dominant power. The centre was held by the traditional rivals of the al Sauds, the al Rashids.

On January 15, 1902, under cover of darkness, a small raiding party of about twenty men scaled the mud-brick walls of Riyadh and hid in a private house overlooking the Mismak fortress. Their leader was Abdul Aziz ibn Saud, twenty-six years old, six foot two inches tall and son of the Saudi emir. When the unsuspecting governor and his entourage strolled out of their stronghold the next morning, the intruders were waiting for them. After a fierce skirmish, the fort and the town were theirs. The old fort, now a museum, is the model for the centennial poster. The point of a spear that broke off during the battle is still there, embedded in one of its massive wooden doors.

Abdul Aziz went on to consolidate his victory, first over the central Najd, then east to the Gulf, and finally west to the Red Sea. By 1932 his sovereignty extended over most of the Arabian Peninsula and the borders of the modern Kingdom had, in large measure, been established.

He ruled for almost fifty years, long enough to oversee the start of the oil age and the changes it would bring. He was, according to all reports, a leader of immense charisma, vision and wisdom. In a land divided by ancient rivalries and tribal allegiances, he was able to impose a sort of unity.

From the earliest days of his rule, he used marriage alliances to cement his power and to co-opt his enemies. One of his first acts after taking Riyadh was to wed the daughter of the town's religious leader in an attempt to win the support of his influential faction. She was not his first wife, nor was she his last. The King's virility was legendary, and contributed much to his mystique. He fathered forty-three sons and an unknown number of daughters. Today his direct descendants are said to number 20,000. He has been succeeded as king by four of his sons in turn: Saud, Faisal, Khalid and Fahd.

All over the Kingdom, the walls of every public office and many private ones are graced with the official portrait of the old King. His face is long, his nose aquiline, his lips full; he has a dark moustache and a goatee beard. He appears to be leaning back into his chequered head cloth; the black and gold *iqaal* that holds it in place suggests a crown, and enhances his regal bearing. His expression is shrewd, slightly amused.

The portrait of the current King, Fahd, appears to one side of his father. The costumes and the beards are similar, but Fahd's face is round and fleshy, with dark circles under the eyes that signal his ill health. To the other side of Abdul Aziz sits the portrait of another of his sons. With his long face and shrewd expression, the regent, Crown Prince Abdullah, bears more of a resemblance to his father.

The old King's shoes will be hard to fill. His sons and grandsons are blessed with riches and influence that he could only have dreamed of, but the times they face are more complex and challenging by far.

At the dawn of the modern era, Saudi Arabia was a land with few natural resources. Although control of the great overland frankincense and spice caravans had once brought the Arabs wealth, by the dawn of the twentieth century such trade had all but disappeared, and they had endured centuries of poverty in one of the harshest environments on earth. What little foreign income they earned came from taxes on pilgrims and from exports of dates and horses.

Our Western dreams of oriental luxury – the odalisques reclining on velvet cushions, the eunuch slaves waving peacock-feather fans, the exquisite refinements of the Arabian Nights – have little place in desert Arabia. They belong further to the north, if they belong anywhere at all, to cultures that were heir to the refinements of Byzantine or Persian civilisation. The desert Arabs lived by a more austere aesthetic.

Many still followed a nomadic way of life, grazing herds of camels, sheep and goats across their traditional tribal lands, raiding the herds of rival clans. Others lived a more settled existence in oases and villages, where they engaged in trade and agriculture. Because of a disdain for manual labour, few practised specialised crafts. Almost everyone was illiterate.

They measured their wealth in livestock, in men's weapons

and in women's jewellery. Some were so poor that they owned nothing but the clothing they wore. Men were admired more for what they gave away than for what they owned.

It was said of Abdul Aziz that he gave everything away, insisting that 'hoarded money never does anyone any good'. Amongst the Bedouin who flocked to his tents for a share of his largesse, the King's hospitality was legendary, and did much to win their allegiance. The social contract he established with his people paired open-handed generosity with absolute authority. It set the pattern for all subsequent Saudi governments, and still prevails today.

At the start of the oil era, Saudi Arabia had none of the apparatus of a modern state: no roads, no hospitals, no schools, save for the *madrassas* where boys learned to recite the Quran, and only a rudimentary bureaucracy. Jeddah, its most important Red Sea port, was a simple facility that served the needs of pilgrims, while its main Gulf port, al Uqayr, consisted of nothing more than a customs post, a *caravanserai* and a fort. The discovery of oil was to change all that.

In the 1930s, when oil revenues began to trickle into Arabia, no distinction was made between the wealth of the state and that of its ruler. Abdul Aziz took personal possession of all the petroleum income. He insisted that the Americans pay him in gold bullion. According to one popular story, he stored the sacks of gold under his bed, and when he ran out of space, stored the surplus under his treasurer's bed. By the time the King died in November 1953 the al Sauds were already wealthy.

The oil boom of the early 1970s hit the country with the force of a tidal wave. As annual revenues passed the US$20 billion mark, the Kingdom was suddenly awash with money, and the main problem facing her rulers was how to distribute the wealth through an unstructured economy. A succession of five-year plans was implemented to facilitate the process.

In the heady days of the boom, development proceeded at a breathtaking pace. Housing, hospitals, schools, public buildings, power plants, roads, bridges, ports and industrial centres arose from the bare desert. Foreign experts flooded in to manage the projects, and foreign workers to provide the necessary labour.

With them came a steady succession of scammers and swindlers, ready to take advantage of the naïve Saudis. A British engineer once told me that when tenders were called for the construction of a major highway, the successful consortium simply picked up their US$7 million payment and disappeared.

Money flowed out to the people in welfare payments and subsidies. Farmers rode in on their camels from the desert, abandoned the animals in holding paddocks attached to Toyota dealerships, and drove away in brand-new pick-up trucks. Young men were sent abroad to study at government expense. A rapidly expanding public service guaranteed jobs for them on their return. Saudi businessmen took advantage of rules banning foreign ownership by forming lucrative partnerships with outsiders wishing to trade in the Kingdom. Often nothing more was required of them than to sign the registration papers and collect their cut of the profits. By 1980, the per capita income matched those of the developed world, and the nation's ports were clogged with cargo ships carrying construction materials and luxury goods. It was as if an entire country had won the lottery.

In the centenary year of 1999, when King Fahd escaped the heat of the Saudi summer by moving his entourage to his home in Spain, he took with him 200 tons of luggage, 400 retainers, and twenty-five Rolls Royces and limousines. Fortunately he did not have to pay excess baggage. A dedicated fleet of eight aircraft, including five 747s and an Antonov cargo plane were employed to carry him and his court.

In Riyadh, Prince Mohammad, the son of King Fahd, was building a palace for himself. It was an exact replica, down to the elaborate carving on each piece of stone, of Spain's glorious Alhambra palace: the crowning architectural achievement of the Moors in Andalusia. By the year 2000, the project had been seven years in the making and had already cost US$800 million. The prize for the most expensive residence, however, goes to another son of the King, Prince Abdul Aziz, whose Jeddah palace (one of several he maintains) cost him US$2.7 billion.

The wealth of the Saudi royal family and the profligacy of its spending is legendary . . . fabulous . . . stupendous . . . in fact, it is hard to find words to describe its scope.

Many Saudi citizens, too, have become rich. They have replaced scarcity with abundance and have grown to love luxury. Some are fantastically wealthy. They live in grand villas with servants to see to their every need. When it's time to redecorate, they fly in teams of interior designers from Paris. They drive their Cadillacs and Mercedes to shopping malls full of Western consumer goods. Their wealth keeps the major couture houses of Europe afloat. Their investments buoy up foreign stock markets. They travel abroad in five-star style, and send their children abroad to be educated at the best private schools. They maintain fully staffed houses around the world, each one ready, down to the fresh flowers in the vases, to receive them at a moment's notice. I met women who spoke casually of their Spanish mansions (it is said that the Saudis are reclaiming Andalusia through real estate purchases), or of their apartments in London or Geneva or Florida.

Even for those who do not enjoy such wealth, life has changed utterly. Within the towns, the mud-brick houses clustered around a mosque and a *souk* have been abandoned in favour of modern dwellings of stone and concrete, with air-conditioning, plumbing and satellite dishes.

Almost all of the Bedouin have abandoned their desert tents for life in the towns, leaving Baluchi and Sudanese shepherds to watch over their flocks. In the 1980s it was estimated that only 5 percent of Saudis still maintained a wholly nomadic existence.

'My grandfather and my grandmother miss the old ways. They still like to take their tent out into the desert,' one of my students, Ghada, told me. She was a plump, sweet-faced girl who listed chatting on the Internet as one of her hobbies. 'But my father and my sister and I hate to go outside. We spend all of our time indoors.'

'What, even in winter?' I asked.

'Yes, even in winter. We never go out.' There was poignancy in her answer.

Traditional Arabia lives on in the hearts of its people. 'What does a man need to live for a day?' Geoff once asked his students, and the answer came back without hesitation, unanimously: 'Seven dates and a glass of milk.' 'It takes two days for a man to die of thirst in the desert,' they added, 'but on the first day, he will be very sick.' Their grandfathers would have known firsthand these equations of survival.

Wealth has brought many benefits to the people. Public spending on education has seen literacy rates rise to equal world standards. Through the introduction of modern medical facilities and universal health care, the incidence of infant mortality and of infectious diseases has fallen dramatically. However, the Saudis now face epidemics of a different sort: along with plenty, they have inherited all the degenerative diseases of the developed world.

'When I first came here thirty years ago,' said Sam, a Physical Education teacher at the university, 'the boys would come in straight from the desert. Their bodies were as lean and as hard as wire. We'd throw them into the swimming pool and they'd sink like a stone. These days they're all overweight and they all float.'

By the year 2000, the national diabetes rate was estimated at 17 percent, up from 2.2 percent in 1970, with similar trends in obesity and cardiac disease (*Arab News*, November 11, 1999).

In place of their old resilience and fierce independence, the Saudis have grown used to handouts, servants and pampering. 'Back then,' said Sam, 'they were men at fifteen. Now they're still children at twenty.'

The change that most disturbs the national psyche, however, arises from their exposure to foreign influences. 'We find teen-age boys wearing reversed baseball caps and speaking with one other [sic] in the manner of black Americans,' wrote Asrar Wa'il Islam (*Arab News*, May 1999). 'And schoolgirls changing their hair colour to blonde, like Lebanese TV broadcasters and Hollywood stars.' In the pages of the local press I detected a fear that traditional culture was being contaminated by Western ideas and Western immorality; that in the deluge of consumerism and

outside influences swamping the country, the Saudis may lose
that which makes them essentially Arab.

The House of al Saud has a stranglehold on power. The princes
and their cohorts hold office as cabinet ministers, provincial gov-
ernors and ambassadors. They head the armed services. They sit
on the boards of major companies. They control the media. They
decide who will be appointed to the *ulema*, the powerful ruling
council of Islamic scholars.

Foreign analysts and Saudi-watchers like to keep an eye on the
royals, trying to assess the stability of their regime and its chances
of survival. According to these experts, the al Saud family costs
the country dearly. Some 40 percent of national revenues is
believed to disappear directly into royal pockets each year. It is
said that even the lowliest prince is on the public payroll with a
monthly stipend of about US$4,000, while senior princes get
over US$130,000 per month. Defense Minister Prince Sultan's
expenses budget is said to run to as much as US$20 million per
month. In addition, many of the princes are said to be engaged in
corrupt dealings worth billions of dollars in total.

Commentators say that while greed and corruption have
undermined the legitimacy of the al Sauds, they are more deeply
compromised by their embrace of a Western lifestyle. The suspicion that they have abandoned the precepts of their religion, that
they indulge in drugs, alcohol and other forms of immorality is
scandalous in the eyes of their pious subjects.

Even more serious has been their reliance on US military
might to prop up their regime. In a society where hostility to the
West is entrenched at all levels, this is seen as an affront to both
religious and national sensibilities. The agreement to station US
troops on the holy soil of Saudi Arabia in the 1991 Gulf War
caused outrage, and has not been forgiven. It is said to have been
the key factor that drove Osama bin Laden to embark upon his
jihad against the West and against the House of al Saud.

The old social contract that granted the ruler absolute power
sits uncomfortably with the aspirations of citizens in a modern

state. The royal *majlis*, the open court in which the sovereign receives his people and in which every citizen can directly approach their ruler with a personal request or grievance, still operates. It serves the useful function of keeping the rulers in touch with the public, while allowing them to appear at their best, as benevolent patriarchs. However, while it is often the forum for robust, astonishingly critical self-expression, few would claim that the *majlis* is a reasonable substitute for political rights and true freedom of speech.

King Fahd is said to be deeply unpopular, his reputation tarnished from the beginning by his days as a young playboy, by his lavish lifestyle and by the greed and corruption of his sons. He is also so ill that his position as ruler is largely symbolic: all of the day-to-day business of running the country has devolved to his regent, Crown Prince Abdullah. But while the Crown Prince is widely respected for his modest lifestyle, his abilities as a leader and his willingness to tackle the nation's problems, his succession to the throne is far from assured. Speculation is rife that following the death of the King, Abdullah will face challenges from his powerful half-brothers, Prince Sultan and Prince Naif. Whoever wins the throne is likely to enjoy only a short reign. Abdullah is in his late seventies, and all of the sons of Abdul Aziz are now old men. The path of succession to the next generation is as yet unclear.

If the analysts are to be believed, the royal family faces unprecedented challenges to their power and multiple sources of instability.

Within the Kingdom, I detected little hint of disquiet. It was as if we lived in a bubble of courtly benevolence, loyalty and stability. The image of the princes that sits foremost in my mind is one that appeared almost every night on television: a senior prince attending an official function. He is greeted with almost fawning deference by a welcoming committee. They kiss his shoulder, his robe. He half raises his hand, as if in blessing. They are surrounded by grinning subordinates, thrilled beyond measure to be in such exalted company.

Only the rumour mill gave us hints that the royals might not be as universally respected as the official line would have us believe.

Through it we heard reports on the serious state of the King's health. We heard about the kickbacks, bribes and sweetheart deals that the princes demanded in their official and private business dealings (one very senior prince was known universally as 'Mr Ten Percent'). We even had it on good authority that the princes had the bootleg alcohol trade sewn up, and were making obscene profits smuggling truckloads of Johnnie Walker into the country.

Naturally, I was curious about the royals: the rumours only served to pique my curiosity. With so many princes and princesses about, Geoff and I had high expectations of meeting one of them. We knew that, although princes from the more powerful branches of the royal family usually travelled abroad for their studies, lesser princes sometimes enrolled at KFUPM. Geoff had noticed their cars, parked with the engines running, in the English Language Center car park. This was a sure sign that the air-conditioner was on and that, behind the darkened windows, a driver was seated waiting for his master to finish the day's lessons.

I was not entirely surprised when Geoff came home from work to announce that he had a young al Saud in his class. Immediately I was filled with unseemly curiosity: I wanted to know all about him. Geoff fed me a few unsatisfying snippets of information: the prince was quiet; he was not a strong student, but was very polite. One day when the prince and his best friend were busy looking at photographs rather than paying attention to the lesson, Geoff demanded to see the pictures. To his surprise, the boys proudly handed over snaps of a pet hunting falcon that one of them had just purchased at a price of SR40,000 (US$10,000), and that he kept in an air-conditioned cage.

Unlike his classmates, who lived in the rather grim campus accommodation known as 'the student lines', the prince had taken a room in al Khobar at a five-star hotel. Towards the end of the semester, he invited Geoff to join him there for lunch. Geoff went off with instructions to note every detail so that he could give me a blow-by-blow account of the occasion.

The prince had picked Geoff up in his car.

'What sort of car?' I asked.

He looked nonplussed. 'It was an expensive car . . . a luxury car,' he said. 'Not a Holden.'

He had been more interested in how the drivers of other expensive-looking cars had waved to the prince as they passed by. 'My cousin,' explained the prince. 'My uncle.'

As they entered the hotel dining room, the prince whispered a discreet word to the maitre d', and everything swung into smooth, deferential, but unostentatious action. They were shown to a table. They ordered scaloppine.

'Was it a private room?' I asked.

'No, it was semi-private, but we had the place to ourselves.'

They talked. Geoff said that he was careful not to ask any questions that might embarrass the prince. The prince, for his part, was easy to talk to.

'He didn't big note himself at all,' said Geoff. 'He had beautiful manners.' And though he was quite frank with Geoff on certain matters, and although Geoff shared some of those confidences with me, because I cannot divulge them without revealing the identity of the prince and his family, I feel obliged to show him the same courtesy. My lips are sealed.

Despite his comfortable circumstances, the young prince was far removed from the power centres of the al Saud clan. He was just another descendant of Abdul Aziz, whose numbers these days are said to include princes who are astronomically rich as well as those of modest means, arch religious conservatives along with liberals who follow Western ways, and, because many have married promiscuously, princes who would pass for Africans, Asians or Northern Europeans.

To mark the Kingdom's centenary, the leading princes of the House of al Saud stepped up their official engagements. All over the Kingdom they were visiting institutions, opening exhibits and delivering speeches. In the Eastern Province, we were to receive a visit from the most powerful man in the land, Crown Prince Abdullah. This was to be a very big deal indeed.

The preparations began weeks in advance, and by the time the

Prince arrived in April, they had reached a frenzy. First to come
were the squads of road workers out on the highways, busy with
bitumen and gravel. Next came the maintenance crews to paint
the buildings and fix the cracks in their facades. Gardeners
planted lawns and beds of flowers. Each tree was trimmed.
Strings of coloured lights picked out the centennial motif on
the fronts of office buildings. On the day before the Prince
appeared, teams of cleaners were out scouring the sides of the
official route for litter, and banners and bunting appeared on
overpass bridges.

The Prince's schedule was packed with engagements that
ranged from visiting a school for handicapped children, to
opening a new patriot missile installation. He was also to visit
KFUPM, where he would inspect the research centre and be
received as guest of honour at an official function.

The big day arrived. Thanks to the efforts of its maintenance
teams and gardeners, the university was sparkling. The courtyard
at the main gate had been washed down and the fountain was
splashing merrily. A welcoming banner hung across the
entrance. The marigolds and periwinkles were in bloom and the
lawns freshly watered. Outside the research centre, road
workers had dug up the cul de sac entrance and transformed it
into a drive-through road so that the Prince's car would not have
to reverse out.

In the afternoon, teachers returning from their classes brought
word to Ferdaws of the air of excitement up on the *jabal*. Excitement and tension: security was at fever pitch. The approaches to
the university had been closed to all but official vehicles. Even
the main highway had been shut down, and would remain closed
for the duration of the Prince's visit. There were soldiers, police
and paramilitaries everywhere, and sharpshooters lurking in the
shrubbery.

The university auditorium had been decorated with enough
imported flowers to give a serious boost to the economy of the
Netherlands. The dignitaries were assembled, waiting for the
Prince to arrive: the dean, the faculty heads, the directors and
the VIPs. But after all the anticipation, the visit turned out to
be an anticlimax. The Prince was late. Very late. After he had

been welcomed effusively and had delivered a ten-minute
address, he left.

'It seemed like he was hardly there at all,' said our friend Selim,
a senior lecturer who had been part of the audience.

Next day, when Geoff came home from the *jabal*, he brought
me a bunch of red roses that he had salvaged from the auditorium. By then the Prince and his entourage had moved on to
other official engagements.

Public celebrations of any kind, other than religious ones, are
rare in Arabia, but for the centenary great things were afoot. In
January the annual Janadriyah cultural festival featured fireworks, folkloric dancing, a military parade and a twenty-kilometre
camel race run over four days and involving 800 camels. Princes
of the royal blood came together dressed in sumptuous traditional
robes to perform *ardha*, the warrior dance of the Najd. The King
Abdul Aziz Historical Center, incorporating a museum, the
nation's first public libraries (including one for women), and
palace restorations, was inaugurated in Riyadh. Also in Riyadh,
an international conference on Saudi history was scheduled, and
more than 100 books and five documentary films on the theme
of the Kingdom's first 100 years were published. Photography
exhibitions and art shows were held in the major cities. Special
stamps, coins and currency notes were issued. Over 100 planes,
including Abdul Aziz's original Dakota DC-3, took part in a spectacular air show in which parachutists jumped from planes
bearing portraits of the old King, the current King and the
national flag. A cyclist set off to ride 3,000 kilometres around the
Kingdom in his own personal tribute.

But the highlight of the celebrations was the staging of an
operetta written by one of the princes, the Prince Edward of his
clan, to glorify the conquests of his grandfather. The show
involved teams of performers, thirty-five horses, fifteen camels,
sound effects, a laser show, fireworks and gunshots. Nothing like
it had ever been seen in the Kingdom before.

It might all have been happening on another planet: so far as
I could tell, women were absent from all of these events. In the
Arab News I read occasionally that a princess had sponsored a
women's poetry reading in Riyadh or an art show in Jeddah.

Everything else, all the displays and events and performances and congratulations, were for men only. But then, few women had been invited to play a role in the momentous events of the past 100 years. Why should this year have been any different?

In the seclusion of my living room, I watched the centennial year unfold. What changes, I wondered, will the next lunar centenary bring?

8

HEAT

The door finally opened and we stepped out into a smothering blanket
of humid heat. I literally gasped for breath and, turning, saw that
the girls were doing the same and looked as shocked as I felt.
FRANCIS MEADE, Honey and Onions

Many an Arabian traveller's tale begins with the protag-
onist stepping down from a ship or a plane into a
furnace blast of hot air. My own arrival at the start of winter
was far less confronting.

November in Dhahran was pleasant. A mild humidity suffused
the daytime heat, and in the afternoon a breeze blew in from
the Gulf to freshen the air. The evenings were soft and balmy, the
sunny mornings enlivened by a chill wind from the north. The
resilient desert plants had absorbed enough water from the morning
dew to put on a spurt of growth, and covered the land with a palette
of sage green and russet.

December was cooler. Tender green leaves appeared on the
ficus and acacia trees that dotted the campus, and beds of
petunias burst into bloom. Now and then, pairs of long-tailed
green parrots flew squawking across the sky. Saudi men
exchanged their white cotton *thobes* for fine woollen ones in
shades of brown and grey.

January was cooler still. Overcast skies replaced the perpetual
blue, and at times a misting rain fell. Sprays of yellow blossoms

appeared under the crowns of the date palms. In the evenings we wore light wraps, and slept under a blanket. I reversed the cycle on the powerful air-conditioning system in our apartment. A flick of the switch, and warm air started to blow from the vents, bringing with it the tang of baking dust. That night I awoke from a disturbed sleep, to realise that the pungent stink filling my nostrils was not a dream. It was a dank, animal smell, like long-overcooked meat. Leaving Geoff to continue his peaceful slumbers, I stepped into the courtyard, inhaling. The night air smelled of nothing more than dust and dew. Sure now that the stink was blowing in through the heating vents, I turned off the switch and went back to bed, convinced that I had been inhaling a dead rat. The next day, our maintenance workers discovered a mash of baked mushrooms in the pipes.

In February it rained, great torrents of water that fell from the skies in sheets for days at a time. Everywhere roads flooded and ceilings leaked, but the locals spoke of the good weather. Driving around in our Honda sedan (purchased at bargain price from a departing expat) became an adventure. Its previous owner had washed it regularly in salt water, so that it had developed an alarming case of rust. As we swished along the road, rainwater flowed in through the gaps around the sunroof and formed a reservoir that we could hear slopping about over our heads. A turn to the right brought a torrent of rusty water down upon me. A swing to the left, and it was Geoff's turn. After the first shock, we were helpless with laughter, and wondered who amongst our friends we should ask out for a ride.

March was pleasant. With the end of the rains, heat returned to the Gulf. The date palms were laden with bright yellow bunches of tiny embryonic fruit: nourishment for the flocks of birds that stopped over on their annual migration from an African summer to a European one. At sunset, as the voices of the *muezzins* calling the faithful to prayer floated out across the still air, we took long, rambling walks around the campus. From the eastern rim of the horizon, bands of oyster-shell pink and mauve mounted up into a sky whose vaulted dome above us was fading from azure to gold. Darkness and quietness settled upon the nearby towns. A scattering of green neon lights appeared, each one marking the site of a minaret.

That year the annual *haj* holidays fell in March, and Geoff applied for the exit visas that would allow us to escape from the Kingdom. I could only be thankful that the swathe of red tape he did battle with to obtain them was secret men's business. All went well, so that on a clear morning we were able to drive onto the King Fahd Causeway that stretched out over the sparkling waters of the Gulf to Bahrain. Looming up from an island midway across we saw the twin spires of the Saudi and Bahraini customs posts jabbing like needles into the air from their saucer-shaped bases.

'Minas Tirith and Minas Morgul', said Geoff, referring to the towers of Tolkein's *Lord of the Rings*, and there was something mythic about them. When we had cleared customs and driven through to the other side, we both breathed a sigh of relief.

Bahrain's pearly white silhouette grew larger as we approached, resolving itself into domes and building blocks and green groves of palm trees. The traffic was orderly as we drove into the capital, and the sight of women driving was wonderful to my eyes. We booked into a hotel on Government Avenue, and ordered drinks from room service. It was the best gin and tonic I've ever tasted.

Manama has all the accoutrements of a modern city, but has managed to preserve some of the air of a traditional Gulf town. Nestled amidst the glass towers, the Bab al Bahrain, or city gate, still stands in its white fortress walls. Behind it are the narrow alleyways of a crowded *souk*. In the old residential areas we came upon houses still sporting the square wind towers that are the traditional cooling systems of Arabian buildings, and in the harbour, shipbuilders were still constructing wooden *dhows*.

Bahrain has a marvellous museum where we explored the archaeology of the Dilmun age, and even more wonderful ancient temple sites and fields full of burial mounds. It has old fortresses, wildlife parks and beaches, and verdant oasis groves. We visited all these attractions and loved them, but the best thing of all about Bahrain was its air of freedom.

Women were walking around in Western dress, drawing barely a sideways glance. Around hotel pool sides, British tourists lay on lounge chairs in tiny swimsuits, braising their oil-drenched skins to a nice shade of lobster. We ordered bacon every day for breakfast. We downed red wine in an Italian restaurant, and margueritas (rather too many) in a Mexican one where there was no sign of a family room. In the hotel bars, Saudi men occupied the bar stools. At the cinema, where we went to see *Titanic*, Saudi families made up most of the audience.

After a week, we went home. This time, as we passed through Minas Morgul on the causeway, I felt as claustrophobic and nervous as if we were truly heading into Mordor. In our luggage on the back seat of our car, as audacious as the ring Frodo carried to Mount Doom, lay a smuggled package of Bahrain's finest bacon. 'Whew!' I said in relief as we cleared customs, but Geoff, who had lately been making a sport of defiance, was cackling in triumph.

April was hot. Day by day, relentlessly, the temperature rose. The desert plants were drying out and dying back: only the succulents still looked lush under their layer of dust. The tamarisk and ficus trees started to shed their leaves, and even the eucalyptus looked more ragged and spare than usual. Because I disliked its artificial chill, I resisted turning on the air-conditioner. Now we took our walks late at night. Even at our gentle strolling pace we worked up a sweat in the sapping humidity. We took our tent down to the beach for the last camping trip of the season. At sunset, as we swam in the tepid waters, a pod of dolphins gambolled past us and slipped away. I gazed after them wistfully: to my eyes, they were freedom itself.

By mid May we were turning the air-conditioner on every morning as the daytime temperature rose above 40 degrees. One by one my pot plants gave up the ghost and draped themselves limply over the sides of their containers. Beneath the crowns of the palm trees, huge clumps of dates were swelling to maturity.

Our lives became more nocturnal, although the expat tennis tournament was still raging out of doors in the heat of the day. Yes, it was hot, the players admitted, but they were determined to complete the playoffs. And besides, they added, you get used to the heat.

We'll see about that, I thought.

On a trip to al Khobar, our trusty Honda seized up and was towed away. We resigned ourselves to life without a car with little regret. By now it was too hot for trips to the beach or the desert, and all our other needs would be met by the shopping bus or by taxis.

As the mid-year break approached, talk amongst the expats turned to how each of us would be spending our three-month summer vacation. Many planned to splurge part of their savings on sightseeing holidays, and for weeks everyone traded guide books and travel tips for faraway places. The teachers were a well-travelled lot. No matter what the destination – Zanzibar, Samarkand, Papua New Guinea, Tierra Del Fuego, the Arctic circle – someone had been there and could give others the lowdown.

For those who just wanted a place to hang out for the duration, Thailand was by far the most popular choice: its special mixture of a relaxed atmosphere, friendly people, fine food and budget accommodation (to say nothing of its seedier attractions) made it the perfect antidote to Saudi Arabia. Indeed, some expats saw Thailand as their second home, and spent every vacation there.

Almost everyone planned a trip home for at least part of the vacation. Men living apart from their wives and children longed to be reunited with them. Couples looked forward to spending time in the private retreats – a croft in the Hebrides, a flat in Cyprus or a villa in Spain – that they were financing with their Saudi earnings.

In the teachers' offices, big red crosses marched relentlessly across the wall calendars, checking off the days. Schemes were being hatched to secure exit visas that would enable an early departure from the Kingdom. Some teachers booked taxis to pick them up directly from their classrooms on the final day. Many were determined to spend not one moment more than was necessary in the Kingdom, and the end of term would see a stampede to the airport.

We chipped in to buy gifts for those of our friends who were preparing for their final departure: fragments of Bedouin jewellery and miniature silver *dhows* mounted on black velvet and framed were popular choices. We wrote goodbye messages on the giant cards that were circulating Ferdaws: 'We'll miss you', 'Stay in touch' and 'Don't spend it all at once'. A rash of parties broke out to farewell the dear departing. Amongst those on the way out were Yuko and her American husband Larry. They were a popular couple, and everyone felt sad to see them go, knowing that our tight little community would miss Yuko's bright smile and Larry's easy cowboy manner. 'Come and visit us in Australia,' Geoff and I urged them, without much hope that we would ever see them again. At Yuko's farewell tea party, the women spoke of the strange nature of expat friendships: so easily formed, so intense, and so fleeting.

For teachers who agreed to work through the summer running catch-up classes for students who had failed their exams, the financial rewards were generous. That year, Geoff decided that he would volunteer. Besides, we both had a perverse desire to experience a summer in the Gulf. First, however, I needed to get back to Australia. My father was about to celebrate his eightieth birthday, and, having missed far too many family milestones through my travels, I was determined to be there.

A few days before the end of term, we farewelled each other at Dhahran airport. Our parting came as a wrench: we had been constant companions over the past few months. I was sorry to be leaving Geoff there to face the heat and dust alone, and sorry for myself as I faced my solitary journey. My sadness didn't last for long. Two hours later, as I boarded the flight in Riyadh that would take me out of the Kingdom, I could hardly contain my joy.

On the Saudia flight I was surrounded by high-spirited Indonesian maids who had completed their two-year contracts and were heading home accompanied by their agents, two jovial Saudi gentlemen. Some of the bolder maids spent the first hours of the flight directing a stream of cheeky repartee in Bahasa and

Arabic at their escorts. They had their fellow maids shrieking with laughter. The agents took it all in good humour; they seemed to be enjoying themselves too.

As the plane droned on into the night the maids settled into slumber. Hours later, as we drew near to morning and to Singapore, they roused themselves from their sleep, brushed their hair and freshened their faces. From their bags they produced tiny jewellery boxes and tissue-paper packages, and drew out bright gold chains and pretty droplet earrings. They dressed themselves up in this well-earned finery and, proudly turning their heads this way and that, studied the effect in little hand-held mirrors. My thoughts turned to Annie and the maids who had shared my first night in Arabia, and I wished them as happy an outcome.

Melbourne was in the early throes of winter: grey, windy and wet. Up in the hills at my parents' home, the gardens and lawns and the misty forest backdrops were impossibly green and lush. It felt miraculous to walk upon moist earth.

Just two days after my arrival, on the very day of my father's birthday party, I came down with influenza. I hadn't come all that way to miss the celebrations, however, so I dragged my aching bones and shivering muscles and throbbing head along to the local lawn bowls club where the party was to take place. Throughout the afternoon, I sat miserably in the corner trying to fend off the greetings of octogenarian family friends by issuing warnings of contagion. 'That's all right, love,' they said blithely as they planted kisses on my cheeks. 'We've had our flu shots.' As I lay groaning in bed for the next week, I could only hope that these shots had been effective.

My illness cut into the plans I had made for my trip home. I did manage some family visits and a trip to the cinema. I went shopping in the city, and ordered a glass of wine with my lunch. I hopped onto trams and trains with a wonderful sense of freedom. I felt empowered as I drove a borrowed car. And yet, as I stood in city streets surrounded by rushing men with pinched, intense faces and busy women dressed in their own version of black, I felt detached. My thoughts turned to my slow and languid days in the Gulf. I thought of Geoff, and wished I was by his side.

Midnight at Dhahran airport. Geoff was waiting to pick me up. Although the arrivals board announced that my flight had already landed, it had not yet left Riyadh: arrival and departure notices were posted according to the timetable rather than to reality. When the plane finally got in at three a.m., I was not on it. Geoff later admitted to a sudden suspicion that I had reneged on my promise to return, but, in fact, Saudia had shipped me to Jeddah instead of to Riyadh, and I was spending a sleepless night on a hard chair in the departure lounge there. It took Geoff another hour to have Saudia trace me through the computer system; only then could he go home to snatch a few hours of sleep.

I staggered into Dhahran after nine a.m., beside myself with exhaustion, to find a tired and anxious Geoff waiting for me. As we fell into each other's arms, I wasn't sure who was the more relieved at our reunion.

This time, as we emerged from the airport, I really did experience a sauna blast of hot and steamy air that took my breath away.

'Bloody hell!' I gasped.

'Yes it is,' replied Geoff.

By late June, Ferdaws was strangely empty. Most of the Western expats had gone off on vacation. Only a few hardy souls – those who had decided to teach through the summer, and those with nowhere else to go – were still in residence. Life for them had shrunk back to a circuit of air-conditioned apartment, air-conditioned car, air-conditioned classroom and, occasionally, air-conditioned supermarket. There was a sense that everyone was pacing themselves, conserving their energy.

It was hot. For several days a heat wave pushed temperatures up to a sultry 48 degrees. The fierce sunlight had bleached and cauterised the rubbish that had been left lying about in the desert. Underneath the surface, however, hot sewage steamed and stewed in the pipes, and unspeakable odours arose from the vents. A burning *shamal* wind blew down from the north, filling the air with sand and dust. I gave up my fifteen-minute walk to the Co-op for supplies, and took the shuttle bus instead. The graffiti scratched into the walls of the bus shelter read 'ICE', 'ICE', and again 'ICE'. I tied my scarf over my face outlaw-style as a shield, and understood the utility of the veil. As much as possible, I stayed indoors.

In my absence, al Shula Mall, centre of life for expats in al Khobar, had burned down. There was some irony in this, given that the word *shula* is Arabic for 'flame'. The fire had burned for three days, casting a pall of smoke into the air that could be seen for miles around. Rumour had it that when the fire engines turned up, their crews had swung into a courtly routine of hand clasping, embracing and kissed greetings, before they stood back and watched the complex burn. But then, perhaps there was nothing they could do: there was only one small pressure hose on each side of the building. Without al Shula Mall, al Khobar seemed to have lost its centre, and we had even less reason to go into town.

The date harvest was in full swing. Ripe bunches dripping with sweetness hung in red, brown and yellow clusters from the palms. Everywhere great heaps of the early maturing varieties lay drying, spread out on the ground on woven grass mats. Fresh dates were on sale in the supermarkets: there seemed to be hundreds of varieties. The girls brought bags of them to class: little bombs that were half toffee sweetness and half astringent crunch. We washed them down with *ghawa*, the bitter Saudi coffee brewed from lightly roasted beans and flavoured with cardamom and saffron. They presented me with gifts of dates from their father's orchards. The papers reported that King Fahd had donated a ton of dates to Muslim prisoners in US jails. 'What the . . .!' I imagined them saying as they received this gesture of largesse. Did they look for a hacksaw in their packages?

In the late evenings Geoff and I still managed our walks, plodding resolutely around the Ferdaws circuit, swigging draughts from our water bottles, collapsing in relief when we finally made it back to our front door. The old-timers cheerfully predicted that it was going to get a lot worse. 'Wait till the humidity comes up,' they said. I wondered what they meant. It already seemed unbearably steamy to me.

Then, one afternoon late in July, I looked at our windows, saw moisture streaming down them, and thought that it was raining. But it was not rain: a blanket of fog had rolled in from the Gulf to drench us. Outside the air was hot and soggy and reeked of wet dust and rotting straw as the desert vegetation soaked and mouldered in the wetness. Beyond the fence, the highway street lights were on and the cars driving past were batting their windscreen wipers.

Every day now the thermometer climbed into the mid-40s, and the nights were not much cooler. When I met, Lillian, one of the other summer wives, at the Co-op, she told me that she had passed out while waiting for the shuttle bus a few days earlier. We agreed that the weather had become dangerous.

'You think this is bad,' said one old hand. 'Wait till you see August.'

When classes ended in late July, it was Geoff's turn to fly home to Australia. He needed the break. The summer had taken its toll on him; he was worn out by the heat and by teaching. As I had already used up my free annual airfare, and as I was committed to teaching a class at the Women's Charity Center, it was my turn to remain in the Kingdom. He left for the airport eager with anticipation. I was filled with apprehension as I waved him off. Spending a month alone in the Kingdom promised to be an interesting experience, to say the least.

By mid August the humidity was hanging about like soup, and the heat was fierce: a roasting 45 to 48; even, on one memorable day, 50 degrees. Fifty degrees in the shade, that is. My worst torment was walking to the laundry. Although it was only fifty or so metres away, with the sun beating down and the heat radiating up from the footpath and out from the walls, it was like a voyage through Hades. I would look over the top of my clothes basket, fix my eyes on the laundry door and will myself to keep going. Safely back in my apartment, I would lie spread-eagled on the terrazzo floor, soaking in the coolness.

By now, everyone with any sense had left. There were so few people about that I felt as if I had taken a vow of silence.

Mahmud still picked me up twice a week to take me to my English classes in Dammam, but I no longer waited for him in the car park. Instead I stayed inside near my front door until the sound of his horn summoned me, and then made a carefully timed dash through the heat to the coolness of his car. Apart from the cashiers at the Co-op, he and my students were my only social contacts.

The girls spent their days sleeping, often arising just in time to come to class. 'How did your grandparents cope before they had air-conditioners?' I asked them, and they told me that they had just got on with what they had to do.

Out on the Dammam Road building site, the Bangladeshis were still working in the sun. I tried to imagine how they must be feeling, and failed utterly. Just looking at them was painful. But for me, the hardest part of the summer was not the heat: I spent very little of my time out of doors. The real problem was the crashing, lonely, continuous, indoor boredom.

Towards the end of August, a refreshed and re-energised Geoff arrived back to rescue me from my world of silence. I fell upon him with relief: for days, I simply could not stop talking.

Teachers were slowly checking back into Ferdaws. Everyone had photos to show and stories to tell of the places they had visited. Nobody seemed to be particularly happy to be back, and there was much speculation about who amongst the brethren was most likely to fail to show, or to 'do a runner'. Several new teachers arrived with their families, all looking dazed and confused. Geoff realised that he was now regarded as an old hand, although he confessed to feeling almost as bewildered as he had in the beginning.

Until classes started up again, there was nothing for us to do. Trapped indoors by the heat, we were developing a bad case of cabin fever. In desperation, we decided to risk the catastrophic temperatures and take an excursion to the port of Uqayr.

The day was like every other day in August – a scorcher so hot that it felt dangerous to be outdoors. We rented a car and set off with the air-conditioner at full blast, praying that we would not have a breakdown or a flat tyre.

Now that the Kingdom was almost completely nocturnal, the

traffic was light. We had an easy run down to the outskirts of al Hasa, and then out to the serene aquamarine waters and sandy white beaches of the Gulf. At the side of the road, a herd of camels lay sweltering in a shallow bog. Others stood with their heads buried in thickets of wild date palms, slowly munching.

For the first half of the twentieth century, Uqayr was the gateway to the al Hasa oasis and to the nascent Saudi state beyond. It was here that the British negotiated treaties with King Abdul Aziz in 1917 and again in 1922 to oppose the Ottoman Turks and to draw the borders between Arabia, Iraq and Kuwait. Photographs from the 1930s show the port as a collection of low buildings that included a *caravanserai*, a customs house and a fort. In the wide open space surrounding them, bundles of goods are stacked in piles ready to be loaded onto waiting camels.

The old buildings were still there, but now they were crumbling and deserted, save for a few Indian fishermen who were sheltering from the midday heat in one of the ruins. We wandered through the blue-painted rooms of the customs house, picking our way over piles of rubble. Old electric fans still hung from the ceilings like bent and battered dragonflies. They conjured up images of the bureaucrats who had once laboured beneath them to chronicle the Kingdom's imports. The wooden jetty where *dhows* had once anchored had been replaced by a metal one, but no boats were moored there. A modern security post stood off to the side, bristling with telecommunications equipment. The old port's only function these days is as a military outpost.

We sat in the shade of an arched doorway to eat our lunch, sweltering, melting, enduring. On the drive home, we were elated. We had braved the midsummer heat. We had survived!

Back at KFUPM, in confirmation of Noël Coward's lyric about mad dogs and Englishmen, our friend Francis was jogging around the Ferdaws circuit. Sweat hung from his eyebrows and coursed down his face. His clothing was soaked, his arms and legs were awash. Drops of perspiration splashed onto the footpath in his wake. As we drove past, he waved cheerfully.

There was change in the air. A new men's college was about to open in Riyadh, offering its students the KFUPM foundation year curriculum. As part of the deal, the university had agreed to supply a number of experienced teachers for the college's first year of operation, and was looking for volunteers. By way of incentive, they offered a generous salary bonus, and promised good housing and conditions.

Geoff and I talked it through. By reputation Riyadh was a con-servative town, and a far more difficult place for Westerners than the Eastern Province. Old-timers warned us that the teething problems of any new venture in the Kingdom would be horren-dous, and advised us not to go. But we wanted to see more of Arabia. We were bored with the featureless landscape and the bland modern cities of the Eastern Province. And so, along with several other residents of Ferdaws, we applied, and were accepted.

Saying farewell to our KFUPM friends was difficult, especially for Geoff, who, in his three years of residence, had formed strong friendships. But it was not just emotional baggage that we had accumulated: we needed to rent a pick-up truck to carry our belongings across the desert to our new home.

We set off in the early morning along quiet roads, armed with a hand-drawn map of Riyadh, instructions on navigating to our new college, high hopes and trepidation. Soon we had left the ruined landscape of the Gulf far behind. In front of us the terrain sloped steadily upwards and the highway draped itself across the desert like a strap of soft black liquorice. Heavy trucks lumbering along in the outside lane settled their wheels into deep ruts that other trucks had pressed into the melting asphalt. Lakes of shimmering mercury appeared in the distance and dis-solved as we approached. We passed over gravel plains and salt flats, through low white hills where camels and goats grazed on dry vegetation, and through a belt of sculpted, toffee-coloured sand dunes.

Three hours into the journey, the first of the landmarks on our map appeared: a series of huge telecommunications dishes perched high on a hill. We came up over a rise to see Riyadh spread out below us, a carpet of low-rise buildings dissected by mighty freeways. In the distance, two lone skyscrapers poked up through a haze of brown dust and smog. Closer, the domes and minarets of substantial mosques were the dominant structures. Far away on the other side of town, the tiny, floating specks of white that glinted in the sunshine were planes floating down towards the airport.

Our road took us past a sprawling camel market where disdainful-looking beasts penned in small enclosures stood motionless in the heat. I could never have imagined such a variety of the beasts: small camels and big camels, black camels and white camels, brown camels and tan camels, camel camels.

To my delight, I noted that some of the buildings were of traditional mud-brick construction. With their massive wooden doors and crenellated walls, they were perfectly designed to resist an armed assault. However, these were not tribal strong-holds, but rather fancy Arabic-themed restaurants, their purpose revealed by the strings of coloured lights draped over their walls and the welcoming billboards raised on their flat roofs.

Like the fringes of al Khobar, the outskirts of Riyadh were in the grip of a construction boom. The desert was studded with the grey concrete shells of new villas and apartment buildings, while recently completed ones faced in sandstone and marble stood behind high concrete walls with gates of wrought iron and opaque glass. We passed plant nurseries displaying greenery and fountains and giant Chinese ceramic planters, showrooms full of luxury furnishings, neighbourhoods crammed with dusty townhouses and apartments and rows of small shops, all shut-tered and barred after their morning's trading.

The capital was a big town that made al Khobar seem like a sleepy backwater in comparison. Mercifully, because by reputa-tion Riyadh drivers were even more reckless than their Eastern Province counterparts, the traffic was light. Despite this, the occasional maverick driver, the unfamiliarity of our surroundings and our general apprehension about Riyadh made navigating the alien streets stressful, and we sighed with relief when at last we pulled into the driveway of the college.

The campus was ringed by a substantial concrete and metal fence that stretched away into the distance, surrounding a dusty paddock and a series of three-storey buildings. Geoff parked under a shade awning and went off to report, while I stayed in the car with the air-conditioner running, sure that my presence would not be welcome. To my surprise he came back immediately with an invitation for me to go in and meet the dean.

In the lobby, two guards sat smugly at a reception desk as workmen wheeled furniture and boxes of equipment past them. Off to the side, the dean's office was a cool oasis of luxury furnished with a huge timber desk, deep armchairs, soft carpets and lush green indoor plants. He was an imposing figure in an immaculate white *thobe*. I was a hot and dusty woman with limp hair and swollen feet in a polyester *abaya*, but he welcomed me with consummate grace, inviting me to rest in a comfortable chair while he summoned his assistant to bring coffee and dates.

My visit with the dean filled me with optimism about our move to Riyadh. How pleasant his kindly solicitations were. How reassuring. Perhaps everything I had heard about Arab hospitality was true: that they are a people at their very best when they are playing host. What a shame it was that we had so little contact with them, I thought. Now I had high hopes of breaking out of the comfort zone of my expat circle; of making contact with the real Arabia.

Half an hour later we were back on the road again, this time following the two young Arabs who had been delegated to guide us to our new home. Geoff struggled to keep them in sight as they sped off through the city. We were both, by now, completely disoriented.

Eventually we came to a high earthen embankment topped with acacias and tamarisks. Behind it lay Riyadh's Diplomatic Quarter. Our road snaked around through a dizzying clover leaf to bring us up to the entrance, a gap in the embankment where security guards checked our papers and waved us through. In front of us, in the middle of a roundabout, a battery of flagpoles arose from beds of ornamental greenery, and water cascaded from a fountain. We followed our guides down a shady avenue of arching date palms, past imposing embassy buildings set amidst flourishing landscaped gardens.

Up ahead, covering an entire city block, the walls of a substantial sand-coloured building reared up. Only an occasional arch or series of squat columns or a decorative motif of little triangular indentations in its walls interrupted the blank face it presented to the outside world. It looked like a cross between a traditional mud-brick fortress and a giant sandcastle. This was the al Kendi complex. Located smack in the middle of the Diplomatic Quarter, it was the hub of the precinct's commercial and public activities, and our new home. We followed our guides into an underground car park, and then up an elevator to an apartment on the second floor.

We stepped through a blue-tiled alcove to the entrance: a heavy wooden door patterned with metal studs. Inside, the air was blissfully cool. Our two young guides showed us around with obvious delight. Two sitting rooms (a his and hers) each furnished with soft couches and low tables, a blue-tiled, high-walled private courtyard, a formal dining room and a modern kitchen. I tasted the tap water: it was not salty. After the spartan pleasures of Ferdaws, it was all quite luxurious, and I smiled my approval to the young men. They both beamed. One of them pulled open the door to the refrigerator. It was stocked with pita bread, cream cheese, cucumbers, tomatoes and fruit. Upstairs we found two bedrooms and two bathrooms, and a laundry furnished with a new washer and dryer. A set of steps led up to a searingly hot rooftop terrace.

Our powerful air-conditioner was set to arctic, and soon we were reaching for our sweaters. At night cold air rippled from the high wall vents and out across the bed. We woke with teeth a-chatter. The dry air fizzed with static electricity. Every time we touched a wall or a door handle a blue spark crackled out. The ones that snapped from the light switches were the most lethal: strong enough to bruise an unwary finger.

Outside the air was smelter hot: the evenings were no cooler than the days. It was said that sometime between three and four in the morning the temperature dropped slightly for about twenty minutes. I found this hard to believe. Our out-of-door excursions were limited to desperate forays down to the mini-mart one floor below us for supplies.

There was no sign of our colleagues, or of anyone else for that matter. After a few days without human contact, we decided to brave the heat and go in search of them. Downstairs a long arcade bordered by low arches and shady recesses curved from one end of al Kendi to the other. Except for a few panels of shade cloth, it was open to the sky. As we toiled along swigging from our water bottles, heat radiated up from the tiles under our feet and out from the surrounding walls. We tried to breathe shallowly so that the air did not burn our windpipes. It was hell, but we were coping.

In the distance we saw another Western couple, and as they drew closer, we recognised Sam, who had come over from KFUPM to be the new college's PE instructor, and his wife Margaret. They had been out for a walk, inspecting the local sporting club about fifteen minutes away.

'You are brave,' I told Margaret. She smiled wanly. Her face had taken on a blotchy appearance. She seemed distressed, and complained of dizziness. In alarm, we settled her onto a stone slab and fanned her with our hands. We gave her some of our water to drink, and poured the remainder over her burning head. Sam went to get his car so that he could drive her the few hundred yards back to their apartment at the other end of the complex. He seemed to be impatient at her frailty, but then, he wasn't wearing an *abaya*.

Cooped up in our apartment again and bored to distraction, we decided to risk another walk. That evening after sunset we made our way out of al Kendi and set off down the palm-lined avenue. We walked carefully, conserving our energy, gulping water every few steps. My *abaya* was a torment and a danger. Now I truly understood what it was like to be a member of the weaker sex.

A security guard stationed outside one of the embassies beckoned Geoff over as we made our way past him. While I waited, propped up against a dusty palm tree to conserve my energy, they engaged in an earnest exchange.

'What did he want?' I asked on his return.

'To sell me a bottle of Johnnie Walker Black Label,' laughed Geoff. 'Five hundred US dollars.'

The guard had chosen the wrong person to make his pitch to. Geoff had little interest in alcohol, and even less in spending that kind of money on it. I, on the other hand, might well have been tempted.

9

RIYADH

Everything was ruled from that unlovable baked-mud metropolis
with its science-fictional new atmosphere of over scale modern
architecture and quaint old Arabian ways.
PETER THEROUX, Sandstorms

One by one the men who were to form the teaching staff at
the new college trickled into Riyadh and took up residence at al Kendi. Leading the move from Dhahran was the 'Wing
Commander', the British director of studies. Next in command
was Sam, the gung-ho PE instructor. Two Englishmen, a reclusive
New Zealander, a Palestinian lecturer in computer studies and
Geoff completed the ex-KFUPM contingent. A Palestinian maths
lecturer had been recruited from Riyadh, and from outside
the Kingdom came the Scottish Terrier, the Quiet Irishman, the
Brother from New York, and Ridwan, an Australian convert to
Islam. Geoff's American teaching partner Bob was the last to arrive.

On the family side, the group consisted of: English Margaret;
Ridwan's Indonesian wife Yanti and her ten-year-old son; Palestinian Ayishah and her two baby girls; the devoutly religious
Iman, also a Palestinian, and mother of three small children; and
Abeba, the regal young Ethiopian wife of the Brother from New
York, who was expecting her first child. Much later we were
joined by Eun Yong, Bob's Korean wife and mother of six-month-old Julia.

This, then, was our community: thirteen men, most of them marked either by age or eccentricity or both; seven women from vastly different backgrounds; and seven small children.

The women got together over morning tea to compare interests and resources. Ayishah and Iman expected to be kept busy with their children, and Iman had her religious studies to attend to. Abeba professed herself to be happy playing on her computer and listening to music. Margaret and Yanti found that they shared an interest in needlework, and made plans to join the local American quilting bee. Margaret planned to look for work as a primary school teacher, while I would try to find work teaching English. We promised to keep each other company and to support each other, but as I joined in the dandling of babies and the talk of shopping and families and cooking, I wondered if they were feeling as dismayed as I was.

The college provided a minibus, proudly emblazoned with its logo, and a Pakistani driver, the courteous and obliging Abdul Latif, to ferry the teachers to and from work. When it was not being used on college business, the bus was available for our use. Our first shopping trip into Riyadh took place on Thursday morning (the first day of our weekend) at the end of the first week of term. Almost everyone – husbands, wives, children, bachelors – turned out for the occasion.

Abdul Latif took us to the Euromarche supermarket, but a cry of protest arose from the troops. 'Take us somewhere where we can do some real shopping,' they ordered him. And off we went across town to al Shula Mall, sister of our deeply mourned al Khobar establishment. 'Not a shopping mall,' exclaimed the dissenting voices. An increasingly resentful Abdul Latif drove on, sitting huffily over his steering wheel.

Eventually we came to an area of narrow streets, traffic jams and crowds of third-world expatriates. Abdul Latif pulled into a dusty car park surrounded on all sides by three- and four-storey buildings tenanted by small traders, and decorated with billboards advertising everything from gold jewellery to fish. This was

Batha, downtown Riyadh, the market centre of town. 'This is more like it!' said the Terrier.

Geoff and I, not really needing to shop, headed off to explore. Beyond the car park and the shops piled high with Western consumer goods, we wandered into a low building dissected by a grid of narrow lanes: the tent-makers *souk*. Its stalls were filled with massive rolls of canvas and bolts of heavy tapestry woven with the Saudi national emblem: a pair of crossed swords under a palm tree. Tailors were bent over industrial sewing machines stitching together swathes of cloth panels. Some of the booths featured demonstration models: doll-size tents that were everything in miniature that the modern Bedouin could desire. But the tents from this market were unlikely to be pressed into service as desert dwellings for nomadic sheep and camel herders. They were destined to become pavilions in the gardens of urban villas.

In the heat of that first morning, we didn't explore far beyond the tent-makers quarter. On subsequent trips, Riyadh's sprawling covered markets were a never-ending source of delight. They were not particularly exotic. They had little of the glamour of the fabled bazaars of Marrakech or Cairo or Damascus. It would have been easier to find a set of nylon underwear in them than an oriental treasure. But the *souks* of Riyadh were everyday, working markets, catering to the needs of the residents of the city and not to the whims of a passing tourist trade. I never tired of wandering through their endless arcades, never tired of anticipating what lay around the next corner. And at times, when rays of sunlight came streaming down into a narrow, receding alley, illuminating bearded old men in white turbans and loose cotton robes, and women draped in voluminous black, the scene had a restrained and timeless beauty all its own.

The new college was meant to be a showplace, and it was. Everyone was impressed by the facilities: the fine classrooms and lecture theatres, the computer labs, the spacious library, the board rooms and reception areas, the staff offices, the cafeteria, the swimming pool and the gymnasium. A string of dignitaries, including Prince Salman, Governor of Riyadh, came to inspect the campus, and Geoff reported that the dean and the sub-dean were aglow with pride as they played host to their visitors. Their largesse rained down upon the teachers, and upon their families too. They had lodged us in prestige apartments and had spared no expense in furnishing them. There were frequent enquiries as to our happiness.

The Wing Commander and Sam persuaded the deans that what was really needed was for the college to host a slap-up dinner to welcome the faculty. Riyadh's luxurious Equestrian Club would be just the place, and wives were to be included in the invitation.

On the night of the great event we were all dressed up in our very best. As we climbed down from the bus, the dean and the sub-dean stood at the head of a reception line and shook our hands as if we were diplomats arriving at a formal welcoming ceremony. They had not brought their wives.

Pre-dinner drinks (glasses of fruit juice) were served in a luxuriously appointed salon. Half an hour later we were ushered into a spacious private dining room, where, on a long banquet table, fine china, silver and glassware sparkled on starched white tablecloths. In the background, a smaller, round table was similarly set. In retrospect, I am almost certain that the round table was intended for the ladies, but if so, it was an arrangement that the Westerners chose en masse to ignore. The early arrivals staked out their places at the main table, couples firmly in pairs, while those slower off the mark, men and women alike, had to settle for the round table.

An elegant Western meal. Silver service from Indian waiters with just the right degree of obsequiousness. We progressed through hot bread rolls, consommé, entree and main, dessert, coffee and dates. Our hosts were graciousness itself, the conversation flowed easily. I found myself seated at one end of the main table, next to the sub-dean. He was an affable and charming dinner companion. 'You must come and meet my wife,' he told me towards the end of the evening, and I felt enormously complimented, although I knew that it would never happen.

At the end of the evening, we drifted out, well satisfied, to the minibus. The two deans and the other dignitaries lined up to bid us farewell with handshakes and smiles. All had gone well. And yet I had the distinct impression that although they felt that they had done what needed to be done, both deans were relieved that this particular piece of Western folly was over.

Geoff came home from work with exciting news. The father of one of the students had invited the entire college, staff and students, to a weekend picnic at his farm outside Riyadh.

'Are our families invited?' he had asked.

'Yes, yes, everyone!' he was assured.

'Are you sure wives are invited?' I demanded, not convinced.

'Yes, that's what they said.'

I still had my doubts, but not enough of them to miss out on the chance to sample some Arabian hospitality.

To our surprise, our enthusiasm for the event was not shared by most of the other teachers. Some had already made other arrangements for the weekend; others decided that they simply weren't interested in spending any of their spare time at a work event.

'Will we be paid to go?' they asked ungraciously.

On the morning of the picnic, only Geoff, Bob, and the two Palestinian teachers showed up. I had feared that I would be the only wife, and was quite prepared to return home if that was the case, but when we arrived at the pick-up point, Ayishah and Iman were there with their children.

Our arrival at the farm caused some consternation: our host had not expected wives after all. When everyone else piled out of the bus, we were asked to stay on board with the children while suitable quarters were prepared for us.

Some time later we were ushered into a large enclosure surrounded on three sides by high green hedges. A pavilion took up the fourth side – a semi-permanent tent-like structure erected on a concrete base. It was furnished with low couches and carpets and a machine that dispensed cans of cold Pepsi and 7-Up. The forecourt was a well-watered lawn of tough green grass bordered with beds of marigolds. Around the edges of the enclosure, children's playground equipment and outdoor furniture stood in beds of sawdust.

For our entertainment, the household servants had laid a large oriental rug on the grass, and now a squad of them arrived bearing a collection of stuffed animals. First, to the delight of the children, came an aging lion. His mane was almost worn away, his papier-mâché snarl was cracked askew and straw was bleeding from his enormous front paws. Next came a family of red deer: a buck with large antlers, a doe, and two spotted bambis.

Having seen to our comfort, the servants abandoned us. Seven-year-old Mohammad immediately attempted to climb onto the back of the largest deer. To our horror, one of its delicate front legs broke with a loud crack, and the animal buckled underneath him. For the rest of the day it lay stiffly on its side, gazing at us mournfully through glassy black eyes.

Someone brought us a printed flyer that outlined the activities that had been planned for the men and boys. First they would be taken on a tour of the farm. Then they would attend a traditional *majlis*, or formal reception ceremony. Later there would be a friendly game of football. Eagerly we scanned the program for the item of most interest to us: lunch. It would be served at two.

Unfortunately, all three of us had skipped breakfast that morning. By ten-thirty we were anxious with hunger, the children were getting cranky, and lunchtime seemed a very long way off. Iman dispatched young Mohammad to the outside world to secure us some sustenance, and, after a considerable wait, a servant brought us a tray loaded with a pot of *ghawa* and some dates. With this we had to be content.

We wandered about the garden. We amused ourselves on the swings. We watched the children playing. We sat about in the pavilion attempting to communicate in my minimal Arabic and Iman and Ayishah's somewhat more functional English. The children threw tantrums that their mothers ignored, save when they interfered with their own conversation. Iman took out her Quran and worked on memorising it. I imagine she made considerable progress over the course of the day.

From time to time a lone male would wander through our enclosure, apparently unaware that it was off limits. Well before I saw him, as if alerted by some sixth sense, my companions had detected the intruder's presence and were scrambling to cover themselves.

Just beyond the hedge we could hear the relaxed, happy voices of the men and boys. They seemed to be having a great time. At about three o'clock everything went quiet, and the tantalising smell of freshly cooked rice and barbecued meat filtered in to torment us. We were, by this time, light-headed with hunger, and still no food came. Had we been forgotten?

The smells faded. Outside, the masculine voices returned with laughter and cheers and the thud of boots hitting a football. And finally we women were summoned to a room adjoining the enclosure where a banquet was laid out for us. The main table staggered under plates piled high with rice, barbecued chickens, kebabs and minced lamb *kofta* on skewers, grilled fish, *tajines* of rabbit and goat and chicken. The side tables held huge bowls of green salad, *tabbouli*, wrapped vine leaves and *hummus*, and piles of flat bread. It was more food than we could possibly eat, despite our hunger. We wandered around the tables, helping ourselves to a bit here and a bit there.

'Picnic very beautiful,' said Ayishah, impressed by the spread. But I was resentful that our banquet, all served at room temperature, was quite obviously the leftovers from the men's meal.

And so the afternoon dragged on. Late in the day, Iman abandoned her Quran and went outside to play on the swings. She was soon swooping energetically back and forth. But suddenly she came flying off the seat, ran behind the slide and flung herself down onto her hands and knees, face buried in the sawdust. Another man had wandered into the enclosure. She remained there, cowering, until I took pity on her and fetched her *abaya*. 'For God's sake, lighten up,' I wanted to say as I handed it to her; but perhaps my face said it all.

At dusk we returned home on the college minibus. The men were tired but happy. It took some time for me to recover from my own foul mood.

Geoff was apologetic.

'I did ask if you could come,' he protested, 'and they assured me that you could.' But by now it was clear that a 'yes' had simply been a way to avoid saying 'no'.

'We should both have known better,' I said.

All September the temperature remained in the mid-40s. Through October, by infinitesimal degrees, it edged lower. Gradually the sun grew less fierce. Or was it simply that we became more inured to the heat and more desperate to get out of the apartment? Whatever the reason, we started to venture out in daylight hours to explore the Diplomatic Quarter.

Those early walks took us no more than a few blocks from al Kendi: all we could cope with before exhaustion set in. We toiled around, content to inspect the various embassies and their carefully landscaped gardens, each one a fine example of how to make the desert bloom.

The security presence was intense. Around the US Embassy, concrete barriers blocked every street, and armed soldiers stopped and checked each vehicle that attempted to pass. Most were turned away.

I had been keen to get some photographs of al Kendi, so Geoff and I went out one day with a camera. Near a roundabout at the far end of the complex I fired off a few shots of the high, blank exterior walls of our home; then we wandered on. In less than a minute a blue and white police jeep roared up and mounted the footpath in front of us, blocking our path. A uniformed officer confronted us and demanded, courteously enough, that I hand over the camera. I complied. He deftly removed the film and exposed the long strip of celluloid. I felt a pang of regret for the shots I had taken of the stuffed lion at the farm picnic. How naïve I had been to even think of taking photographs so close to the US Embassy.

Gradually we extended our walks out into the residential zones of the Diplomatic Quarter. Setting as our destination one of the many public gardens that dotted the precinct, we trudged off doggedly along dusty footpaths across tracts of bare desert. The gardens were laid out, Islamic-style, with geometric symmetry. Fountains splashed gently into reflective pools bordered by stone ledges and clipped box hedges. Crunching gravel pathways led around regular beds of flowers and shrubs, and into shady palm groves. The effect of all this formality was deeply restful. It was lovely to sit quietly in one of the bowers along a garden's edge, watching small birds flit back and forth through the foliage, until we had recovered our energies for the walk back to al Kendi.

In time, we explored out to the edges of the enclave. The Diplomatic Quarter is a wedge-shaped piece of land with its sharp end pointing towards the heart of Riyadh. The long, blunt rear edge of the wedge backs onto the Wadi Hanifa, a deep, many-branched gorge that dissects the Riyadh plateau. On the escarpments high above the valley floor stand the crumbling ruins of small watchtowers that must once, not so very long ago, have served to warn the people who farmed the *wadi* of impending raids by hostile tribes.

At first glance the cliffs of eroded sandstone that border the *wadi* looked completely natural, but close inspection revealed that the rocks had been artfully engineered to enhance the natural strata and to form a pathway. As it meandered around the contours of the escarpment, the path branched out onto viewing platforms, around playgrounds and amphitheatres, and into small chambers and picnic areas where a family could sit in privacy. Along its route it passed through formal gardens and informal plantings of native desert plants. It was a beautiful place to walk, even at night, when the path and the recesses in the rock were softly illuminated by low outdoor lights.

Extending back from the Riyadh end of the Diplomatic Quarter, raised embankments formed the two short sides of the wedge, and along the top of these embankments a broad footpath trailed through groves of acacias and tamarisks and around picnic spots offering panoramic views of the city.

I grew to love these paths. In the cooler months of the year I would take Geoff's bicycle out and pedal furiously, recklessly along them. The Diplomatic Quarter was the only place in Riyadh where it was permissible for women to cycle, and even here I noted scandalised expressions on the faces of the Arabs as I went flying past. I didn't care. I was glorying in my own small moment of liberation.

At the new college, the teachers were settling in, friendships (and enmities) were forming and the character of the fraternity was starting to emerge. This promised to be an interesting process, given the rugged individualism of many of the teachers. It was almost as if the college recruiters had gone out of their way to assemble a disparate cast of eccentrics, although a more likely explanation was that the prospect of working at a new college in Riyadh was unlikely to draw in mainstream candidates. I assured Geoff that, despite the odd blend of enthusiasm and prickly sensitivity in his character, he was by far the least eccentric of the crew. He looked unconvinced.

The bus journeys to and from work were a key meeting point for the teachers. The early shift, taking their lead from the Terrier, had embarked on a spirited Chomskean analysis of the Middle East, from which they were soon able to conclude that the key to all understanding was oil. Geoff rode in on the late shift, and reported that the conversation had turned to an exploration of Arabic culture, language and religion, with one of the Palestinian teachers a willing informant. I envied both groups, although each was generous in sharing insights with me. Meanwhile, some teachers were pursuing trajectories so individual as to make sense only to themselves. They avoided contact, disappearing into their apartments or into the depths of Riyadh with barely a trace in their spare time.

In the aftermath of the picnic, the Saudi directors of the college let the teachers know how disappointed they were that so few of them had attended. There was a loss of face involved – the college had wanted to demonstrate its prestigious foreign faculty, and the teachers had let them down. This was the first sign of bad relations. Things were to get much worse.

At first, the irritations were minor, and could be put down to teething problems. Geoff was forced to work extra hours because his teaching partner was late in arriving. Joy at the announcement of a one-day holiday in the first week of semester turned to disgust when it was learned that it would be made up for with a six-day second week. Some management decisions seemed arbitrary and counterproductive. Why, for example, were two shifts needed when there were so few students, so few classes and so many empty classrooms? The answer was that this was the way things were done at KFUPM, and the college was doing things the KFUPM way.

There were complaints about the KFUPM curriculum. The teaching materials were stodgy and overly academic, exploring such fascinations as the fifteen grammatical uses of the word 'if'. The course had been designed to prepare young men for studies in engineering, and had little relevance to the needs of students destined for careers in management. The teachers' initial enthusiasm turned to anger when their suggestions for adaptations and improvements were ignored. They were dismayed that many of the students accepted into the course did not meet the minimum standards necessary for them to cope with the work, and that some spoke no English at all in a college where the medium of instruction was English. They accused the administration of window dressing and of ignoring important educational issues.

Back at al Kendi, some families were unhappy to discover that their apartments had no natural lighting. Everyone was annoyed when telephone connections took months to materialise. A contractual promise of membership in a sporting club was not honoured when the cost turned out to be more than US$2,000 per person.

Soon money matters, some as petty as a failure to reimburse staff for out-of-pocket expenses, became a source of friction. Monthly salary payments were slow to arrive. Some teachers made the bitter discovery that they were being paid less than their colleagues. Those who, like Geoff, had made the move from Dhahran to Riyadh on the promise of salary bonuses, were angered when the bonuses were not paid, and when no-one would own to responsibility for paying them.

Feuding broke out between the deans and the teachers,

between the Wing Commander and his troops, between the teachers themselves. Morale sank to abysmal depths. Private conversations became recitals of complaint. Geoff came home tired and dispirited every day, although a good night's sleep restored just enough sparkle each morning for him to go on. Now we remembered the advice we had been given: Don't get involved in any new venture in the Kingdom.

Perhaps the problems had to do with poor communication and with differing sets of priorities. The teachers wanted to know, letter and verse, exactly what was going on. The administration kept reassuring them not to worry, to be patient, that all would come out right in the end. Given that many of the teachers had more than a passing relationship with cynicism, the sad result was that relations became increasingly poisonous.

Thanks to Abdul Latif and the college minibus, we were beginning to know our way around the city. The word *riyadh* means 'gardens', but in its dusty open spaces and busy thoroughfares full of careening traffic, there was little evidence of the cultivated greenery that had given the town its name. Everywhere rampant commercial and residential developments were threatening to obliterate all trace of the original townscape.

An excursion to the ruined city of Diriyah, just a few kilometres to the north of the Diplomatic Quarter, showed us something of the area as it must have appeared before the modern age. The town, seat of the al Saud tribe and capital of the first Saudi kingdom, was once home to 5,000 residents. In the early nineteenth century the Ottoman Empire reacted to the growing power of the al Sauds by sending an Egyptian army under Ibrahim Pasha against them. Diriyah withstood a six-month siege before it fell to the invaders. Abdullah, the Saudi leader, was taken in chains to Istanbul and later beheaded there.

When we visited, the city was a ghost town of narrow walled streets and crumbling mud-brick residences and palaces. Some of the old houses were still virtually intact, and it was possible to wander into them, to see rooms opening off a central courtyard, and kitchen walls stained black with cooking smoke. Just in time, the civil authorities had come to see the value of preserving their heritage. Restoration work was under way at Diriyah, and already some of the old palaces had been rebuilt.

In Riyadh, too, attempts were being made to preserve the past. Our next excursion was to the King Abdul Aziz Historical Center, an impressive development that lies just a short distance from busy downtown Batha and the city's then most famous landmark, its water tower. The tower is a sturdy concrete column that fans out at its top into a dish painted with sky-blue stripes radiating out from its centre. The structure gives the impression that a flying saucer has just landed in Riyadh.

In contrast, the Historical Center complex contains many fine examples of traditional Najdi architecture. For all their simplicity, these buildings are impressive. Square two and three storey mud brick buildings sit closely together across narrow alleyways, tapering slightly as they rise. The render on the coffee-coloured walls is combed into wave patterns, and the walls themselves are topped with white-painted crenellations carved into stepped triangles. The triangle motif is repeated on the heavy wooden doors in arrangements of brass studs and dots painted in red and black. Murabba Palace, the former residence of the old king, is a modest two storey structure arranged around a very small square courtyard. The upstairs galleries are closed in behind window panels of pale pink and green tinted glass. The complex also includes a new museum, a men's library and a separate library for women (to my great disappointment, it was not yet operating when I visited), and the inevitable mosque.

Geoff and I often went along on the evening and weekend bus runs, using them as a jumping-off point for our explorations. We remained optimistic that amongst the wearying dusty strips of shops and offices we would find something of interest, and at times our faith was rewarded. One night we stumbled into a small outdoor women's *souk* where the veiled traders sat on their mats talking loudly together in harsh-sounding Arabic, at the same time holding out scraps of food to a gang of desperate-looking feral cats. They took almost no notice of us as we lingered to admire the colourful woven baskets that they were selling, or to sift through their strings of beads and their trays of broken fragments of Bedouin jewellery.

Another night, while taking a shortcut through a multi-storeyed car park, we came upon a collection of caged falcons, each standing silently immobile on a small pedestal wedged into a bed of sand, looking for all the world like giant houseflies in their bulging hoods. And once, we wandered into a neighbour-hood of traditional mud houses in which the inhabitants all appeared to be Africans. According to the Brother from New York, who claimed to know about such things, they were the Kingdom's surviving slaves and their descendants.

I was part of a core group of wives who, ruthless in our deter-mination to escape our apartments, showed up for every weekday bus trip to shopping mall, supermarket or *souk*. It was with the women that I first visited the Mismak fortress in Dira Square, now preserved as a museum. We didn't go in. A sign at the door advised us that 'the entrance of women without *mahram* (husband or brother, etc.) is strictly prohibited'.

Dira is also the site of Riyadh's Grand Central Mosque. On weekdays the area outside the mosque seemed innocent enough with its clean-swept paving and ornamental palm trees, although I could not look upon it without shuddering. The place is also known as 'Chop Chop Square'. On Fridays after the imam preaches his sermon, criminals are executed there, and anyone in the vicinity is rounded up to watch. It is reported that Westerners are always placed in the front row of the crowd. We were religious in our avoidance of Dira on Fridays.

In comparison to the cities of the Gulf, Riyadh had more to offer in the way of scenery, resources and places of interest. It was a richer and more substantial town; but it was also more uptight, more austere, and more rigid. In Riyadh, our favourite restaurant turned us out into the street at prayer time. In Riyadh, all the women, Arab and Western alike, wore *abayas*.

One morning, we waited in vain for Abdul Latif and his bus to take us out shopping. The college had received complaints from citizens shocked at the spectacle of women sitting brazenly with their hair uncovered, and worse, of men and women talking and laughing together as they were being driven about. This was not the sort of attention the college wanted. Until it had been fitted out with curtains and darkened windows, the bus would be unavailable.

The al Manahil Women's Center was only a fifteen-minute walk from al Kendi. Inside its walls, away from the busy car park where male drivers congregated to drop women off and to pick them up again, al Manahil was an oasis of shade and luxury. A glade of tall evergreens shaded a broad paved courtyard and a grassy playground where happy toddlers played, each one tended by his or her own Indonesian nanny. When the air was particularly dry, a fine mist would spray from valves high in the trees, softening the parched air with welcoming humidity and easing edgy nerves.

In the light and airy lobby of al Manahil, ladies came and went: to the elegant restaurant, to the Internet café, to the tennis court, the gymnasium and the swimming pool. They might stop to relax on cushioned wicker couches set amidst low tables and potted palms, and to sip coffee and nibble at cakes brought to them by attentive Filipino waitresses, or pause at the music shop to buy a CD, or to inspect the costume jewellery and Italian giftware in the boutiques. In the calm of the salons, teams of hairstylists, beauticians, masseuses and aromatherapists stood ready to pamper them. In the children's restaurant, staff armed with balloons, bubbles and party hats waited for the chance to delight their children.

But the main attraction of al Manahil, the thing that drew women to it again and again, was its classes. From aerobics to swimming, from painting to computers, the centre offered lessons to improve the body and the mind. In an upstairs wing of the building, the British Council had established the women's branch of its English language school, and it was here that I presented myself one morning to enquire about the possibility of work.

In the reception area, happy children were emerging from a classroom clutching pictures they had drawn, and running into the arms of their fond mothers. Standing at her crowded desk, an assertive young Englishwoman was fielding telephone enquiries, consulting her appointment book, complimenting some children on their drawings, and explaining firmly but tactfully to two pearls in their shells why she could not give them a discount on their English lessons. This was Tess, the director of the school. She looked up and gave me a warm smile of greeting.

I was in luck. Soon I was booked for a few hours of teaching every week. What a relief it was to have an escape from the oppression of my apartment, a place I could get to by myself, without having to wait for a shopping bus. What a joy that my social circle had widened to include the staff of the British Council, and that I had the opportunity to meet some of the women of Riyadh. And what could be more pleasant than to spend some time in the ease and comfort of al Manahil?

I met my first class a few days later, a group of seven aged from late teens to late twenties. I began in the usual way, getting them to introduce themselves and to tell each other a little about themselves. When they had done that, one of them said, 'What about you? Tell us about yourself.'

'Well, I . . .' I began, but they interrupted me.

'What do you think of Saudi Arabia?'

'Be honest. Tell us what you really think.'

'Well, I . . .' I began again, about to issue some platitude about it being 'interesting', or 'different'.

'We hate it here,' said one, and looked about for confirmation. The others were all nodding vigorously. 'It's a terrible place for women,' she said.

10

LOVE AND MARRIAGE

Listen! Treat women kindly; they are like prisoners in your hands.
HADITH, AL-TIRMIDHI, 276

When Riyadh families set out for an evening of fun, the al Kendi Plaza was a favourite destination. It was a vast expanse of white marble paving bordered on two sides by cafés, fast-food restaurants and shops. The cafés, taking advantage of the relaxed rules of the Diplomatic Quarter, had installed tables and chairs for al fresco dining. To my knowledge, this was the only place in the entire city where men and women could enjoy such a facility together.

At the close of each day, big family cars filled the street outside the al Kendi complex. Their passengers were hidden behind darkened and curtained windows, but as the cars pulled into the kerb their doors would fly open. Out would spill: little boys and girls; Indonesian nursemaids carrying infants and clutching bags filled with clothes and toys; substantial family matriarchs in full blackout toting capacious black handbags; willowy teenage girls, also in black, but unveiled; lanky teenage boys in jeans and baseball caps; paters familia in crisp whites; and Subcontinental drivers. At the rear of their vehicles the women stood and issued instructions to the men who were busy unloading strollers, tricycles, toys, rugs, picnic baskets and bags of supplies. When all was assembled, each group proceeded en masse into the plaza.

Some families moved to occupy the tables. Others staked out territory at the far edges of the square, spreading out rugs on the ground. Even before they were settled, the children were on the loose. Bandy-legged toddlers lurched off to explore. Small children started to chase balls around, to torment the stray cats lurking hopefully in the greenery, or to pedal their tricycles earnestly about. They were resilient little beings who seldom cried, even when they fell with a splat onto the ground, or when they were bowled over by a wayward football. Their nursemaids followed them around at a distance, ready to pick them up and dust them off, or congregated in twos and threes, no doubt glad of this opportunity for contact with their own kind.

From age five and up, almost every child was mounted on wheels, with in-line skates the most popular choice. I always watched out for my favourite, a tomboy of about thirteen. Not yet veiled, but already swathed in an *abaya*, she would tie her long black skirt up around her waist and fling herself into her skating with reckless abandon, a mixture of ruthless determination and utter bliss on her face. I wondered how long it would be before she was brought under control.

The plaza was filled with big-booted youngsters taking their first slippery steps. Soon they were ready for 'the spillway', a wide marble ramp that sloped down into the plaza from the housing area. Here they hauled themselves hand over hand up the side railings, their feet sliding treacherously out from under them. At the top they paused, waiting a turn to test their wobbly skills on the way back down.

Although they accomplished each descent with loud squeals and screams, the children appeared to be totally fearless. They needed to be. At intervals, a gang of teenage boys would slice through them, racing each other in a circuit that took them out of the plaza through a side arch, across the forecourt of the mosque, through a sharp left turn into the arcade that ran beneath our apartment, then down the spillway and back into the plaza. Nobody seemed to be worried by their antics, but as they charged through the crowd at breakneck speed, missing babies and tiny children by only a hairsbreadth, they scared the hell out of me.

Teenage girls strolled about the plaza in small groups, loitering over the magazine stand and the ice cream cabinet in the mini-mart, or wandering out through the arch to walk about in the gardens around the mosque. Teenage boys cruising in their vicinity jostled each other and talked loudly, so that the girls huddled together and cast scornful glances over their shoulders, or ostentatiously ignored them. Sometimes the two groups lingered in the shadow of the arch leading from the plaza and exchanged words, but then the ever present police would move in swiftly to send the girls on their way and to reprimand the boys.

At prayer time, the men and boys drifted off to the mosque, leaving the women in possession of the plaza. Upon their return, the men attended to the needs of their families. It was the males who were sent to the store for supplies, or who ordered food and drink from the cafés. With these tasks taken care of, fathers settled down with their families to relax and enjoy the evening. They took obvious delight in their children, leading small boys and girls by the hand around the plaza, buying them treats in shops, waiting indulgently in the fun parlour while their progeny were shaken about in toy cars and aeroplanes. Back at their tables they took little ones on their knees and chatted with them tenderly.

And so the families sat out under the night skys, each one a self-contained unit that had nothing at all to do with the other families seated only metres away. Late in the evening they summoned their drivers, who had been lounging on stone benches out near the entrance. The cars were brought around again, and by midnight everyone had packed up and departed, leaving the square deserted.

Deserted but for the cats, and for the janitors who came to sweep up the food containers and lolly wrappers and soft drink cans. By morning, the plaza would be washed clean.

My ideas about family life in Saudi Arabia were formed long before I ever went there, when I read Jean Sasson's *Princess*. I can still remember the sense of outrage I felt at this account of the life of a woman of the House of al Saud, purported to be in her own words. Here were tales of oppression and cruelty, of daughters murdered for family honour, of sadistic and perverted husbands, of women imprisoned in padded cells and left to rot there. Above all, there was the princess's own sense of injustice and powerlessness. 'AN APPALLING INDICTMENT OF THE TREATMENT OF WOMEN IN SAUDI ARABIA' shouted the red-banner words on the front cover of my paperback edition.

The bitter images of *Princess* contrasted strangely with the picture of happy families that I saw unfold before me night after night in al Kendi Plaza. Although the ways of the Saudis who came there were completely foreign to me, there was something so prosaic, so everyday normal in their demeanour. As to the assertive young ladies who came to my English classes, it was hard to imagine them as anyone's victim.

But what was really going on behind those black veils, the darkened car windows, and the high walls and latticed windows of the houses? Only one thing was clear: the family and, by extension the tribe, were of paramount importance in Saudi society. In fact, it was hard to think of any institution that came even close to rivalling them.

'We are a hot people,' one of my students confided, and despite their strict moral code, the Saudis are not prudish. They see no inherent value in celibacy. The sexual urge is frankly and fondly acknowledged by both sexes, and is regarded as part of Allah's divine plan for men and women, so long as it is confined to marriage.

'O Muslim community!' the Prophet is said to have preached. 'Your daughters are like ripe fruit on a tree. Fruit must be picked at its optimum moment; otherwise the sun or other agencies will rot or spoil it. You must likewise give your daughters in marriage at the moment when they are ripe, and neither later nor sooner. If you leave them hanging about too long, their inevitable corruption will be your fault. They are human, and their needs must be met.'

Marriage is regarded not just as the way to individual fulfilment, but also as a means of integrating young people into society, taming their wilder impulses, and promoting social cohesion. It is a 'biological, psychological and social necessity', wrote Dr Tariq Sharif (*Arab News*, July 9, 1999). 'Any delay or failure in finding one's partner disrupts the mental development of an individual, resulting in a sense of isolation, depression and restlessness.'

In May 2000, Saudis were shocked to read that, according to official census figures, over one third of the female population was unmarried. Dark rumblings erupted about the state of modern marriage and the social cost of educating girls. The Central Statistics Department of the Ministry of Planning quickly issued a clarification. The figure was not accurate, they said, because it referred to girls aged from twelve to twenty-five. Only 2 percent of women aged twenty to twenty-five were unmarried, and when women aged over thirty were included in the count, this figure fell to less than 1 percent (*Arab News*, May 9, 2000).

Traditionally girls have married young. The Prophet was betrothed to his favourite wife, Ayesha, when she was nine and he was fifty-four. Until quite recently, according to my students, a marriage age of thirteen was not unusual, and still occurs. Today, however, girls are choosing to finish their education before they marry, and only 16 percent wed before they are twenty (*Arab News*, April 4, 2000). Even so, an unmarried woman of twenty-five is thought to be on the shelf.

According to academic Dr Kamal Al-Sobhi Al-Harbi, for fear of spinsterhood, a woman aged twenty or over should accept any suitor. Her wish to continue with her studies should not be given undue importance. 'There are many girls who miss the train as a result of insisting on this,' he writes (*Arab News*, December 12, 1997).

Although the girl's wishes are supposed to be taken into account when a marriage is contracted, most have little say in the matter. As the mother of one (somewhat reluctant) girl told me matter-of-factly, 'When her brother decides that it is time for her to marry, she will marry.'

Only a few are able to resist the pressure, and they tend to be the highly educated and financially independent daughters of the elite, secure in their professional careers. 'Because of my financial independence and psychological maturity, I am not at all ashamed of admitting that I am thirty-five, and still single,' said one young woman (*Arab News*, July 9, 1999).

Although the girls in my classes valued education and aspired to careers, few of them could imagine a future without a husband and children. 'It is a woman's role to be a wife and mother,' they told me time and time again.

An unmarried woman lacks status and dignity, and even control over her own finances. 'Life is terrible for a girl who doesn't marry,' said one student. 'Maybe her father will grow too old to drive her, and her brothers will have no time because they have families of their own. Then she is like a prisoner in her parents' home.' She was still single at twenty-eight, and her words had the edge of personal experience.

Although bachelors enjoy a freedom that their sisters can only dream of, they can also find that being single is difficult. Society regards them as wild cards, a danger to respectable families and pure young women. Waiters regularly turned single men away when they attempted to sit at the outdoor tables in al Kendi Plaza. When the shopping malls were crowded, young men not in the company of a female relative were barred. Real estate agents refused to do business with them because neighbouring families were apt to complain about their presence. 'As soon as they found out I'm a bachelor,' lamented one young man, 'they rejected me straight away.' (*Arab News*, May 6, 1999)

One of Geoff's students, a young man of eighteen, was already married. His family had arranged a match for him after he had become obsessed with a young woman and made a nuisance of himself by calling her and following her around. The marriage was seen as a way of keeping him out of trouble.

Despite the risks attached to being a single male, men tend to wed later in life than women, not least because of the financial burden of marriage. According to the youths in Geoff's classes, the price of a Saudi bride is US$100,000, made up of a $20,000 dower to be paid in cash or jewellery (for poor young men, there are popular charities that sponsor the payment of dowers), wedding ceremony expenses and the cost of providing his bride with a house and furnishings. She, however, is under no obligation to contribute financially to the marriage, or even to do the housework if she chooses not to. Her role in the transaction is to provide companionship, sexual partnership and children.

Because of the disparity in their ages, men and women might approach marriage with wildly differing expectations. Men marry when they feel that they are ready to settle down and enjoy a home life; to trade freedom for responsibility. Many young women, however, see marriage as a means of escape from the stifling restrictions of their parental home, and as a pathway to personal freedom and power. But they may well find that they have traded one set of controls for another.

Almost every Saudi marriage is arranged. Far from being horrified at this, the girls I knew were content to let their fathers choose their husbands. 'Of course he will make the best choice for me,' said one. 'He loves me very much, and he knows my character better than I know it.'

In choosing a husband for their daughter, families are advised to consider factors such as the prospective groom's religious observance, his character, his education and income, and whether he will require his bride to live far away from her family. The girl should also be consulted as to her wishes and expectations (*Arab News*, December 12, 1997).

A man who is seeking a bride might rely on the recommendation of a third party – a friend or a female relative, for example – to find a suitable match. Perhaps some of my students were scouting for sisters-in-law amongst their classmates. If so, I never knew about it, although I was always impressed with the courtesy with which they treated each other. In other parts of the Arab world, the basis of choice might be as simple as liking the look of a girl. 'His mother and sister saw me out walking and followed me home,' a young Jordanian told me. 'Then he came and talked to my father.' Her marriage seemed to be as happy as most.

A man who belongs to a good family and has an assured income is likely to have his suit accepted. On the other hand, rejection can be brusque. One of Geoff's acquaintances told of how his first proposal was turned down because the girl's father thought his lack of a beard indicated that he was not sufficiently devout.

Most couples have little chance to get to know each other before they wed, and while they might be committed to marriage, they have no commitment to one particular partner. This can lead to some very strange nuptial ceremonies, which are reported in the press to the delight of everyone.

Here are some of my favourites:

A groom brought his wedding to a halt when a disagreement arose with his bride. Feeling loath to waste the money he had spent on the ceremony, he asked if any of the other young ladies present would be willing to marry him. He chose one of the three girls who volunteered, and the wedding went ahead with a new bride in the starring role.

A man arranged a marriage contract with the father of a girl, his only contact with her family. On the day of the ceremony, unsure of the exact address of his bride, the groom went to her neighbourhood and made enquiries. He was directed to a house where a wedding was scheduled. He didn't know anyone there, and they didn't know him, but on his arrival, the ceremony began. It was interrupted when the bride's father showed up and demanded to know who the impostor was. He was, of course, in the wrong house (*Arab News*, December 17, 1999).

A husband divorced his new wife while the wedding party was still in progress, because she dared to criticise his mother's dancing. 'If my wife talks to me like this now when she hardly knows me,' said the groom, 'what will she say in the future?' (*Arab News*, August 6, 1999)

At a group wedding organised by a charity for poor young people, some brides were mistakenly paired up with the wrong partners, because all the grooms were related and had similar names. Fortunately one of the brides realised the mix-up as the couples were on their way to their bridal chambers (*Arab News*, August 8, 1999).

A father registering the marriages of his three daughters mixed up their names, so that the youngest daughter ended up married to the middle daughter's fiancé. In order to rectify the mistake, the couple would have had to divorce, and then to observe the stipulated waiting period before the bride could marry her own fiancé. Everyone praised the common sense of the youngest daughter when she solved the problem by agreeing to the first marriage. 'It is Almighty Allah who destined me to marry this man,' she said. What her older sister said was not recorded (*Arab News*, December 12, 1999).

When it came to selecting husbands for their daughters, I felt sure that most families chose with care and sensitivity, and that the resulting unions worked very well. Not all girls were so fortunate, however. Ignorance of a bride or groom's character and a cavalier attitude to a daughter's happiness could lead to disaster in individual cases.

One woman confided to a friend of mine that she had not wanted to marry at all, but under pressure had consented to wed a man from a family that she knew to be progressive. She was dismayed to find that her husband was the one member of his family with deeply conservative views, and chafed within the confines of her marriage.

On February 11, 2000 the *Arab News* ran the story of Kamilia (not her real name). The daughter of a very poor family, she had been married at the age of sixteen to an old man who subsequently imprisoned her on the third floor of his house. Although he was kind to her, she later found out that he had two other wives and sixteen children, and was deeply in debt. Left to herself most of the time, 'to overcome loneliness' she gave birth to six children within seven years of marriage. When her husband wanted to marry off their nine-year-old daughter to a forty-four-year-old man so that he could settle his debts, Kamilia asked for and was granted a divorce. She remarried, this time to a fifty-two-year-old man, but he divorced her when his first wife found out about the marriage and objected to it. Now this young

woman found herself alone and unsupported with six children
to care for.

The Saudis look upon Western marriages and their basis in
romantic love with horror. They defend their custom of arranged
marriage by reference to an ideal: a match made by caring parents
taking full consideration of a daughter's needs and wishes. Such
a marriage cements family bonds and offers both partners sexual
fulfilment, the joy of children, and eventually companionship,
serenity, comfort and even love. No doubt many Saudi marriages
approach this ideal, and even I could see some advantage to their
methods. A focus on the institution of marriage, rather than upon
personal romantic fulfilment, might relieve the partners of the
pressure to be all things to each other, and to find fulfilment, in
one another alone. Perhaps if their expectations are less than
exalted, any disappointment may be less bitterly felt and the
union may prove resilient.

But in the press I read tales of greedy fathers selling their
daughters into marriage and then pocketing their dowries, of very
young girls wedded to very old men, and of the ruin of virgins
taken as wives and then divorced or abandoned.

The official line that a woman's role was to be a wife and
mother was trumpeted everywhere, yet I met young women
who were as ambivalent about marriage as I had been at their
age. What happens to the square pegs? I wondered. How much
unhappiness do they endure in their unwished-for marriages?
I could only be grateful that no man had had the power to turn
me into a tradeable commodity, and that I had enjoyed the
freedom, for better or worse, to make my own choices and to
control my own destiny.

A beginner's English lesson. The topic was 'My Family'.

We looked in our course book at a picture of a young woman
with her parents and her sister. Then we played the cassette.

'Hello. My name's Susan. I have one sister. Her name is . . .'

We discussed the picture again, and made a vocabulary list:
mother, father, sister, brother . . .

Next up was a diagram: a family tree. We worked through it together, eliciting the vocabulary.

'Catherine is Susan's . . .?'

'. . . sister!'

We added other family words to the list: husband, wife, son, daughter, uncle, aunt, cousin ...

I drew my own family tree on the board, and stuck some photos of my relatives on it in the appropriate places. Then I invited the students to gather around and ask me questions about them.

'Who is this?' said Sara, pointing.

'She is my niece,' I told her.

'Who is this?'

'He is my brother-in-law.'

'Teacher, you no have children?'

'No.'

They exchanged glances, then regarded me with grave sympathy.

Next it was their turn to show their photographs. 'This is my niece,' said Karima, offering a picture of a small child. 'She very nice girl. Very ugly.'

'Yes,' I confirmed, remembering that Saudis describe their children as ugly to ward off the evil eye. 'Very ugly.'

'Noura,' I asked, 'do you have any brothers?'

'Yes, I brothers.'

'How many brothers do you have?'

Noura screwed her face up in concentration. She counted on her fingers. She conferred in Arabic with the other girls. Sheika answered for her.

'Teacher, she has thirteen brothers, but the mother different.'

We added half-brother to the vocabulary list.

The girls practised asking each other questions. 'How many mothers do you have?'

'I have three mothers.'

I handed out markers and sheets of butcher's paper. 'Now please draw your family tree, just like this one,' I said, indicating the simple chart I had drawn on the board. I should have known it wasn't going to be quite so straightforward. Soon the girls were lost in concentration. Their diagrams sprawled out in ever-branching webs that filled their sheets of paper and threatened to stray off across their desktops.

'Teacher, this man is my sister's husband,' said Farida, pointing to a node on her tree.

'Yes, he is your brother-in-law,' I said.

'No, teacher, he is my cousin.'

Some 39 percent of Saudi marriages are between first cousins, and more than 50 percent are kept within the family. So common is the practice of marriage between cousins that a wife addresses her mother-in-law as *marat-ammi*, literally 'wife of my uncle'.

One of my students, Leila, told me how she had come to marry her cousin. 'I was sixteen,' she said, 'and he was thirty. He was an engineer. He was educated in the USA, and he was already very successful. My father thought that he would be a good husband for me, so he talked to him about it, and he agreed.'

'How did you feel about it?' I asked her.

'It was no problem. I knew that my father would make the best choice for me. But for my husband it was terrible, those early days. I was just a child, and I was very spoilt.'

Although some of my young students professed themselves to be less than enthusiastic about the idea of marrying a cousin ('I don't like any of them,' said one), it is the option that most families prefer. This is hardly surprising, given the importance of privacy in Saudi culture. Intra-family marriage avoids the unpleasantness of admitting a stranger into the bosom of the family, and reduces the risk of any nasty surprises that such a stranger may bring. Families may also have a tempering influence on the behaviour of partners: after all, if a husband mistreats his cousin, everyone in the family is likely to know about it. But by far the most frequent reasons I heard given for the practice were that it builds clan cohesion and keeps the family fortune intact.

Marriage to a first cousin does increase the risk of genetic disorders in children born to the couple, and although, according to some medical opinion, these risks might be exaggerated, for some families they are real enough. One woman I met had three blind daughters, and in the *Arab News* (February 4, 2000) I read of couples with up to seven children all born with impaired sight or hearing. My students often made mention of afflicted children or siblings.

'It is God's will,' they would tell me resignedly.

These days, however, many cousins seek genetic counselling before they consent to marry.

One of the first Saudi women I met was Warda, my upstairs neighbour back at KFUPM, whose husband was a research student at the university. I had been quite unaware of her existence until the day she knocked on my door and, to my surprise and delight, invited me to visit her. A few days later I made my way upstairs to join her in her living room.

For once there was no Danish furniture in sight. Instead, Warda's apartment was furnished with soft, cream-coloured sofas and luxurious woollen wall to wall carpeting. We sipped coffee from tiny gold cups, and nibbled on sweet honey and semolina biscuits. Khalil, her one-year-old son, worked his way back and forth between us on chubby legs, his hands gripping the edge of the low, glass-topped table.

Warda was just twenty years old, and had been married for two years. She brought out her photo album and proudly showed me snapshots of her honeymoon in Europe, of her husband and of young Khalil. Every few minutes her mobile phone would ring: a cousin or girlfriend calling to chat. How did she spend her days? I asked her. She said that she played with her child and cooked for her husband. She professed herself to be perfectly in love, perfectly happy.

A woman gains status through parenthood, and especially through the birth of sons. She is even honoured with the name of her firstborn son: Um Abdullah (Mother of Abdullah), or Um Mohammad (Mother of Mohammad). Women without children are to be pitied.

For men, children are proof of virility. I had heard that they regard the birth of a daughter as a disappointment; that they had been known to divorce a woman who bore them no sons, or to take another wife. Despite this, I saw only affection in the way fathers treated their daughters, and the girls who came to my English classes left me in no doubt that they enjoyed loving relationships with their fathers.

'Children are God's gift,' my students told me, and God has been generous to the Saudis. They have one of the world's highest birth rates, with an average of 6.25 live births per woman. Family planning, regarded as an attempt to interfere with God's creation, is not popular in the Kingdom.

However, an expat obstetrics nurse at King Faisal Hospital in Riyadh told me that many women feel under pressure to produce babies in order to please their husbands. 'It's not unusual to see women in with their fourteenth or fifteenth pregnancy,' she said. 'I've got a patient at the moment who's in for her fifth caesarean delivery. After the last one, we persuaded her to have a tubal ligation, because another caesarean is almost certain to kill her, but her husband refused to sign the consent form. He says he wants just one more baby, and she's prepared to indulge him.'

In April 2000 a ground-breaking operation was performed by an all-Saudi team of doctors at the King Fahd Hospital in Jeddah. In a world first, the team transplanted a uterus into a woman who had been unable to bear children. Sadly, the operation was ultimately unsuccessful, but in those early days an outpouring of national pride greeted its announcement. It was, said the commentators, proof of the Kingdom's efficiency and potential. I thought rather that it was proof of where the nation's priorities lie.

'Man marries his maid after nine years,' said the headline (*Arab News*, August 20, 1999). According to the story that followed, wives in Taif now feared to keep female servants in their houses, and husbands were threatening to marry maids as a way to stop their wives demanding more servants.

Polygamy in Arabia predates the arrival of Islam. The Quran decrees that a man may have up to four wives at any one time, so long as he is able to care for them adequately and treat them equally. Because divorce is easy for a man, he may in his lifetime have a succession of many wives. The Prophet himself had several, although it is clear that some of his marriages were to cement political alliances or to take care of the widows of fallen comrades.

'These days,' one Saudi woman told me, 'it is very unfashionable for a man to have more than one wife, and only uneducated men do it.'

My own impression was that the custom was still common enough. I was told of families where the husband kept one permanent wife, but married and divorced a series of other wives for variety; of others where the husband often travelled abroad, and each time married a different local woman for the duration of his visit. While this form of temporary marriage is not approved of, there was little official criticism of the practice.

The vagaries of polygamous marriage are a rich source of copy for the nation's press. Here are some examples from the pages of the *Arab News*:

In Jeddah, a first wife had a falling out with her husband's second wife, and by way of revenge printed up invitations to his supposed third marriage. The second wife, upon reading one of these invitations, collapsed and had to be taken to hospital (June 14, 1999).

Again in Jeddah, in an unusual display of filial devotion, an eighteen-year-old son supported his father's second and third marriages by helping to arrange the ceremonies, and by trying to pacify his distraught mother (August 10, 1999).

In Al Baha, a husband who beat his first wife when she quarrelled with his attractive new wife was in turn beaten by the outraged family of the first wife (January 27, 2000).

Two themes underpin the black humour of these reports. The first is the difficulty experienced by hapless husbands in managing more than one passionate wife. The second is the sense of insecurity that wives feel in face of the threat that their husband will remarry.

She has good reason to feel insecure on that count: if she makes too strong an objection, he might just divorce her.

'Of the things which are lawful, the most hateful to God is divorce,' says the Hadith (AD 13:3), but Islam allows couples to escape from an unhappy marriage and to start afresh. The common belief that a Muslim man can divorce his wife simply by repeating three times 'I divorce you' is false. In fact, he only has to say it once. And although Islamic law outlines certain formalities that must be observed before he can send his wife back to her family, in essence a man can obtain a divorce very easily. He has no need to justify his decision.

A woman who wishes to terminate her marriage has a far more difficult path to follow. She must apply to a court of law for a divorce and must give a legally acceptable justification for her suit. In the eyes of the law her word will carry less weight than her husband's. Even if she complains of neglect or physical abuse, the magistrate will be loath to break up her family if her husband expresses remorse for his behaviour and promises to reform. And, in fact, many women are completely dependent upon their husbands, and have no other choice than to endure even an abusive marriage.

In Islamic marriage the wife does have property rights. The dower that her husband pays is hers to keep as a form of insurance against the possible failure of her marriage through divorce or the death of her husband. The Arabian women that I met took these rights very seriously. When thieves broke into a friend's house, for example, she insisted that her husband immediately replace her stolen dower jewellery. The system doesn't always work, however. Some husbands cheat their wives of their dower; some wives never see their dower because their families have kept it, and most dowers would not keep a woman for long anyway. Because women have so little opportunity to support themselves through paid employment, divorce may well equal financial ruin.

Given how difficult it is for women to live independently, it is inevitable that in order to preserve their marriages they should feel under pressure to please their husbands, whether this means bearing them children, putting up with another wife, or gratifying their sexual demands. The obstetrics nurse from King Faisal Hospital in Riyadh told me that one of the most common operations performed in her department was post-natal reconstructive surgery. This had nothing to do with the women's own comfort, she said. They wanted to 'make themselves tighter', because their husbands had complained that they were too loose. In one case, the woman had given birth only two weeks before.

The percentage of marriages that end in divorce is unknown. I have seen estimates ranging from 20 percent to as high as 70 percent; it is unclear whether these figures include marriages that could be considered to have failed because the husband has simply neglected or abandoned his current wife in favour of a new one. One veteran teacher told me that he had lost count of the number of boys from broken homes he had seen in his classes. Typically, although by law it is the father who has responsibility for and custody of children past the age of seven, they had been abandoned along with their mothers. As a result, he said, many boys suffered from poverty and hunger, and their mothers were forced to rely on charity to survive.

The Pakistani maintenance worker dismissed his assistant, and asked for a drink of water. He took the glass I brought him, and settled down in an armchair in my living room to drink it.

'Very big problem here in Saudia for me, madam,' he said with a sorrowful face and a conspiratorial air.

'Oh?'

'Yes, very big problem. The Saudi women are giving me big problem. I go to fix their apartment, they say "please look in my bedroom". It is terrible.' He waited for my reaction.

'Oh,' coldly.

'Yes. Their husband, you know, he does not . . .' An expressive wave of the hand. 'You know. So the women, they are crazy. They make me . . .' Another wave of the hand.

'Then they are calling me, calling me. "Something is broken, you must come." Very dangerous for me. But what can I do?' He spread his hands out, palms up, in a gesture of helplessness, and licked his lips. 'Because they like me very much.'

By now I could see where the conversation was headed. I went to the front door and stood waiting for him to leave.

Even back in Australia I'd heard tales of the wicked ways of Saudi women. On my last trip home a Melbourne taxi driver, a recent immigrant from Ethiopia, had told me about a man from his village who had gone to work in the Kingdom, and had come home to his friends with stories of Saudi women pursuing him, seducing him, tearing his clothes off, refusing to take no for an answer. 'It was terrible for him,' he said, 'those Saudi women . . .'

I'd clucked sympathetically, trying not to laugh.

If the official line is to be believed, Saudis adhere to a perfect system of morality in which men and women never meet outside the family and passion is played out only within the confines of marriage. It was no surprise that everyone acts with modesty and decorum, at least in public. To be caught committing a sexual transgression is to risk dire punishment, even death.

Because her family's honour rests upon her purity, a woman must be pure beyond reproach. She must be publicly invisible, because to be otherwise gives her a reputation. It is a deadly insult for one young man to ask another, 'How's your sister?' Such a question implies that the girl is known about and talked about. The correct form of enquiry as to the well-being of a man's family is, I am told, 'How are those who stand behind you?'

A woman can never allow herself to be left alone with an unrelated man. According to an oft quoted Saudi proverb, in such a situation, a third party is always present, and that one is Shaitaan, the devil himself.

But: 'Arab women are flirtatious,' said one of Geoff's colleagues. 'They really take a good look at you from behind those veils.' And Geoff confessed that he, too, had felt the gaze of dark eyes upon him.

My students told me of girls who passed their time in their bedrooms randomly dialling phone numbers in the hope of finding a man to talk to, and of women who paid taxi drivers for the use of their mobile phones so that they could call their lovers. They even told me of 'very bad girls' who, when they were supposed to be attending classes at university or visiting their female friends, were, in fact, keeping trysts with their lovers.

'What will happen to them if they are caught?' I asked. The girls shook their heads and would not speak.

'It depends on the family,' said one finally, but another added darkly, 'This is a dangerous country.'

'When I worked in a hospital south of Jeddah,' a New Zealand nurse told me, 'every week we'd find one or two newborn infants abandoned on the doorstep. The *muttaween* would come round and pressure us to say that these babies looked like Asians, and should be registered as the offspring of naughty housemaids,' she said, 'but they looked like Arab babies to me.'

Despite these stories of misbehaviour, I had no reason to believe that the vast majority of Saudi women were not pure in thought, word and deed. I was not so sure about the men. For them, a smorgasbord of opportunities for dalliance exists outside their already flexible marriage arrangements. Within the family home there are maids to be exploited. The existence of brothels in the major towns is an open secret. Homosexuality is forbidden absolutely, yet almost every male expat can tell tales of being propositioned by a hopeful Saudi male. In the fleshpots of the world, their reputation for venality is unsurpassed.

I was left with the question: Just how bad are things for Saudi women, and what do they think of their plight? Unlike Jean Sasson, I had no princess willing to confide in me. It seemed indelicate to probe my students for information on such private matters, and they were hardly likely to confide in a foreign teacher whom they met with for just a few hours each week. Indeed, whenever our conversations veered towards a sensitive area, I came hard up against their natural reserve. Their usually animated faces became expressionless, they fell silent. I respected their privacy and backed off, reassured by the affection with which they spoke of their fathers, whom they invariably described as 'wise' and 'kind'.

My suspicion was that Saudi marriage and family life, when it works, can be very good indeed for a woman, but that when it goes wrong, it can be hell.

Expat medical workers assured me that it was common to find women in their hospital wards who were the victims of beatings. I heard anecdotal evidence of honour killings: stories of murdered young women found buried in sand dunes. Articles appeared in the *Arab News* with the titles 'Standing up against domestic violence' (May 14, 1999), 'Housewife beaten to death in Jizan' (November 10, 1999), and 'The problem of women abuse' (March 31, 2000).

Judging from these newspaper articles, a certain level of violence was endemic in society. I read about wives beaten by husbands, children beaten by mothers, husbands beaten by fathers-in-law, servants beaten by mistresses or masters, students beaten by teachers, teachers beaten by students. 'A Saudi living in the United States was recently sentenced to serve a jail term for beating his wife,' read one report (*Arab News*, July 25, 1999). 'It never occurred to him that what he viewed as teaching his wife some good manners would land him in jail in a foreign country.'

'When I first came here in the early seventies,' a veteran expat told me, 'the government had given all the farmers pick-up trucks. You'd be driving along the road and you'd see a farmer in his truck with his sons by his side. His wife and his daughters would be in the back with the sheep and goats.'

It seemed to me that while the material status of Saudi women had improved, in social status they were still little better than children, or worse, chattels. Sometimes I wondered if the only real change that had occurred in the past thirty years was that their families were now rich enough to buy cars that could accommodate an entire family.

The Saudis, and Muslims in general, dispute the idea that their religion places women in an inferior position. Didn't the Prophet himself put an end to the practice of killing baby girls? Didn't he urge his followers to treat women kindly? Didn't he establish property rights for women that were not matched in the West for centuries? Men and women are equal in the eyes of Allah, they argue, but by nature different, with different roles to play. Men are rational beings who are naturally suited to lead their families. Women are emotional creatures whose happiness lies in accepting their God-given role as wives and mothers.

Rebellion against this divine plan can only lead to unhappiness and social decadence. For proof of this, Saudis look to the West, which is constantly held up as an example of moral decay. 'We keep our women at home and call it protection,' wrote a correspondent to the *Arab News* (March 24, 2000). 'They have brought their women, half-naked, on the streets and call it freedom.' From the reports they read in the press and no doubt from the sermons they hear preached in the mosque, Saudis could be forgiven for thinking that Western society has surrendered entirely to promiscuity, unmarried teenage pregnancy, rising divorce rates, declining fertility rates, abortion on demand, pornography, HIV-AIDs, drug abuse and crime.

The reason for the rot is clear: 'These reports of dysfunctional Western families is strong evidence of the havoc played by the destructive slogans of the feminist movements,' wrote Dr Asem Hamdam (*Arab News*, May 6, 1999). 'On the other hand, Islam has made the relationship between husband and wife above material considerations and has also provided it with a stronger base which holds it together with greater strength.'

Despite its flaws, the institution of the Saudi family is robust. Saudis look to their families for companionship, friendship and entertainment. They rely on family connections and resources for support, and are bound to their clans in a complex web of favour, opportunity and obligation.

I could see that the young women who came to my classes were often bored, frustrated, and impatient; some were even rebellious. But they were not seeking massive change. For them, family was everything; they would have it no other way. They were proud, and offended by Western stereotypes that classed them as victims.

'Do you think it's fair that men have more power than women?' I once asked a class.

'It is better that men lead,' they told me. 'Women are very emotional.'

'But of course you are,' I wanted to say. 'It's the only weapon you've got.'

After a class at al Manahil one day, a student, Samira, introduced me to her mother. To my delight, the two women asked me to visit them.

At last, I told myself, I'll get to see inside a Riyadh villa, and get a taste of real family life.

Samira came to pick me up in the family's huge American station wagon. I joined her in the back seat, where she sat fully veiled. Her two young brothers had come along for the ride, and a Filipino driver was at the wheel.

The family home in a western suburb of Riyadh was an imposing two storeys of pale stucco surrounded by a high concrete fence. The heavy security gate led into a grassy fore-court where a couple of date palms stood next to a swimming pool. We entered the house through a pair of huge doors made of frosted glass and wrought iron.

The boys disappeared into the house as we were hanging up our *abayas* in the hall, and Samira's sister Haifa and her mother Ruqayyah appeared. They made me welcome in the Saudi way, with a light embrace and phantom kisses on the cheeks.

The women led me into an enormous room that was luxuri-ously fitted out with crystal chandeliers and thick Chinese rugs. Around the walls, baroque gilt chairs upholstered in tapestry provided seating for fifty or sixty. 'This is our *majlis hareem*, where we receive our visitors,' Ruqayyah explained. 'The men have one just like it on the other side of the house.' We spread ourselves out over four of the chairs, and a servant brought tea and a small dish of sweet dates.

'See, my daughters are wearing the traditional Arab dress for you,' said Ruqayyah, and the girls shyly modelled their elegant caftans, Samira in black with elaborate white embroidery, and Haifa in gold upon brown. Ruqayyah had opted for a casual look: a pair of black stretch pants and a T-shirt.

She was a woman of about forty-five, still attractive. As we sipped our tea, she told me about her life. 'I married my husband when I was sixteen,' she said. 'As soon as we were married we moved to the USA so that he could continue his studies. At first I felt very unhappy there; I was so cold and lonely and everything was strange. I had no-one to talk with, I was by myself all day in the house. I couldn't go out.'

She gave birth to her first child alone in America, aged just seventeen. 'That was terrible. At home my mother and my sisters would have been there to help me. There I was completely alone, with no-one even to speak my language.'

In time she learned to adjust, even to enjoy the American lifestyle. She learned to speak English. She got her driver's licence. She found female friends there. 'I still call my friend in Florida,' she told me. 'I miss her very much.'

Later we moved to the dining room, where a table lay groaning under dishes piled high with steaming food. There was a *biriyani* made of rice and camel meat; peppers and aubergines stuffed with mince, pine nuts and herbs; a kind of handmade, whole-wheat pasta; a starchy dish of mashed potato mixed with chicken; a pot of *molokia*, the viscous green soup that so many of my students claimed as their favourite dish; bowls of the fava bean stew known as *foul*, and of *hummus* and *tabbouli*.

'My daughters have spent all day cooking for you,' said Ruqayyah. 'They want you to try the real Saudi food.' The two girls smiled modestly. They had prepared enough food to satisfy the appetites of all sixty possible occupants of the *majlis hareem*, and now handed me a large plate, inviting me to help myself. Feeling under pressure to do justice to their efforts, I gave myself a generous serving. The girls and their mother looked disappointed.

'Have some more,' urged Haifa.

'Have you tried this one?' asked Samira.

'You must have some of this one,' said Ruqayyah, and she scooped a stuffed vegetable onto my plate.

The food was delicious, and I ate as much of it as I could before I pushed my plate away. My hosts looked doubtfully at me. They had eaten very little. I couldn't tell whether they felt insulted that I hadn't eaten enough, or shocked at my greediness.

After the meal, we retired to a spacious family room that was comfortably furnished with low couches and tables. A servant brought us *ghawa* and sweets. Now the conversation turned to family life in Arabia. Ruqayyah talked freely, generously indulging my curiosity.

'Our family is from the Najd,' she told me. 'We are the true Arabs. The names of our fathers are written down in family books that go back to before the time of the Prophet, peace be upon him.'

'The *abaya* is comfortable for us,' she said. 'It makes us feel safe. But some families are so strict that the wife never unveils, not even before her own husband.'

'These days, only uneducated men take a second wife,' she said. 'But you know, there are some wives, when they get tired of their husband's "strength," who try to arrange a new wife for him.'

'It was my dream to go to college and get my degree,' she said, 'but my husband would never allow this for me. But my daughters are educated. They will marry when their education is finished.' I glanced at the girls. They both looked squeamish.

'In the family,' said Ruqayyah, 'fathers have all the power. Do you know, if a father wants to kill his son, he has that right.'

I listened avidly, fascinated. After so many months of feeling shut out by the shyness and reserve of the Saudis, I was astonished by her frankness. I wished the night could go on forever. There were so many questions I wanted to ask.

Samira placed some rose-scented incense in a censer and set it alight. The fragrant odour curled up and wrapped itself about us. We chatted on, until the phone rang and Samira took the call.

I overheard an impatient male voice at the other end. She answered back just as sharply and then hung up. 'That was my father,' she said. 'He and my brothers are in the other half of the house, in the library.'

Suddenly I remembered my Arabian etiquette. After the coffee has been served and the incense has been lit, it's time for the guest to go home.

11

GOD'S COUNTRY

*If we look around, we see that everything – including the sun, the
moon and the stars, the high hills and the mighty oceans – are obeying
a Law – the Law of Allah.*
GHULAM SARWAR, Islam Beliefs and Teachings

F rom the tall, narrow windows of our apartment we looked
out onto the huge mosque that lay at the heart of the
Diplomatic Quarter. Like the rest of the al Kendi complex, it was
built in the austere style of the central Najd desert: a crenellated
sandcastle with walls rendered in pale tan. Its minarets were two
soaring but solidly square towers, fifty metres tall. Five times a
day the *muezzin* climbed to a microphone in the nearest tower to
call the faithful to prayer.

'*Allah akbar*,' he chanted in the early hours of the morning
when the world was still dark. 'Allah is most great . . . Come to
prayer . . . Praying is better than sleeping . . .'

His amplified voice was sonorous and rich. For the first few
days it jolted us awake, but later it insinuated itself into our
dreams and became our early morning lullaby. Did anyone
respond to this predawn call? Perhaps, like me, they simply rolled
over and went back to sleep.

His later summonses, spread throughout the day and evening,
drew a steady stream of men to the broad, arched entrance of the
mosque. From my high window I watched them slip out of their

shoes, place them in neat pairs against the wall, and disappear inside.

Prayer is the second of the five pillars of Islam. (The others are the profession of faith, almsgiving, fasting and pilgrimage.) Muslims still pray in the manner taught to them by the Prophet 1,400 years ago. First come the ablutions: ritual movements to cleanse the face, the hands, the lower arms, the feet and the hair of the head. These gestures are performed without the benefit of water when none is available. Thus purified, the men form themselves into orderly lines facing towards Mecca and the Kaabah. The imam, who is not a priest but a scholar and the leader of the congregation, chants the prayer, which is also the first Surah of the Quran.

'In the name of Allah, Most Compassionate, Most Merciful,' he prays. 'Praise be to Allah, Lord of the universe. Most Compassionate, Most Merciful. Master of the Day of Judgment. You alone we worship; You alone we ask for help. Guide us in the right path; the path of those whom You have blessed; not of those who have deserved Your wrath, nor of the strayers.'

'Glory to my Lord the most great,' the congregation responds. 'Glory to my Lord the most high.' 'God listens to those who thank Him.' 'I bear witness that there is no god but Allah.'

No doubt prayer has benefits for the physical body as well as for the spirit; in terms of suppleness, a congregation of Muslims would put one of Christians to shame. Muslims do not so much say their prayers as perform them; standing, kneeling, and bowing down in submission. The foreheads of the most devout are callused from touching them to their prayer mats.

In the mosque, each man prays alone before Allah, and each is part of the brotherhood that is that congregation. Arabian women stay at home to perform their prayers. They are part of a wave of supplication that sweeps around the world every day, triggered by the rise of the sun. It begins in a ripple of concentric circles around the Kaabah, then, following the dawn, sweeps west over the Arabian Peninsula and on into Turkey and the Balkans. It eddies into Europe and fades there, but across North Africa it carries all before it. On the other side of the Atlantic it is picked up by immigrants and converts in the Americas. Over the vast emptiness of the Pacific it registers barely at all, but as the sun rises over the southern Philippines, over Malaysia and Indonesia, it picks up momentum. Up it rolls through Sri Lanka, Bangladesh and India. In Pakistan it crests in a mighty surge that washes over Central Asia and the Middle East, back to Mecca, to where it all began twenty-four hours earlier. Another day has begun.

If there is power in prayer, then this is powerful stuff.

'I am so proud to be Muslim,' said Khalifa, one of my students at al Manahil. 'So proud to live in this country where God chose to send his messenger. And I am proud of my language, Arabic, because this is the language that God chose to reveal to us the Holy Quran.'

Islam was everywhere. Mosques peppered the landscape so frequently that every man was within easy walking distance of one. Just outside the Diplomatic Quarter the ornate, tiled domes of three cathedral-sized mosques sat side by side. There were others just as opulent nearby.

Islam informed the way people dressed, the way they inter-acted, the way they thought. It permeated every conversation, touching it with courtly formality. *Alhamdulillah!* May God be praised! *Allah yubaarikfi.* May God bless you. *Insh'Allah.* If God wills it. *Wallahi!* By God!

Saudi television served up a steady diet of prayers and sermons, recitations from the Quran, and live telecasts of pilgrims circling the Kaabah. Local articles in the press were imbued with Islam, and each Friday the papers featured pages devoted to the religion. In the *Arab News* this took the form of feature articles, photographs of mosques, and regular 'Guidance from the Prophet', 'Islam in Perspective' and question-and-answer columns. Each printed reference to the Prophet's name was followed by the acronym PBUH – Peace Be Upon Him. The same blessing was intoned after every spoken mention of his name.

The Saudi state and Islam are so closely intertwined as to be inseparable. The king is blessed, *bismillah* (by the grace of God), with the title 'Custodian of the Two Holy Mosques', the Grand Mosque of the Kaabah in Mecca, and the Prophet's Holy Mosque in Medina. These are the most holy sites in all Islam. The state's constitution and its legal system is Sharia, the system of laws set out in the Quran (the Islamic holy book, or bible) and the Hadith (the collected sayings of the Prophet). The national flag bears the Quranic inscription *'ilaha il-Allah; Mohammad rasul Allah'* – There is no god but Allah; and Mohammad is His Prophet – in elegant Arabic calligraphy, white on a green background, underscored by a drawn sword. This is the first pillar of Islam, the avowal of the faith that, in the centuries of the Muslim conquests that followed the death of the Prophet in 632 AD, was enough to spare the life of an infidel who recited it.

The state runs to an Islamic calendar that dates from 622 AD, the year that marks the beginning of Islam as a mass movement, when the Prophet fled from Mecca as the persecuted leader of a minority sect, and was welcomed into Medina as both the religious and the political leader of that city. The calendar has currently advanced to the fifteenth century. The months pass in lunar time according to the waxing and waning of the moon, slipping forward by eleven days each solar year. The days move to the rhythm of prayer.

At each call from the minaret, everything pauses. Television programs are interrupted, businesses pull down their shutters, men head to the mosque, hostesses take time out from entertaining, long distance travellers pull to the side of the road.

In the West prayer tends to be a discrete practice confined to churches and to private spaces, while public prayer is the province of mystics and crackpots. Amongst the Saudis, it is a routine activity that comes as naturally as eating or sleeping. I was always amazed to see teenage boys, rough truck drivers, and hardened security guards kneeling to pray in the open air. Once, on a train journey from Dammam to Hofuf, when we found ourselves in seats facing a small open area at the front of the carriage, a carpet was unrolled at our feet, and a succession of people came to pray – first the men and boys, then the women in their veils, then the male stragglers. We felt like intruders, and squirmed in embarrassment, but the locals paid us not the slightest heed.

'Write a paragraph describing the person you most admire,' I instructed my class. Nine out of nine students wrote about the Prophet Mohammad, and I made a note to myself that the next time I set this assignment, I would ask them to write about the living person they most admire.

I could see the appeal of Islam: the simplicity of its five pillars, the grace and purity of its traditional arts and architecture, the poetic beauties of the Holy Quran, evident even in translation. I liked the absence of an elaborate hierarchy of priests, and the sense of community and brotherhood (I use the term advisedly), overriding race, colour and class. I was sure that the act of submission to the will of the Almighty brought with it a deep sense of peace, and that there was satisfaction to be gained in adhering to a path of obedient righteousness. It was hard not to be impressed by the piety of the Saudis, and by the depth of their conviction.

For many Muslim expats, the attraction of a work contract in Saudi Arabia was in being able to live in the heartland of their religion. They embraced Saudi conservatism so completely that even the more liberally minded locals flinched at their fervour.

To Western expats, however, the local version of Islam seemed to be intent upon squeezing all the fun out of life. Loud public laughter was out – considered vulgar and unseemly. Music, with the single exception of martial songs, was un-Islamic, as was dance. Public entertainment didn't exist. Flirtation was, of course, completely out of the question – young people must do without it, on pain of public flogging. Even colour was subdued. I don't think I ever saw a bright red car in the Kingdom. For cars, only muted and quiet tones exhibited the proper degree of modesty.

It was as if the walls of a nunnery had been broken down, and the whole society had become infected with a censorious piety. We grew weary of the need for constant circumspection, weary of the condescension shown to non-Muslims, weary of the suspicious wariness with which we, as infidels, were regarded.

'Don't judge all Muslims by the Saudis,' urged the broad-minded, both Muslim and non-Muslim.

The third pillar of Islam is almsgiving, or Zakat, and the fourth is fasting. Both are observed during the month of Ramadan.

My first experience of a Saudi Ramadan was in the Eastern Province. The university had us on written notice: public consumption of food or drink during the holy month was a crime. Anyone caught drinking, eating or smoking in public during daylight hours would find themselves with a fast (no pun intended) ticket out of the country, and could expect no support from the administration. To assist staff in their observance, all of the water coolers on the *jabal* were removed for the duration.

While expats awaited the onset of Ramadan with, at best, resignation, Muslims looked forward to it with keen anticipation. Mosques were cleaned and furnished with new carpets. Strings of coloured lights were wound around lampposts, draped over the facades of buildings, and strung up in shopping malls. Shopkeepers decorated their stores with banners and bunting, filled them with merchandise and advertised Ramadan specials.

'Ramadan is the best time of the year,' one of my students assured me, 'because all my family is together. The best memories of my childhood are from Ramadan.'

No-one could tell us exactly when the holy month would begin. By mid December, all eyes were raking the evening sky for the first glimpse of the new moon, at this stage a barely visible sliver, that would signal its onset. Finally, on December 18, the calm of the evening was shattered by an outburst of explosions. Ramadan had begun, and revellers were letting off an arsenal of firecrackers to celebrate.

The next morning, highways were empty of cars, shops failed to open, and restaurants and cafés remained closed and shuttered. Banks and other commercial establishments announced reduced daytime trading hours. Throughout the month, the days remained quiet and subdued. Official press announcements were at pains to tell us that Ramadan should make no difference to our work schedules, that offices and businesses should maintain their services as normal. But, in fact, the whole population had become nocturnal. Only the Bangladeshis seemed to be keeping to their normal schedules.

Ramadan, the month in which the Quran was revealed to the Prophet, is celebrated with gratitude to Allah, fasting, prayers and repentance. During Ramadan Muslims try to do righteous deeds, to cultivate piety, charity, mercy, forgiveness and patience, and to refrain from disputes, hatred, violence and fighting. Eating, drinking, smoking and sexual activity is forbidden from sunrise to sunset for all adults bar invalids and travellers. Truly devout believers even abstain from swallowing their own saliva. The fast is rigorously observed, at least in public. Non-observance is illegal.

As each day drew to a close, the longing for sunset was palpable. In the late afternoon the air filled with delicious cooking pot odours. Small children in their Friday best clothes appeared around Ferdaws carrying trays of homemade pastries, sweets and steaming pots of food as gifts to their neighbours. The call to prayer was the signal for the start of *iftar*, the meal that breaks the fast. Traditionally *iftar* begins with a sweet drink made of dried apricots called *qamar-ad-din*, or 'moon of the religion'; it presages a night of feasting.

Once, on a trip to Egypt, we saw tents in the streets where diners sat waiting to be served free meals at the end of the day. In Dubai, we saw men and boys crowding around neighbourhood bakeries for freshly baked bread to take home to their families. Perhaps there were Ramadan activities to be seen in the streets of Saudi cities too, but, marooned in my apartment, all I saw were the hurtling cars that crowded onto the freeways at sunset, their drivers desperate to get home in time to break the fast with their families.

We should not have been so surprised at the sudden obsession with food. The shops were filled with Ramadan offerings: trays of sweet pastries, cakes and confectionary, mountains of dried dates, figs, apricots and nuts. Newspapers featured Ramadan recipes from around the world, and columnists grew lyrical with nostalgia about Ramadan feasts their mothers had prepared for them in childhood. Most families increased their monthly food budget by between US$800 and $13,000, and at the end of the month hospitals reported a rise in admissions of patients with diseases caused by overeating.

Ramadan ended as it had begun, with the first sighting of the new crescent moon, signal for the celebration of Eid Al-Fitr. In Eid, Muslims congratulate each other on their observance of the fast, and also fulfil their obligation to give a portion of their wealth to the needy as Zakat. In Saudi Arabia, Zakat takes the place of taxes, although its payment is a matter of conscience, and there is no formal national system for its collection and distribution Some Saudis donate money to mosques or to charities (since September 11, 2001, however, there have been many questions raised about the destination of money collected in this way). Some purchase rice at Zakat centres that undertake to distribute it to poor countries. Some give directly wherever they see a need, perhaps to the beggars that congregate around the Zakat centres. In 1999, the authorities estimated that over SR100 million, or US$31 million was paid in Zakat (*Arab News*, January 16). However, the spirit of charity was not without its limits. In a cruel irony, Ramadan was also the time for a crackdown on beggars. In 2000, 930 non-Saudi men, women and children were rounded up by the authorities and deported (*Arab News*, March 23).

For the three days of Eid, a festive mood took hold in the Gulf. Eid was the peak shopping season of the year, a time for Saudis all over the Kingdom to exchange gifts and to fit themselves out in new clothing. In scenes that brought to mind Christmas in the West, shoppers wedged themselves into crowded shopping malls, queued outside the most popular shops, staggered out under the weight of their purchases, and then sat in endless traffic jams on their way home. Their happiness was contagious: we were glad to see the end of Ramadan too.

Although he was born into a pagan tribe, through his contacts with Jewish and Christian traders, the Prophet Mohammad would have been familiar with monotheistic ideas. The religion he founded is an extension of the Judeo–Christian tradition, and Muslims refer to the adherents of all three faiths as 'people of the book'.

Some of the features that today we most readily associate with Islam were adopted from the Judeo–Christian tradition. Christians prostrated themselves in prayer, and Christian women veiled themselves in the time of the Prophet. The ram's horn summoned Jews, and wooden clappers summoned Christians to prayer; Mohammad substituted these with the human voice. The first Muslims, like the Jews and Christians of their day, faced towards Jerusalem in prayer until the Prophet directed them to face the Kaabah instead.

Muslims believe that the Prophet was the divinely inspired messenger of God, instructed by the Archangel Gabriel, whom they know as Gibrail, to proclaim His word, as revealed in the Holy Quran. His followers regard Mohammad as the last of the great prophets of the religions of the book, starting with Adam and continuing through Noah, Abraham, Moses and Jesus.

In addition to the Quran, Muslims recognise the Torah, the Psalms, and the Gospels, but believe that over time these texts have become corrupted by human interpretation. Claiming divine instruction, Mohammad reinterpreted the sacred writings of the Jews and Christians. Jesus, he said, was not divine, but a human prophet of God. He was born not in a stable, but under a date palm. He could not have turned water into wine, because God has decreed that alcohol is *haram*. Jesus was not crucified: God would never have allowed this to happen.

Because he was the latest of the prophets, Mohammad is regarded as the final word of God, and his followers refer to him as the 'seal of religion'. They expect no further prophets.

Muslims do not see their faith merely as the last of the religions of the book: they also claim it as the first. The Arab tribes, according to the Prophet, are descended from the patriarch Abraham through his firstborn son Ismail; some even claim Adam as the first Muslim. By this reasoning, they believe Islam predates both Judaism and Christianity as the original and purest form of monotheism; the one true religion. This is also why Muslims often speak not of conversion to Islam, but of reversion.

Amongst the Western expatriate community there were very few reverts. We had more than our share of dabblers in Eastern religion: our Buddhists and our Hindus and our New Age pantheists. Somehow, though, when it came to Islam, few showed any interest at all.

We did have men who had professed the faith in order to marry a Muslim woman. Some were sincere, others Muslim in name only, and at least one still regularly attended Friday mass. We had women who had married Muslim men and reverted. They were, if anything, even more committed to their new faith than those born into it. But when it came to embracing Islam purely as a matter of spiritual conviction, I can think of only one example from our circle: the Welshman known to his colleagues as Taffy Abdullah. I met him only once. In his white *thobe* and his red and white head cloth, with his black-draped wife keeping a modest distance to the rear, he seemed more Arab than the Arabs, and was just as enigmatic.

We were given every encouragement to revert. The Saudi state had established *dawa* centres that disseminated Islamic teachings. Government presses churned out an endless supply of foreign language religious literature. Geoff's students showered him with pamphlets: 'The Life of Mohammad'; 'Jesus: a Prophet of Islam'; 'Islam Beliefs and Teachings'. When I asked a Palestinian friend a question about the Quran, she immediately set about procuring a handsomely bound English translation of the holy book for me. The state even offered financial rewards for any non-believer prepared to embrace the faith.

Their efforts were mostly in vain. Although the press regularly reported on the reversion of small numbers of Filipino maids and nurses, the rigours and austerities of Islam had little appeal for Westerners.

Geoff and I were touring the excellent Islamic collection of the new National Museum in Riyadh. We gazed at artefacts from the time of the Prophet: shards of pottery and tiles from ancient mosques. The pilgrimage gallery had a wonderful collection of early photographs of the *haj*. A black silk cloth, richly embroidered with gold calligraphy, that had once been draped over the Kaabah was there (the cloth is replaced each year), as was an elegant set of doors wrought in precious metals that had once graced its entrance. We studied a relief map of Mecca that was as close as we were ever likely to get to the holy city.

We wandered into the gallery devoted to Mohammad ibn Abd Al-Wahhab, the eighteenth-century religious reformer who established the prevailing Saudi school of Islam. Written in enormous letters on a banner that stretched along the entire wall of the chamber was a quotation from the great man that summed up the essence of his philosophy.

'Every innovation is an error,' it said.

The iconoclast Al-Wahhab was born in the year 1703 of the Western calendar, at a time when traditional superstitions and idolatrous practices such as the worship of trees and visits to the graves of saints had again taken hold amongst the Arabs. He urged an end to such practices. 'Mud alone cannot save you,' he told his followers.

He advocated a return to the simple purity of Islam as revealed in the Holy Quran and in the Sunna, or observed practice of the Prophet. All things not contained in the original texts, and any interpretations that had emerged since that time were to be rejected. There was no room for pluralism in the faith: truth, he argued, is monolithic. The Wahhabi approach has been described, at its best, as 'sublime minimalism'.

Al-Wahhab and his ideas might have disappeared if it had not been for a fortunate alliance. In 1744, turned out of his tribal lands after he had caused a woman to be stoned to death for adultery, he took refuge with the al Saud clan. He convinced their leader of the righteousness of his cause, and of the need for a renewed commitment to *jihad*, or holy war. Together Al-Wahhab and the al Sauds launched raids on Mecca and Medina to purge them of idols. Together they forged the first Saudi kingdom. Each side of the alliance was integral to the success of the other, and the intertwining of the fortunes of their descendants continues to this day. The zealous austerity of Wahhabi Islam is the public face of Saudi Arabia.

An insistence upon the unity of Islam and a strict rejection of interpretation has given the Saudi community strength and cohesion. But there has been a price to pay for unity, measured in terms of oppression and rigidity. Expats and their bleatings about personal loss of liberty are, in the great scheme of things, hardly important. Far more serious is the repression of minority beliefs. The large Shia communities of eastern Arabia and the Hashemites to the south are regarded as heretics, a stain on the unity of the faith. Their relationship with the Saudi state is uneasy.

Even within the mainstream Sunni community, the pressure to conform is intense. The penalty for apostasy, or renouncing the faith, is death. The story of two young men who, upon returning to the Najdi town of Buraydah at the completion of their studies in California, confessed that they were no longer convinced about Islam, is perhaps apocryphal, although we heard it from an expat who lived in Buraydah at the time, and had it confirmed by a Saudi friend. The horrified families of the youths consulted with the local imam, who agreed that firm action would have to be taken. Acting upon this instruction, the fathers arranged for their sons to be murdered.

'What is your ambition? What do you want out of life?' Geoff asked an eighteen-year-old student in a conversation tutorial.

'I want to be more obedient,' the young man replied. Under the circumstances, this seemed like a reasonable ambition.

'Cover your hair!'

An angry voice just behind me as I wandered through Riyadh's al Akariya shopping mall. I turned to see a slight, hard-faced man glaring at me, although not quite directly (to look at a woman is considered *haram*). With his straggly beard, a white kerchief covering his head, and his skinny legs poking out from his short *thobe* (cut a pious seven inches above his ankles), he was instantly recognisable as a *muttawa*. I grabbed the scarf that was draped across my shoulders and yanked it up over my hair. Satisfied, the *muttawa* strode away.

'You can take it off now,' said another voice just behind me. An American woman, grimacing in distaste as she removed her own scarf.

The *muttaween* are employed by the wonderfully named Committee for the Promotion of Virtue and the Suppression of Vice, and are recruited by a process that is so dependent upon nepotism that it has been described as 'a nice little family business'. Their function is to enforce public standards of decency. They have the ability to issue fines, to order public lashings and to send people to jail. Although their dress suggests that they have given up on material goals in favour of spiritual ones, the generous government funding they receive allows them to live well, and to be kitted out with new Range Rovers and mobile phones.

As far as I could tell, Westerners, and all we stood for, were their worst nightmare, and they were ours. Pork eaters, alcohol drinkers, fornicators: the West was the source of all abomination in their eyes. Most of all, we were not Muslims, and our very presence in the land of the Prophet was a violation of its purity. Confrontation was inevitable. The *muttaween* made it their business to challenge every instance of un-Islamic behaviour they came across. Dress infringements, although a persistent aggravation, were only the beginning. On rumours of Christian services, social functions and alcohol, the *muttaween* would try to gain entry to our compounds to root out un-Islamic behaviour. They patrolled the streets to make sure that our favourite restaurants were closed for prayers. They challenged couples out in public together, demanding to see proof that they were married to each other. Those who were not risked charges of fornication or prostitution and the possibility of severe penalties.

We heard tales of *muttaween* whipping the ankles of women whose *abayas* were too short, or striking their uncovered faces. One report had them involved in a fracas with an American man in the al Akariya shopping mall, in which the man was tipped over the top floor railing to his death three floors below. Another had them confiscating the favourite toy of an inconsolable

American toddler – the object of their ire, the tot's stuffed pink pig. But every Westerner's favourite story (again perhaps apocryphal) was of the female American GI stationed in the Kingdom during the Gulf War who, when challenged, pulled a gun on her tormentor and ordered him to 'Back off!'

Folk wisdom said that, because men are not supposed to look at women, the best strategy for a Western woman harassed by a *muttawa* over matters of dress was to challenge him: 'How dare you look at me?' Our embassies advised us to avoid trouble, but that if arrest was likely, to insist on being arrested by the regular police rather than the religious ones.

Recognising that confrontation was in nobody's interest, the Saudi authorities took discreet steps to keep Westerners and *muttaween* separate. The Diplomatic Quarter was a *muttawa*-free zone; the security personnel who manned the entrances were under orders to keep them out. Similarly, the security guards of the larger Western compounds were able to deter *muttaween* intruders most of the time. Less clear was how a whole city, al Khobar, remained free of them. We assumed they had been paid to stay out.

At first I thought that the *muttaween* had been created specifically to torment Westerners. Only gradually did I come to realise that they were the scourge of Saudis as well. The religious police spent the bulk of their energies wandering the shopping malls to clamp down on teenage flirtation, roving the streets to ensure that all businesses observed prayer time, rounding up men and driving them to the mosque for prayers (they often included dark-skinned Western men in their sweep), making sure that everyone was observing Ramadan, and harassing female students as they came out of school. Saudi women, in fact, complained that the *muttaween* were harder on them than they were on their Western sisters.

As befits a family business, there were female *muttaween* too, including one particularly pious young lady in one of my English classes. It was only after the course finished that I learnt of her status. On our last evening, the women sat for a test, and as they finished, they withdrew to a room across the hallway for a party. The lady *muttawa* was the last to finish, and as soon as she had handed in her paper, she went home. The rest of the class welcomed me to their party, and urged me to try the delicious cakes and pastries and the coffee that they had brought. Their conversation, in Arabic, sounded annoyed, and I asked them why.

'If we knew that Miriam was not coming,' one of them explained, 'we could have had music.'

In April 2000, Amnesty International published a report that was critical of human rights and religious intolerance in the Kingdom. The report was greeted with outrage. 'The Arabian Peninsula is the cradle of Islam,' said Sheikh Saleh bin Mohammad Al-Lihayda, Chairman of the Supreme Judicial Council, 'and despite this fact, the Kingdom does not force any non-Muslim expatriate to abandon his religion, even if it is wrong.' (*Saudi Gazette*, April 9, 2000)

By no stretch of the imagination was there freedom of worship in Saudi Arabia. Public observance of any religion other than Islam was illegal. Officially, expatriates were free to worship in their own way, as long as they did it in private. However, any outward display of non-Muslim religious affiliation was banned, and the religious police had been known to seek out Christian worshippers in private houses and to arrest them. Although the Saudi press was quick to report on instances of 'Islamophobia' and of discrimination against Muslims in Western nations, they showed no such sensitivity to the rights of non-Muslims in their own country.

Like many Westerners of my generation, I would describe myself as a lapsed Christian. If pressed, I might give as reason for abandoning the faith the abuses committed in its name by missionaries and zealots in times past, or its rigid dogmatism today. But the truth of the matter was that by the time I arrived in the Kingdom, religion had ceased to have much relevance to my life. In its place, I espoused humanist values and championed secularism. It was only through others that I came to experience the sting of religious intolerance. And it was through others that I came to realise that Christianity was not only alive and well, but creative and diverse within the Kingdom.

Joseph, a South Indian shop assistant whom Geoff had befriended, was a devout Christian. One day, he had been sitting outside his housing unit quietly reading his Bible, when a Muslim neighbour came along and confiscated the book. Geoff, who was becoming increasingly offended by the religious intolerance that surrounded us, set about securing a replacement copy of the Bible for his friend. In gratitude, Joseph invited us along to his weekly prayer meeting. It was, of course, a clandestine affair. Every few weeks, he explained, its location had to be changed so as to avoid detection.

At seven o'clock on a Thursday night, Riyadh's downtown Batha area was humming: gridlock traffic in the streets, gridlock pedestrians on the footpaths, Geoff and I hovering in a side street just off the main road.

'Mr Geoff!' said a nervous voice behind us. It was Joseph. 'Please follow me.'

He led us into the cramped lobby of a rundown apartment building, and into its battered lift. We emerged on the fourth floor into a dark, narrow hall, and were quickly ushered into one of the apartments.

Safely inside, Joseph introduced us to our host and hostess and their children, and to the other Christians who were gathered there.

On the living room wall was a large wooden cross, and a paper banner that read 'Jesus is Lord'. There were stacks of song books, and a guitar leaning on a chair. Joseph handed us each a cushion and invited us to sit down. We took our place on the floor at the back of the room. A little girl brought us each a can of Pepsi.

A steady trickle of new arrivals: men, women and children. They looked at us with a puzzled curiosity that verged on edginess, but, after explanations in whispered Tamil, greeted us warmly in the same way that they greeted each other: 'Welcome, Brother! Welcome, Sister!'

The congregation, grown to about forty strong, settled themselves onto the floor around us in the small living room. Bibles emerged from capacious handbags. Song books were distributed, and some of the ladies used them to fan themselves. The host, who was also the pastor, picked his way through the crowd to the front of the room. He knelt under the cross, facing us, his hands raised in the air. We mirrored his pose.

The prayer was fervent, and very long. It moved seamlessly from English into Tamil and back into English.

'Praise Jesus!' chanted the pastor.

'Praise Jesus!' echoed the congregation with one voice.

'Grant us your blessings, Lord!'

'Bless us, Lord!' 'Thank you, Jesus!' 'Hallelujah!' came the replies.

It was hard to tell where the prayer ended and the first hymn began, but suddenly the pastor was strumming the guitar, and everyone was singing. The first hymn led straight into the second; at the end of the third, an elder stepped forward to lead us in another long prayer. Then a worshipper called out the number of the next hymn, and off they went, singing lustily again. We were all still on our knees. My prayer was that the neighbours could not hear us, or if they could, that they were not Muslims.

We had planned to stay for a few hymns and then make a polite withdrawal in a pause between them. Now I realised that there would be no 'between'. The congregation was settling in for a song and prayer session that would go on through the night without pause. There were over 500 songs in the photocopied song book, and prayers without number on the tongues of the faithful. Our fellow worshippers were working themselves into a state of rapture.

I nudged Geoff in alarm. 'My knees!' I hissed. But it seemed like hours before we staggered to our feet and made our apologetic escape, preferring the risk of eternal damnation to the agony of continued kneeling. Our fellow worshippers seemed surprised at our departure, but didn't pause in their singing. They were just warming up.

Our visit to Joseph's congregation had aroused my curiosity about Christianity in the Kingdom, so that when Geoff came across a discreet, delicately coded reference in an expat newsletter to a weekly Christian service in Riyadh, we determined to take ourselves along to it.

This time the congregation turned out to be a respectably dressed crowd of ordinary, mostly Western men, women and children. Save that the service was held in a recreation room next to a swimming pool, we could have been at church somewhere in the leafy green eastern suburbs of Melbourne. As the lady vicar welcomed us, volunteers were busy arranging the chairs and handing out hymn books.

That morning, we were led in worship by a highly reverend gentleman visiting from the headquarters of the Middle Eastern branch of the Anglican Church, a man of mixed Anglo–Lebanese background. His sermon addressed the relationship between Muslims and Christians, and the need to search for common ground. He reminded us that Christ was not, in fact, an Englishman, and suggested that, in terms of culture at least, he might have found more in common with our Saudi neighbours than with us. I was impressed that he was able to deliver some of his illustrations of this message in both English and in fluent Arabic.

As he held the communion chalice over his head and the congregation lined up, I gazed at this impressive figure in his white and gold robes, and wondered how he had obtained a visa.

Travel broadens the mind, they say, by teaching us about other cultures. It also has a way of bringing us smack up against our own cultural assumptions; of making us question things that we would otherwise take for granted. Living in an Islamic theocracy had the effect of making me re-examine my own religious beliefs.

I found that there was much that Islam and Christianity had in common. Both were monotheistic and patriarchal by nature. They shared the practices of fasting, prayer, pilgrimage and almsgiving. The Saudi system of Sharia law, with its stonings and beheadings, had an Old Testament feel to it. When I read about Abraham and Jacob in my contraband copy of the Bible, they sprang vividly to life as Bedouin tribesmen. From doctrine to architecture, aspects of the religions that had once seemed to contrast now revealed themselves to me as continuities. Even Muslim ideas about women, viewed in historical terms, were familiar.

Despite my resolve to be broadminded, however, I found some features of Islam to be confronting. Although Christianity has had its share of holy wars, worldly princes and bloodshed, I had come to regard them as aberrations of the faith. I found it hard to reconcile Mohammad's roles as man of religion, secular ruler and military leader. I grappled with the contrast between the Christian injunction to 'turn the other cheek' and the Islamic idea of *jihad*.

I began to question the contribution that these religions had made to the societies that had nurtured them. How much could the static nature of the Islamic world be ascribed to Islam, with its insistence upon orthodoxy and obedience, I wondered, and what had the Christian faith contributed to the Western dynamic? I became aware of how many of my attitudes were informed by Christianity, and how firmly Western culture, for all its secularism, was based in the Christian tradition.

I can't claim that I was reborn into the faith of my forebears by my time in Saudi Arabia, but I did take a renewed interest in it and, ultimately, learned a new respect for it.

As an expat Westerner, I could not help but be aware that I was heir to centuries of confrontation between East and West. I was embarrassed by the behaviour of my forebears; an avowed apologist for Christian bigotry, for the excesses of the crusaders, and for the injustices of colonial and post-colonial interference in Middle Eastern affairs. And yet it came as a shock for me to realise that, for many in the Muslim world, the wounds of conflict still run deep. In Arabia, the crusades still rankle. The loss of Andalusia in 1492 is still mourned; the capture of Constantinople by the Muslim Turks thirty-nine years earlier is in no way seen as a fair trade.

More disturbing was a consistent and all-pervasive anti-Westernism. Western culture was denounced in the press and from the pulpit as the root of all evil; an abomination. Western society was depicted as violent, dangerous and licentious; Western ideas, such as globalisation, feminism, liberalism and democracy, as threats to Islam.

'The enemies of Islam are in a state of general alert to spread false beliefs and vague notions to undermine the religious faith,' warned Sheik Dr Abdul Rahman Al–Sedeis in his Friday sermon from the Grand Mosque in Mecca on May 5, 2000, giving voice to a general view that the threat from outside was not just a passive one. On the contrary, the West was seen to be actively plotting against the Islamic world.

In a mindset that reminded me of the American cold war propensity to see a communist under every bed, some Muslims cultivated a paranoia that thrived on hostility to the West, and everywhere saw evidence of Western–Zionist subversion.

In the summer of 1999, students at a Saudi Islamic college discovered to their horror that if they read the 7-Up brand name on soft drink cans backwards, it looked like the word 'Allah' in Arabic. Despite urgings from the Ministry of Commerce, the Pepsi company refused to change the way the name of the drink was written (*Arab News*, November 25, 1999).

Again in 1999, another group of students staged a protest against the Coca-Cola company. The circulars the students distributed outside mosques and schools alleged that the company was engaged in a Zionist plot against Islam, because its familiar logo could be read backwards as 'No Mohammad, no Mecca'. The Ministry of Information promised to look into the matter, although what action they planned to take against a company that was not permitted to operate in the Kingdom was unclear. For some of the locals this was going too far: one *Arab News* writer headlined his column 'Yes to Islamic zeal, no to neurotic obsession' (November 11, 1999).

Each modern border conflict, whether in Kashmir, the Balkans or the Sudan, reinforced the conviction that the Muslim world was under attack from the West. When Indonesia withdrew from East Timor in 1999, a cartoon in the *Arab News* (September 25) showed that country as a barefoot soldier with blood spurting from the stump of his recently severed arm. Above him, a disembodied arm labelled 'United Nations' wielded a bloody machete.

No mention at all of Indonesia's shameful record of oppression in the province, nor of the carnage left behind following its withdrawal. It was enough that territory previously in the Muslim orbit had been lost.

Deepest of all wounds was the bleeding ulcer of the Palestinian–Israeli conflict, each instalment of which brought renewed outrage and despair. The USA's continuing support of Israel and apparent blindness to Palestinian suffering convinced the Arabs that they were the victims of an Israeli Zionist plot that controlled Western governments, the Western media and Western corporations.

More moderate Saudis who did not subscribe to conspiracy theories still felt misunderstood by the West and misrepresented by Western media, which an *Arab News* editorial (November 18, 1999) accused of 'crass ignorance and insensitivity', and of perpetrating an 'anti-Islamic bandwagon' that exists 'like a virus throughout all Western society'. 'Islam is constantly presented in the darkest of guises,' the same editorial protested. 'If it is not being associated with terrorism or cruelty, it is suggested that it is socially backward, that it degrades women – and this from a society where murder is rampant, a society which is being overwhelmed by drugs and which has long been inured to pornography . . . If there is not Islamophobia in the USA, what there is [is] a self-evident mountain of ignorance . . .'

Given the depth of anti-Western sentiment in the Kingdom, it was perhaps surprising that Geoff and I lived as untroubled an existence as we did. Although we often felt that our presence was an irritant to the Saudis and an impurity in the pure heartland of Islam, most of the time we were treated with courtesy and kindness, or at least with forbearance.

But not by everyone. Often it was hard to ignore the feelings of disdain and disapproval that emanated from the strict (not necessarily Saudi) Muslims around us. Strict Wahhabi Islam teaches its followers that good Muslims should have nothing to do with unbelievers, that they should accept neither employment nor advice from them, should avoid any form of friendship or conviviality with them, should not smile at them, wish them well on their holidays, or even eat their food. As one imam declared,

Muslims should 'harbour enmity and hatred for the infidels and refrain from taking them as friends'.

In the face of this intolerance, we grew less tolerant of Islam.

The most holy site in all Islam is the Kaabah, the black draped cube in Mecca that Muslims direct their daily prayers towards. Underneath the embroidered black cloth stands a simple, one-room temple made of stone and wood, approximately twelve metres square. Although it has been reconstructed several times in its history, most recently in 1996, it is an ancient site of worship.

Before the time of the Prophet, the Kaabah was the key pagan shrine of the Arabs, and was filled with images of their gods (including one of the Virgin Mary) and with heathen idols. It was already the focus of pilgrimage for the tribes: for one month each year all feuds were suspended so that the Arabs could journey in peace to Mecca and sacrifice to their gods.

At first Mohammad and his followers did not bow down towards the Kaabah, but like the Jews and Christians of their day, turned towards Jerusalem in their prayers. When Mohammad turned towards Mecca instead, he claimed to have been directed to do so by Allah Himself. Whether he was divinely instructed or not, it was an inspired political move. By placing the Kaabah at the centre of Islam, Mohammad gave his teachings a distinct Arabic identity and overcame the resistance of the Arab tribes who worshipped there. In 630 A.D., the eighth year of the Muslim calendar, the Prophet entered the Kaabah on pilgrimage and cast out the idols that were housed there.

Muslims believe that the Kaabah was raised by Abraham and his son Ismail. It stands near to the sacred well of Zam zam, where Muslims say that Ismail's mother, Hagar, found the water that saved her life and that of her new-born son, following their flight from the tents of Abraham and from the jealous rage of his wife, Sarah.

The Kaabah was, Muslims claim, the first temple ever dedicated to the worship of the one God. Some even say that its first builder was Adam, and that Abraham merely restored Adam's work. In the corner of the base of the temple is a sacred black stone, most likely a meteorite, that is believed to be the only remnant of Abraham's original temple. Over the centuries it has been almost worn away by the kisses of pilgrims.

The pilgrimage to Mecca, or *haj*, is the fifth pillar of Islam, and is required of all Muslims at least once in a lifetime. It takes place in the month of Dhur Al-Haj, the last month of the Muslim year, between the eighth and the thirteenth days.

By the sixteenth century, when European eyewitnesses observed the great convergence, the *haj* was already an event of massive proportions. From Damascus came 40,000 pilgrims mounted upon 30,000 camels; 20,000 pilgrims came from Cairo accompanied by 100,000 camels; Persian Shias came by way of Baghdad; Indians and East Indians took sea passage, and then joined Arabs from Yemen, Muscat and the Gulf making their way overland to Mecca on camels, on donkeys and on foot.

The journey involved considerable hardship, and often required all the worldly resources that individual pilgrims could muster. They endured swindlers, bandits, pirates, Bedouin raiders, storms, drought and thirst on a journey that could take years to complete, and from which many never returned.

Today most pilgrims arrive by jumbo jet. The journey is both faster and safer than it has ever been, but it is still a mammoth undertaking, and there is an ever-present danger that things may go badly wrong. The death of 251 people in 2004, crushed by a surging crowd, was just the latest in a string of disasters. 'The *haj* is like a war,' says *haj* historian Dr Fouad Angawi, and certainly the Saudi Government prepares for it as if for a military campaign. The facts and figures for the March 2000 pilgrimage, gleaned from the pages of the *Arab News*, tell the story:

- 2,682 international arrival flights at Jeddah airport's *haj* terminal
- 586 local flights
- 2.5 million pilgrims (2 million visitors and half a million Meccans)
- pilgrims from 100 different countries and 70 different language groups
- 3,500 translators

- 30 daily classes and lectures to inform pilgrims about the rituals
- an army of volunteer guides recruited to assist the pilgrims
- 1,600 trucks to deliver food
- 750 sales outlets for food
- 350 cold storage trucks, each loaded with 20 tons of food
- 10 million meals distributed
- 35 million bottles of drink
- 10,000 containers at the Grand Mosque for the distribution of holy Zam zam water
- fleets of buses contracted to transport the pilgrims
- tent cities built to house them
- health and safety inspectors hired and trained
- medical teams on standby to deal with burns, sunstroke and infectious diseases; stockpiles of medicines
- wheelchairs and ambulances at strategic points
- police and security personnel for crowd control; surveillance cameras and helicopters to assist them
- cost to the Saudi Government: more than US$1billion
- revenue: no-one was saying.

For most pilgrims, the *haj* is the trip of a lifetime and the defining moment of their faith. Their numbers include the poor, the illiterate, the infirm, the disabled, the elderly, children, and a host of foreign dignitaries. Somehow, all of them will perform the rituals of the *haj*, and perform them all together in strict synchronicity.

Upon their approach to Mecca, pilgrims announce their intent to make the pilgrimage, and dress in *ihram*, the clothing that signifies their equality before God: men in two seamless white cloths, and the women in simple robes. Here alone in all the Kingdom women do not cover their faces, but present themselves openly before Allah. From the time that they put on *ihram*, the pilgrims cannot shave, cut their hair or nails, or engage in sexual intercourse.

At the Grand Mosque on the eighth day of Dhurr Al-Haj, they circle the Kaabah seven times in a counter clockwise direction. Next they run back and forth seven times between the hills of Safa and Marwah, re-enacting the desperate search for water that preceded the discovery of the well at Zam zam. Then they spend the night at the town of Mina, ten kilometres east of Mecca.

The next day they make their way to the Plain of Arafat, where Mohammad delivered his last sermon. Here, in the supreme moment of the *haj*, they stand praying together from noon to sunset, declaring their presence to Allah: 'Here I am, oh Lord, Here I am.' After sunset they head back towards Mecca. They spend the night under the open sky at Muzdalifah, where they collect stones for the next part of the ritual.

In the morning, they move back to Mina, where they will spend the next three days. Here they will 'stone the devil', pelting three stone pillars with the pebbles they have collected at Muzdalifah. Here, too, they will sacrifice an animal.

'We provide sacrificial animals that fulfil all Sharia and health requirements,' trumpeted a half-page advertisement in the *Arab News*, sponsored by the Kingdom of Saudi Arabia Project for Utilization of Sacrificial Animals. 'We would like to inform pilgrims who wish to make use of Al-Badila Modern Sheep Slaughterhouse or the camel & cow slaughterhouse, that both slaughterhouses are open 24 hours throughout the Eid al adhaa days. If you decide that we be your proxy: the price shall be SR340 per head.' (March 1, 2000)

Ten thousand officially appointed butchers were standing by. The main abattoir in Jeddah reported itself able to handle 2,500 sheep, and 250 cows and camels in an eight-hour shift. Each animal would be tagged so that buyers, if they wished, could stand in a special viewing area and identify their own sacrifice as it was performed (*Arab News*, March 19, 2000).

Over the three-day period, the Islamic Development Bank took charge of 450,000 slaughtered sheep, and oversaw the distribution of their meat to twenty-seven countries (*Arab News*, March 20, 2000).

The festival of sacrifice was also boom time for unofficial butchers catering to those who were unwilling to wait in long lines at the abattoirs, or who could not afford the price. The papers reported that there were gangs of roving, knife-wielding butchers, not all of them professional, willing to do the job on the spot. One enterprising soul was caught running a butchery out of a Jeddah apartment. When he was arrested he had already slaughtered ten sheep in his living room, and had another twenty penned and ready to be dispatched (*Arab News*, March 19, 2000).

After the animal sacrifice has been performed, the pilgrimage ends as it began, with pilgrims circling the Kaabah seven times. This is the prelude to a mass exodus from the holy city of Mecca.

In the year 2000, the *haj* went smoothly. Although there were the usual complaints of pollution, traffic gridlock, police harassment and extortion, there were no major incidents. No fires, no riots, no protests, no stampedes, and, apart from the usual *haj* flu, no serious epidemics. Egyptian bus drivers who disputed their contracts were deported en masse, as were hundreds of expat pilgrims unable to produce their *iqamas*. Forty thousand would-be pilgrims were turned away because they did not have the necessary *haj* permits. Sixty *haj* travel agents had their licences suspended after complaints from pilgrims. Three hundred and thirty beggars received jail sentences and lashes (*Arab News*, March 22, 2000).

As the pilgrims headed home, the Kingdom breathed a sigh of relief. Congratulations poured in from around the Muslim world: compliments on the successful management of the *haj*. The authorities could have been forgiven their bout of modest self-congratulation.

Geoff and I called in upon our friends and neighbours at al Kendi, Ridwan and Yanti, who had just arrived back from the *haj*. Both of them were sick with chest infections, and Ridwan was croaking like an asthmatic bullfrog. This was hardly surprising, they said: thrown together with millions of pilgrims from who knows where, everyone gets sick at *haj* time. Ridwan said the ten-hour bus trips to and from Mecca had been hell, and that getting through the *haj* was an exercise in survival.

'When you're circling the Kaabah with 100,000 other pilgrims,' he said, 'it's everyone for himself. But they teach us to concentrate on not hurting anyone else, and then on not responding to provocation if someone hurts you.'

'The first time we did the *haj*,' Yanti said, 'it was very stressful.

I was always worried about where I should go, what I must do, how to stay with the group, and how to stay out of danger. But this time I was more relaxed because I knew what to expect, and I enjoyed it.'

At Mina their group had sat outdoors all night long on mats, part of a crowd one million strong. Despite their sniffles and snorts and hacking coughs, Ridwan and Yanti's eyes were aglow as they spoke of it.

'It was,' said Ridwan, 'one of those moments . . . an epiphany.'

I envied them their experience. What did we have in the West, I wondered, that could compare? I thought of rock concerts and football games, of pilgrims walking to Santiago de Compostela in Spain, of crowds gathered in St Peter's Square in the Vatican. We might have gatherings as intensely felt and as historically resonant, but for sheer scale, nothing comes close to the *haj*.

The Saudis are deeply conscious that they hold a special position in the eyes of Muslims everywhere. They are the custodians of the Kaabah and of the Prophet's Holy Mosque; they administer the pilgrimage; they claim that their language maintains the classic Arabic of the Holy Quran; their strict interpretation of Islam retains the religion in its purest form, or so the Wahhabis like to claim.

Their enormous wealth has enabled the Saudis to be generous on an international scale: they have used their petrodollars to build and maintain mosques and schools and to fund charities and Islamic organisations all over the Muslim world. In non-Muslim countries, too, since the 1970s they have built over 1,500 mosques, 210 Islamic centres, and dozens of academies and schools.

This largesse has not been universally welcomed. Critics have charged the Saudis with using their wealth in an aggressive campaign to promote their own puritanical version of Islam over all other versions of the faith. The Taliban of Afghanistan are only the most notorious evidence of their efforts. From Indonesia to Algeria, cells of Wahhabi-inspired fundamentalists are pursuing their own intolerant agendas, backed with massive infusions of Saudi cash. Wahhabi proselytising has been particularly effective, it is said, amongst Muslims in states that were formerly part of the Soviet Empire in Central Asia, the Caucasus and the Balkans, as well as amongst the small groups of poor and uprooted Muslims living in Western societies.

Islamic fundamentalism thrives on hostility to the West, and it is easy for Westerners to see its spread purely in terms of the threat that this hostility poses. In the Muslim world, however, dissident voices see the issue not only as a clash between Western and Muslim civilisations, but also as a struggle for the future of Islam. Liberal Muslims accuse the Wahhabis of denying the complexity and diversity of Islamic history, and of rejecting the spirit of intellectual inquiry that created the golden age of Islamic civilisation, that extraordinary eighth to thirteenth century flowering of culture that was the result of a blending of Arab, Persian, Egyptian, Jewish and European influences.

'Wahhabism,' writes scholar Ziauddin Sardar, 'has reduced Islam to an arid list of do's and don'ts.'

Isha, the mid-evening and final prayer of the day. A peaceful darkness settled over the land. '*Allah akbar*,' called the *muezzin* into the darkness. His voice floated down to us out of a cut-glass indigo sky. 'Allah is most great. I bear witness that there is no other god but Allah. I bear witness that Mohammad is the Messenger of Allah. Come to prayer . . . Come to success . . . Allah is most great.'

Another wave of prayer surged westward, to be followed by another, then another. More than one billion Muslims, one fifth of the world's population, turning their thoughts towards Mecca.

We had our own mantras. 'Not all Saudis are intolerant,' we repeated, and 'Don't judge all Muslims by the Saudis.'

12

PROGRESS WITHOUT CHANGE

Now, here, you see, it takes all the running you can do, to
keep in the same place.
LEWIS CARROLL, Through the Looking Glass

By late 1999, Geoff and I were doing well in our attempts
to tap into Riyadh's expat scene. This was not a challenging task: the bored foreign community was ever eager to welcome
newcomers, even quiet ones like us. With our new friends, we
were soon enjoying a round of social visits, restaurant meals and
excursions. We had even been introduced to a small private
cinema, where we were able to see the latest Hollywood
movies.

Most of all, we went to parties. Expats never missed an opportunity to celebrate a birthday, an anniversary, an arrival, a departure, or a national holiday – any nation's national holiday. When
there was no occasion to celebrate, we held a party anyway.

I had heard stories of wild parties; parties awash with drunkenness, rowdiness and high jinks. Alas, we were never invited to
one like that. Instead, the ones we went to were tame, friendly
affairs. There was drink, but little drunkenness. The sight of
men and women talking, laughing and dancing together would
have shocked most Saudis, but there were rarely any Saudis in
attendance.

We went to parties where we sat outdoors beside swimming pools, eating by candlelight in canvas pavilions. Parties where we lounged on oriental carpets and smoked fruit-flavoured tobacco through bubbling *sheeshas*. Parties where the guests brought their favourite dance music along, and we jitterbugged and jived into the wee hours of the morning. Parties where we played table tennis and pool. Parties where we rubbed shoulders with ambassadors, surgeons, kitchen workers and smugglers.

Above all, we talked. Bagging the host country is a favourite sport amongst expats everywhere, a response to the 'Them vs Us' mentality that often develops between locals and their long-term guests. Inevitably, our conversations turned to the Saudis and their strange ways.

We listened as mechanics told us about the inefficiency of their Saudi co-workers; as teachers spoke of schools where harsh discipline and rote learning were the norm; as engineers laughed about boondoggling and wastage; as businessmen talked of red tape, bribery and corruption.

Some maintained a positive outlook. 'Look at what the Saudis have achieved in the last thirty years,' they'd tell us.

For others, the country was hopelessly mired in backwardness and contradictions. 'Do you know what year it is here?' they'd ask. 'It's 1420 . . . the Middle Ages. That's all you need to know.'

In my classes, I quizzed the girls about their attitudes to wealth. 'What do your proverbs tell you about it?' I asked, and quoted the saying: 'It is easier for a camel to pass through the eye of a needle than for a rich man to enter heaven.'

They were adamant in their disagreement. 'Riches are God's gift,' they told me. 'Only greed is bad.'

'What would happen if the oil and the money runs out?' I persisted. 'How would you feel if you were poor again.'

'If that is God's will, we will accept it. It is no problem,' they said.

Saudi Arabia still had immense reserves of oil and gas, and with new ones still being discovered, there was no foreseeable danger that the supply would run out. There were, however, signs that all was not well in the national economy.

In 1998, world oil prices dipped in the wake of the Asian economic meltdown, and the Kingdom shuddered. Car dealerships reported that their sales had fallen away to almost nothing. Expats complained that their salaries were not being paid. The women's centres in Dhahran and Dammam where I was teaching English struggled to maintain classes and activities in the face of falling enrolments. Newspapers reported widespread business difficulties, and official sources spoke of the need for collective belt-tightening. Crown Prince Abdullah warned his people that the good times were over, and unlikely to return.

Much of the slowdown may have been due to temporary cash flow problems amongst a people who have never had a culture of saving. Official figures, however, revealed a more ominous reality. Despite decades of massive oil revenues, the national budget had been in deficit for sixteen consecutive years, and the national debt was equal to 100 percent of GDP.

The problem was simple. The Kingdom was still reliant on oil for virtually all of its income. The price of oil, over the long term, was dropping. Analysts had tagged the nation a 'one-string economy', and warned that its reliance on oil for 90 percent of its export earnings made it inherently inflexible and vulnerable to international events that the government could not hope to control.

Public spending on infrastructure projects to support the needs of the population was falling behind. In parts of Riyadh and Jeddah, whole new suburbs were springing up without sewerage and water. In some areas electricity brownouts were a daily occurrence. Even the established infrastructure was falling into disrepair. Many of the nation's roads were in urgent need of maintenance, while massive spending was required to bring schools and hospitals up to standard.

Although the personal wealth of many Saudis was gargantuan, many more were confronted with falling standards of living and, in some cases, desperate poverty. The national per capita income, equivalent to a healthy US$28,600 in 1981, had plunged to less than US$8,000 by 2000. Massive numbers of young men and women were unable to find work. The traditional informal welfare system of family support and state handouts was proving inadequate in the face of these problems. Not all of the beggars on the footpaths of Riyadh and Jeddah were foreigners.

As the Kingdom's centenary passed and the year 2000 approached, all the signs pointed to a need for drastic change. The nation's leaders were aware of the problems, as well they might be. The money supply was drying up, putting the old pact between the House of al Saud and its citizenry under threat.

In the local press, all the talk was of reform as the government cast around for ways to cut costs, raise funds, and diversify the economy. State enterprises were to be privatised; foreign workers to be replaced by nationals; princely stipends to be reviewed. Prices were to rise at the petrol pump. Citizens were called upon to bring their offshore investments home.

The Kingdom's old isolation was to be broken down. In an attempt to stimulate competition, laws would be passed allowing foreign nationals to own property and to set up businesses. Expatriate workers would be encouraged to invest their earnings in the local stock market. The Kingdom applied for membership of the World Trade Organisation.

The time was ripe, and there was every reason for optimism. The Saudi people had already demonstrated their resilience in the face of massive social upheaval. Despite its economic problems, the nation was still awash with money. And yet there was a sense of pessimism in the air; a feeling that the resolve needed to tackle problems was lacking.

'Nobody knows the exact number of unemployed people in the Kingdom,' wrote Abdul Rahman Al-Rashid (*Arab News*, October 24, 1999). 'Nor do we have any idea of the number who will face the threat of unemployment in the next few years.'

Everybody knows, however, that the problem is enormous. A rough estimate is that about 27 percent of the male population is unemployed, and for women the figure might be as high as 95 percent. From 1993 to 1999, the number of working-age

Saudis increased from 7.3 million to 9.8 million. Every year another batch of young graduates comes flooding onto the labour market. With half the population under eighteen years of age, and with the birth rate as high as it is (an average of 6.25 live births per woman), the unemployment problem is a time bomb.

The challenge of accommodating the hopes and aspirations of the young, of finding jobs for them and integrating them into the economy is enormous. The consequences of failure – substance abuse, crime, social disruption, the potential for a rebellion of the frustrated that would threaten the balance of power – haunted the nation's press throughout my stay.

Significantly, the number of locals without work was roughly equal to the number of foreign workers in the Kingdom. The government's solution was 'Saudi-isation': the policy whereby expatriates would be replaced by Saudis in the nation's work-force. With an estimated US$18 billion sent out of the country each year in salary remittances, it was a policy that made perfect sense. Clearly, the jobs would have to come from the private sector, where an estimated 95 percent of employees were foreign nationals. What was not at all clear was whether Saudi workers were ready to take over the jobs of their expatriate counterparts, or whether Saudi employers were willing to hire them.

The state education system had completely failed to equip its graduates with the sort of skills demanded by the private sector. The school curriculum was tired and outdated. With its emphasis on obedience and rote learning, it was churning out thousands of young people lacking in motivation or initiative. There were far too many religious studies graduates, and far too few scientists, technologists and business graduates. Few could operate a computer or speak English, although employers had identified these skills as vital.

A cartoon in the *Arab News* tells the story: a young man bounds up a staircase where each step bears the name of a level in the school system – Elementary, Intermediate, Secondary, and University. At the top of the stairs, armed with his diploma, he has run smack into a closed door tagged 'Employment' (March 1, 2000).

Unrealistic expectations were part of the problem. Young men had come to believe that a comfortable managerial position in the civil service, preferably one with an expert expatriate assistant to take care of day-to-day matters, was their birthright. Geoff's students would often tell him, only half in jest, that all it took to be a manager was a big desk, a big chair and a newspaper. In the eyes of many young Saudis, a job in private enterprise lacked the prestige and the connections of the civil service.

Non-government employers complained that their recruits were often unskilled, had a poor work ethic and lacked any idea of customer service, although in fairness few of them were offered any orientation or on-the-job training, and most had little idea of what was expected of them. Few recruits felt any sense of commitment to their employer; often they simply disappeared from their posts as soon as a better offer came along.

The Saudis have traditionally been loath to accept any work that they consider beneath their dignity. 'To be a clerk, a cashier, a porter, or even a secretary was deemed unfit for a Saudi,' wrote one analyst. 'For years such jobs have been frowned upon.' (*Arab News*, May 26, 2000) In another cartoon, a youth is shackled by a heavy chain to a huge iron ball that bears the caption 'Customs and Traditions'. He is attempting to pull it towards a sign marked 'Industrial Areas' (*Arab News*, October 10, 1999).

For their part, Saudi employers were reluctant to take on their young compatriots. They continued to recruit a willing army of expatriates to staff their businesses. It wasn't just that the foreigners were cheaper. They came ready-equipped with skills; they were thought to be more reliable, more compliant and more diligent than their Saudi counterparts, and they were prepared to take on work that Saudis would not do.

In order to further the goals of Saudi-isation, in the year of the nation's centenary each business was required to meet a compulsory target of 5 percent local employees. State enterprises led the way, with Saudia Airlines claiming 100 percent Saudi-isation by 2000, and Aramco reporting significant progress. Officials confidently predicted that full Saudi-isation would be achieved within ten years (*Arab News*, October 2, 1999).

Despite their optimism, it was clear that for many Saudi

employers, compliance with the law was little more than window dressing. At Geoff's workplace, for example, half a dozen Saudis had been engaged as administrative assistants. They spent their days sitting around, drinking tea and waiting to be sent on errands. Only one of them had been given any responsibilities, and he had been placed in charge of the stationery cupboard. For a few weeks he doled out pens, pencils and whiteboard markers to the teachers. He did not, however, keep records, nor did he reorder supplies when stocks ran low. Eventually, when there was nothing left to distribute, he rejoined his colleagues in the tea room. Any teacher who needed a pencil was advised to take his request directly to the dean.

The situation was not all grim. Private colleges were being established to fill the gaps in the state education system and to address the needs of the private sector. Employment agencies were being set up to help match job-seekers to jobs. Increasingly, young Saudis were to be found working in areas that they would previously have found unacceptable: as shop assistants, hotel receptionists and clerks. Their stories were taken up enthusiastically by the press, which lauded them as examples to others. 'I thought I would try this job,' said one young man employed as a car washer. 'At first it was really a terrible and bitter experience. I imagined everyone was looking at me, that they were sneering at me. But the job pays well . . . I soon found out nobody cares. I was just another person doing just another job.' (*Arab News*, March 4, 2000)

In the early days of the 1970s oil boom, the Saudis turned to the West for the expertise they needed to run their country. Their Western managers enthusiastically embraced this opportunity to build an economy from scratch, obligingly providing them with state-of-the art plans, projects, timetables, budgets, structures and institutions. Nothing could have been more foreign to traditional Saudi ways.

Schedules and punctuality had no place in the life of the nomad; initiative, responsibility and accountability no meaning to a people who worked by consultation and deference to traditional authority. The alliance between Western managers and their Saudi partners and masters was always going to be uneasy: the miracle is that so much has been achieved, despite their conflicting values.

There could be no denying, however, that by the end of the Saudi century, the civil service infrastructure was moribund. Headlines from the *Arab News* tells the story: 'Bureaucratic follies cost people time and money' (September 22, 1999), 'Where is the ministry when action is needed?' (April 29, 2000) and 'What makes bureaucrats the nasty people they are?' (May 25, 2000).

As a result of past guarantees of full employment, the civil service was bloated to saturation point with there-for-life officers. Secure in their personal fiefdoms, they were as notorious for their arrogance as they were for their ability to hinder rather than help. Although some 60 percent of the national budget was going to pay their salaries, no-one believed that they were delivering value for money.

Weighed down by tradition and inertia, the bureaucracies had become nightmare labyrinths of red tape, obfuscation and mis-management. In them, plans were formulated and ignored, decisions were endlessly deferred because no-one was prepared to take responsibility for them, and mistakes were glossed over to avoid blame and embarrassment for those in authority. Even able administrators were stymied by the system. At KFUPM, one director waited until just before he retired to implement a series of brilliant initiatives. It was said of him that he had always wanted to do the right thing, but had delayed acting until he felt sufficiently free of personal obligations.

Corruption was endemic. Private corporations maintained civil servants on their payrolls to ensure that key government contracts came their way. Official business could be accomplished at lightning speed, dragged out indefinitely, or simply ignored, all according to the whim of the official concerned, and everyone knew the value of a well-placed bribe delivered in a suitably respectful manner.

The private sector was beset with its own problems. Saudi businesses, cosseted behind a shield of subsidies, protection, and easy access to funds, were exhibiting all the ills that a lack of competition encourages: poor planning, mismanagement, over-capitalisation and waste.

In an *Arab News* article entitled 'Hail to the Chief', journalist Tariq Al-Maeena described the visit of a new CEO to a manu-facturing plant. His story was firmly placed in hypothetical terri-tory: the 'Nuts & Bolts division' of the ACME Metallurgy company, somewhere 'in the third world'. No-one who read it would have doubted its relevance to Saudi Arabia. The facility, he wrote, was 'plagued by poor performance, the equipment . . . in a high state of disrepair, and employee morale . . . plunged to very near the bottom. Production [was] steadily declining: high quality . . . a thing of the past . . . operating costs . . . on a spiral-ing increase'. In the days before the CEO's visit, the executives embarked upon a program of 'getting things in order'. Along the route he was to take, garden beds were planted, walls repainted, floors re-carpeted, and paintings hung. Doors leading to other areas were closed off. On the appointed day, the CEO completed his visit 'oblivious to the decay festering beyond his peripheral vision' (April 29, 2000).

When Geoff went down to al Kendi Plaza to get a pizza from one of the takeaway shops there, he experienced firsthand the power of connections. He placed his order, and then went outside to wait for it. He sat down on a stone ledge alongside a pair of Pepsi-drinking Arabs. The men struck up a conversation.

'Where your country is?' asked one, with a condescending air.

Geoff said he was from Australia.

'You are working Embassy Australia?' asked the other dis-missively.

'No, I work for Prince Sultan Private College.'

The name meant nothing to them. 'What place is this?' demanded the first.

To help them understand, Geoff decided to give the college its Arabic name. He began enunciating carefully: 'Emir . . . Sultan . . .'

The men choked on their Pepsis.

'You work for Emir Sultan! In his *kasir*!?' they spluttered, suddenly deferential.

Geoff, of course, had never set eyes on Prince Sultan, and would have been hard pressed to discover the location of his *kasir*, or castle. Still the name had worked its magic, and he saw no need to enlighten his interrogators.

For the Saudis, personal connections are everything. With a nudge and a wink from the right person, any door can be opened. At the drop of a name, any problem can be solved. Even expats know that their best insurance against trouble is to have the business card of a prince stashed safely in their pocket, ready to be flashed should circumstances require it.

This is *wasta*, the Saudi system of influence and favour. The term, which means 'custom' denotes an ability to make things happen or to pull strings. It describes a complex web of mutual expectations, credits and obligations.

It is the traditional way. The power of tribal leaders, the loyalty and respect they commanded from their followers, rested on their ability to distribute favours and redress grievances. Those with the closest connection to the leader possessed influence by virtue of proximity, and were in turn courted by those further from the centre of power.

In dealings with officialdom, it paid to have inside contacts. Appointments were made, land grants allotted, contracts signed, all along lines of personal favour. Places at KFUPM, the nation's top university, were hotly contested, but each year several hundred were assigned on the basis of tribal influence to young men who had not passed the entrance tests. Well-connected students could have expulsion orders reversed or poor exam results boosted to a pass. Meanwhile, teachers noted a marked divide between their Sunni and Shia students. The Sunnis, knowing that they could rely on family connections to see them right, tended towards laziness and complacency. The Shias, lacking the advantages of the Sunnis, were diligent students who knew they had to achieve excellent results if they were to succeed in life, and that even then they were likely to be passed over in favour of those with influence.

The system may have worked well enough in the old days, but it sits uncomfortably in the modern state. As the population booms, there are simply not enough resources or jobs to go round. Whether it is about securing a university place, a job or promotion, or a favourable business outcome, those with connections succeed, while those without miss out over and over again.

The cost of the influence system is twofold: the discontent of those outside or at the bottom of the hierarchy, and the all-pervading mediocrity that occurs when opportunity is based upon patronage rather than merit. The end result is cynicism and stagnation.

An expat joke from the late 1990s:

Boris Yeltsin, Bill Clinton and King Fahd have all been granted an audience with God, who tells each leader that he may ask one question.

Yeltsin thinks for a while, and then he says: 'Tell me, God. Will Russia ever again have the power that it had under the communists?'

'Yes, Boris, it will,' says God. 'But not in your lifetime.'

Then Bill Clinton says: 'Tell me, God. Will I ever win respect in the eyes of the American people?'

'Yes, Bill, you will,' says God. 'But not in your lifetime.'

Finally it's King Fahd's turn. 'Tell me, God,' he says, 'will Saudi Arabia ever become an efficient modern economy?'

'Yes, Fahd, it will,' says God. 'But not in my lifetime.'

Two pacts lie at the heart of the Saudi system of government. In one, the people granted absolute power to Abdul Aziz in return for a share of his largesse. In the other, the King agreed to share power with the religious establishment. He retained for himself the right to control the political, economic and military affairs of his realm. To the *ulema*, or council of leading imams, he granted authority over every aspect of social, moral and religious life.

The King was simply continuing a tradition. From the beginning of their alliance in the mid-eighteenth century, the House of al Saud and the Wahhabis had drawn strength from each other. The princes gained legitimacy in the eyes of their pious subjects. The Wahhabis gained protection, influence and power.

The result has been a curious split in the national psyche. In terms of technology and lifestyle, the Saudis have leapt into the modern age, adopting modern advances in medicine and science, embracing the material culture of the West in a buying spree that has lasted decades. At the same time, they have been at pains to resist any contamination by Western ideas. An entrenched conservatism permeates every aspect of life in the Kingdom.

Western religious, cultural and social practices are regarded with an almost pathological suspicion as antithetical to the teachings of Islam, or worse, a conspiracy against it. 'Muslim Ummah,' preached the imam at the Grand Mosque in Mecca, 'is faced with the waves of irreligious thinking and conception and misleading secular ideology that are being propagated under the cover of [the] globalization campaign.' (*Arab News*, May 6, 2000)

For some, the very idea of progress is rejected. Wahhabi religious scholars look back some 1,400 years to the time of Mohammad and of the four righteous caliphs who succeeded him as the golden age of Islam, an age that provides a blueprint for the perfect Islamic state. Any faults or problems in the modern state they attribute to a falling away from the old, simple ideals: the answer is always a return to the old ways. 'The Islamic nation will never return to its' [sic] glorious position of past and return [to] its' legitimate rights unless once again it adheres to its' faith,' preached the imam of the Grand Mosque in Mecca in December 1999. 'We have enough lessons and experiences, the flag of secularism will never succeed. There is only one thing that remains for the Islamic nation and that is a political and social repentance and to go back to its' noble message by which the Muslims can defeat their enemy and restore their glory.'

For every official attempt to move forward – to introduce new technologies, to enhance opportunities for women, to relax the rules, to reform the education system or to diversify the economy – there was a countervailing resistance. 'Progress without change', was said to be the official slogan of one of the early five-year development plans. This may have been just another expat joke, but it seemed to describe the situation perfectly.

Throughout 1999, the world was gearing up to celebrate the new millennium. In the Western media, commentators looked back over the past 2000 years to evaluate our achievements and failures, and to ask the question: 'What does the future hold for us?'

Some of these articles filtered through to the *Arab News*, but not many. Almost the only millennium issue that the Kingdom shared with the West was that of the Y2K bug, as Saudi institutions scrambled to have their computer systems ready before the deadline. Grand Mufti Sheikh Abdulaziz bin Abdullah Aal Al-Sheikh described the millennium as a 'heresy of the unbelievers', and ordered Muslims not to celebrate it (*Saudi Gazette*, December 28, 1999).

Late in December 1999, Geoff and I rented a car and drove down to the United Arab Emirates. Our plan was to meet up in Dubai with some Australian friends, Michael and Kerry, who were passing through the Middle East.

On the way we spent a few days in the pleasant greenery of Hofuf, before tackling the 700 kilometre journey south through barren wastelands and then east along the salt pans that form the northern edge of the Empty Quarter. Although the roads were excellent most of the way, and superb once we had crossed the border into the Emirates, we arrived exhausted in the modern, mega-wealthy oil city of Abu Dhabi.

The next day was December 31. In our hotel room, we turned on CNN to watch the world gearing up for a giant party. In Sydney, where the new millennium had already dawned, there had been a spectacular display of fireworks, and revellers were out in the streets. But outside on the streets of Abu Dhabi, all was quiet. No doubt the local expatriates were having the time of their lives at private parties all over the city, but no public celebrations of any kind were to be seen.

We went to see a film at the local cinema, and emerged from it just as the clock in the lobby struck midnight.

'Happy New Year,' whispered a Filipino attendant as he brushed by us.

Out on the deserted streets, we danced a millennium waltz. Then we went back to our hotel room.

After a day of rest in Abu Dhabi, we drove on to Dubai, an easy three hour journey. Dynamic Dubai is justly nicknamed the Hong Kong of the Middle East. Although it has few natural resources, apart from the small inlet that has always been a centre for trade in the Gulf, it has built a thriving economy based on petrochemicals, aluminium, tourism, banking and entrepot trade activities. Modern ports and cargo terminals, industrial plants, office blocks and infrastructure projects peppered the landscape on the approaches to the city, and everywhere I looked the bulldozers and cranes were at work installing more. Although they were working at a frantic pace, they seemed to be barely keeping up with demand. Dubai's commercial centre is all glitter and bustle.

That night, we picked our friends up from the airport and drove them through teeming streets and flashing neon signs to their hotel. Later we sat outdoors at a terrace café, sipping drinks, talking about their travels in Paris and Cairo, and about our lives in Saudi Arabia.

'It's a wild and crazy country,' said Geoff, shaking his head. Keen to develop his theme, he went on to describe some of the contradictions of the place. I added a few examples.

Michael and Kerry shifted uncomfortably in their seats, and exchanged glances. 'Aren't you being a bit negative?' they suggested.

Perhaps we were. Then again, perhaps we weren't. We pressed our argument.

'The corruption is beyond belief,' said Geoff.

'There'll always be corruption,' said Michael. 'There's corruption in the Victorian public service.'

'The wastage . . .' I began.

'Western societies are the most wasteful on the planet,' Kerry countered.

We persisted through bureaucratic inertia, nepotism, lawlessness and economic stagnation, with our friends suggesting at each turn that things were just as hopeless in Australia.

'Just look at what they've achieved here,' said Michael, with a sweeping gesture towards the broad boulevards and soaring skyscrapers. It was useless for us to suggest that Dubai, with all its sparkle, was not Riyadh.

'Perhaps you've been there too long,' said Kerry.

That, at least, was one thing we could agree upon.

13

THE INFORMATION

[She] is crazed with the spell of far Arabia,
They have stolen [her] wits away.
(with apologies to) WALTER DE LA MARE, 'Arabia'

Back in Riyadh, time began to pass slowly again as our lives fell into a routine. On a typical day, Geoff would get up early, shower and make breakfast for himself long before I awoke. Before he left for work, he brought me a cup of tea and set it down at my bedside. Often the tea turned cold before I stirred myself to drink it.

Eventually I would drag myself out of bed. Out of the window, the same blue sky and the same dusty brown heat haze. I would linger in the shower, enjoying the sensation of wetness, avoiding the day. A stab of guilt over wasting water, and I turned off the taps.

Downstairs for breakfast. As I spooned up my corn flakes, I liked to leaf through a magazine – usually the latest edition of *Emirates Woman* – although I would already have read every article.

Plans for the day? None. No classes to teach. No shopping bus. No tea parties. A little housework perhaps. A load of washing. A few stretches.

Outside I heard Shaheen, the Pakistani sweeper with the face of an angel, swabbing the tiles with his mop. I gave him 5 riyals, and he hauled a twenty-litre bottle of drinking water up from the mini-mart down below, and tipped it into the dispenser on my kitchen counter.

Later I might brave the heat and trudge down to the small supermarket at the other end of al Kendi for some bread and fruit. Maybe drop in on Margaret or Yanti or Eun Yong. Pick up a copy of the *Arab News*.

There were books on the shelf, but I had already read everything remotely interesting, and quite a lot that was not. Briefly I considered a tract by the Dalai Lama, borrowed from the Quiet Irishman, on dealing with anger. How I wished we had his thoughts on handling boredom.

I glared at our smart new touch-tone telephone, and wished it was connected. We had been waiting weeks, but there were always 'technical difficulties'. No telephone, so no email. I could write a letter: 'Dear – not much has been happening here . . .'

Boredom . . . boredom . . . boredom! Excruciating, grinding, pathetic boredom.

At least there was TV. I reached for the remote control . . . settled onto the couch . . . glanced at the clock . . .

Only ten a.m. That it should come to this!

The big screen crackled softly and a picture appeared. The Saudi channel, with the local version of young talent time: a slender youth reading from the Quran. His voice rose and fell, the words flowing resonantly, rhythmically. At the end of his reading, he received congratulations from a panel of bearded judges, and no doubt some comments on the finer points of his performance.

I took aim with my remote.

When King Abdul Aziz tried to introduce radio broadcasts to his deeply conservative Kingdom in the 1920s, he met with strong resistance from the *ulema*, the council of religious scholars. The new medium, they declared, was of the devil's making. The King won them over by broadcasting a reading of the Quran. Could this, he asked them, be the devil's work?

When Crown Prince Faisal wanted to introduce television in the 1960s, he met with similar resistance, and answered it in the same way – by broadcasting a steady diet of prayers, readings from the Quran, and scholarly discussions on religious matters.

Although religious broadcasts still dominate the airwaves, programming is more varied these days. Chat shows, dramas, children's programs, cartoons, cultural programs, sport and news have been added to the mix.

'What is your favourite TV channel?' I asked my students.

'I like the Syrian channel,' volunteered one. 'I like the music, and the actors.'

'I like the Discovery channel,' said another enthusiastically.

'My favourite channel is the Saudi channel,' said a third firmly. 'I like to watch readings from the Quran.'

'I like the Saudi channel too,' said the next girl, and the others echoed her. 'Yes, the Saudi channel.' 'Yes Saudi TV.' 'Me too.'

Was it my imagination, or did the voices lose some of their animation?

The magazine that I chose to accompany my breakfast was a typical Western-style glossy with stories on fashion, health, career and family aimed at modern Arabian women, whether locals or expats. In my edition, the featured health and well-being article was headed 'It really is a case of mind over body'. 'Fascinating new scientific research proves for the first time,' offered the opening paragraph, 'that what we perceive, think and feel can play a crucial role in whether we stay well or become sick.' Photographs of beautiful young women accompanied the article: cultivating tranquillity on a beach, meditating in the lotus position, enjoying an aerobics class. To each photograph the censor had applied his thick black marker. Bare arms, bare legs, bare midriffs and bare décolletages were all obliterated under an ugly black smear. At least this time the ink had been allowed to dry, and the pages were not stuck together.

On the cartoon page of the *Arab News*, each time Blondie appeared in her nightie the censor would draw in a black T-shirt. The sexy blonde secretary in the Beetle Bailey strip regularly had her miniskirt transformed into a maxi, and her bare arms concealed beneath finely drawn mesh sleeves.

In a copy of *Scientific American*, the illustrated pages were removed from an article on the human body. In another, in which an article on human evolution was illustrated by a painting of ape-like creatures wandering through a forest, the breasts of the female ape had been subjected to the black-marker treatment.

I couldn't help but wonder who did this kind of work. Were they volunteers who pitted themselves against a tide of depravity, sacrificing themselves to keep the rest of us pure? And how long did they last in their jobs before exposure to such filth turned them into slavering degenerates?

'This is God's country,' one of my students told me. 'Of course we want to keep it pure.'

Keeping it pure meant keeping out anything that threatened to undermine the local culture, anything that smacked of Western decadence, anything that was ungodly. The list started with alcohol and pork, and went on to include any materials deemed to be obscene, pornographic or offensive to Muslims.

We were warned to expect rigorous searches of our belongings at customs, and the confiscation or destruction of any book, magazine, video, CD computer program or work of art that did not pass inspection. One of Geoff's American colleagues at KFUPM, a new arrival, was distraught that his family Bible had been confiscated. An English friend complained that not only had his *Steel Magnolias* video been seized, but that he had incurred a SR6,000 (US$1,600) fine for attempting to import pornography.

'It is extremely saddening,' wrote Dr Abdul Qader Tash in his 'Straight Talk' *Arab News* column, 'to see the moral degeneration of the media in many Arab and Muslim countries. Woman – her voice, picture and physical features – has become the most primary means of attracting and seducing people. The figure of women, displaying all those features that decency demands should be kept covered, have come to be accepted as a mark of

sophisticated marketing technique of goods and services . . .'
(February 6, 1999)

It was not just the female form which offended. In Jeddah,
when the Ministry of Commerce confiscated T-shirts and other
clothing printed with objectionable slogans, the Committee for
the Promotion of Virtue and Prevention of Vice issued the following list of words and phrases they deemed to be objectionable:

vixen	chorus girl	Christmas
nude	buy me	Cupid
whore	I am trash	Bible
hussy	pussy	vicar
kiss me	vice	atheist
I am ready for sexual offers	bawdy	Madonna
lust	eccentricity	dram
adulteress	flirt	spirit
bastard	socialism	brandy
charming	Christian	tippler

Even Nike, the Greek goddess of victory received a mention
(*Arab News*, May 25, 1999).

My daily crossword puzzle in the *Arab News* regularly had
some of its clues expunged. The missing words could be guessed
by filling in the cross clues: 'sow', 'pig', 'ale', 'loo', 'Zeus', and, in a
strike against astrology, 'Leo'.

Reviews of Arundati Roy's Booker prize-winning novel referred
to the work as *The . . . of Small Things*. Christian crosses were
banned, as was the very word 'Christ'. The exercise class I
attended was listed as a 'Stretch and Relax' class: the word 'yoga'
was unacceptable.

Any foreign comment on Saudi affairs was unwelcome.
Robert Lacey's book, *The Kingdom*, despite its sympathetic por-
trayal of the rise of the House of al Saud, was banned because
of a number of perceived slights, including that it was thought to
insult the nation's founder, Abdul Aziz, by suggesting that he
became a little senile in his later years. The *Lonely Planet* Arab
Gulf States guidebook was conspicuously absent from the travel
shelves of the few Western book shops. Magazines like the

Economist and *Time* often appeared with whole sections ripped out. A search of the contents page would reveal a missing article about Saudi Arabia.

Flick. The BBC World Service. News on the hour, round the clock; but not much had happened since the last time I tuned in. Still the same long lines of miserable Kosovan refugees trudging across a frozen landscape.

Next up, 'Hard Talk', featuring Tim Sebastian's interview with Xaviera Hollander. I had already seen it three times.

One evening late in July 1999, just before we moved to Riyadh, I was at a party at Ferdaws. Just after ten, the wife of one of the teachers arrived, straight from her shift as a nurse at the Aramco hospital, with a horrifying tale to tell.

In Qatif, a large tent accommodating the women and children of a wedding party had caught fire and collapsed. The hospital's emergency department had been overwhelmed with victims suffering from burns and smoke inhalation. Every hospital in the region had been mobilised to help with the crisis. Already the number of fatalities stood at thirty-seven.

Over the next few days, the local papers carried heartrending reports of the tragedy as the death toll mounted. Eventually it reached sixty-seven, and included the young bride. Over a hundred were injured, some of them seriously.

I looked for reports of the wedding fire on the BBC news. There were none, although a bus crash in India with only half the number of casualties received full coverage. As far as I was able to tell, the event was not reported at all in the international media.

Not that the Saudis would have minded. Their love of privacy makes them more than happy to be ignored by outsiders. So great was their distaste of foreign scrutiny that there was little or no Western media presence in the Kingdom: no reporters, no wire services and apparently no local journalists prepared to sell stories to outside media services. The Saudis were even sensitive about expat photographers trying to snap local colour, fearful that they would capture images of beggars or squalor that would show the Kingdom in a bad light. 'Foreigners may take photographs of these [negative aspects] and carry them to their homes or publish them in their newspapers,' wrote one *Arab News* correspondent (April 21, 1999), giving expression to the general squeamishness about both outsiders and images.

One of the self-improvement activities I had planned as a way of filling my days in the Kingdom was to become a more proficient photographer. To this purpose, I arrived armed with a brand new SLR camera and a selection of books of instruction. I soon learned that many sites – mosques, bridges, desalination plants, embassies, military and telecommunications installations – were off limits for security reasons. Everywhere else, Saudis regarded cameras as an unwelcome intrusion, offending both against the right to privacy and the Islamic prohibition on depiction of the human face, so that any attempt to photograph people was likely to cause hostility. My album is filled with endless shots of buildings, palm trees and desert. There are hardly any of people.

The great irony was that in the absence of direct reporting, the stories about Arabia that were reaching the outside world tended to be either negative, sensational or both, and to make the Saudis appear monstrous. Human rights abuses, the maltreatment of women, religious extremism, judicial executions, official corruption and profligate spending are part of the truth, but not the whole of it. Missing were accounts of the wider social context, the positive aspects of life in the Kingdom, and the ordinary, everyday lives of the people.

Flick. A Middle Eastern drama – probably Egyptian. I once watched one of these all the way through, although it was in Arabic. It told the story of a childless, but nonetheless happily married man. His mother, desperate for grandchildren, nags him into taking a voluptuous neighbour, who has been flirting outrageously with him, as his second wife. Suddenly both wives are pregnant, and both of them with twins! Soon the hero is inundated with squealing children, enduring the nagging of both his wives and his mother, and struggling to make ends meet on his humble salary. In the last scene, he commits suicide by leaping from a bridge into a river. Until this tragic denouement, I had been convinced that I was watching a comedy.

In April 2000, the *Arab News* celebrated its twenty-fifth anniversary. The *News*, a tabloid with a circulation of over 50,000, was the Kingdom's first English language daily, founded in a Jeddah garage in 1975 by two Saudi brothers, Hisham and Mohammad Ali Hafiz. Its mission: 'to project Arab and Islamic views in a clear and forthright manner' (April 20, 2000).

It was not the only English language daily in the Kingdom. Nor did it, by international standards, offer cutting-edge journalism. But somehow the *News* became my paper of choice, and an hour spent browsing its pages was often the highlight of my day.

The readership of the *News* was made up largely of expatriates, and the paper catered to their needs. International news purchased from the wire services, lifestyle articles reprinted from American magazines, and coverage of the activities of local expatriate sporting and business clubs made up a large part of its daily fare. A regular column offered legal advice to foreign workers having problems with their contracts. Letters to the editor engaged in passionate debate about such things as the merits of the Pakistani or Indian cricket teams, or the taxation policies of the government of the Philippines. No doubt it was expatriates who directed most of the questions to the paper's resident expert on Islam. Questions like: Is it permissible for a man to urinate standing up? (Answer: Yes, it is.) And: Is it permissible for a man to sleep with both his wives at once? (Answer: It depends.)

The front page led with reports on the official engagements of the country's rulers. King Fahd, Custodian of the Two Holy

Mosques, sent cordial greetings to his excellency the Emir of
Dubai, and received gracious thanks in reply. Crown Prince
Abdullah received a delegation from Daghestan. Minister of the
Interior, Prince Naif, addressed a meeting of the Gulf Coopera-
tion Council. This information came directly from the Ministry
of Information, and was presented without analysis or criticism.

After the official news and headline stories from international
wire services came stories of day-to-day life, some amusing, some
tragic: children lost and found, family squabbles, police investi-
gations, crimes petty and serious, the inevitable executions.

It was the *Arab News* that, for several weeks in late 1999,
brought us the unfolding drama of a young man condemned to
death for accidentally killing his friend. Although the family of his
victim were entitled to demand his execution, by law they could
agree to give up this right in exchange for blood money. When
they decided that the price of their mercy would be an unprecedented SR5 million (US$1.3 million), things looked very black
indeed. Fortunately, *Al Madinah* newspaper stepped in to launch
a public appeal. It played out in the press like a hospital
fundraiser. 'Nine days to execution and not enough money', read
the December 1 *Arab News* headline. Happily, the young man
was eventually spared.

A regular column, 'From the Local Press', featured translations
and cartoons from other Saudi publications. From it I learned
about the everyday concerns of the Saudis: the shortcomings of
the state education system, the problems of youth unemployment, the high costs of medical care, the corruption and obfuscation rampant in the public service bureaucracies, the
uneasiness caused by rapid social change.

The *News* had its own stable of journalists and columnists.
One young Saudi wrote about Filipino affairs with genuine affection for the Pinoy community, and took his countrymen and
women to task for their cavalier treatment of Filipino housemaids
and sevants. Female writers spoke eloquently about the achievements, aspirations and frustrations of Saudi women, and while
they were careful not to offend community standards, they were
persistent and forthright advocates for reform. Conservatives
wrote about the need to adhere to tradition.

It was the *Arab News* that brought home to us the true extent of public outrage, frustration and bitterness caused by the unresolved Palestinian crisis. While every writer decried the double standard in the West's treatment of Palestinians and Israelis, many went further, and saw persecution and conspiracy. The Western media, the British parliament and the US congress were all under the control of the Zionists. Day after day the political cartoons showed Uncle Sam and the United Nations as puppets manipulated by a Zionist master, Peace as a dead white dove, and Islam as a hapless Arab, powerless to do anything about it.

On the darker side, the *News* revealed a persistent strand of anti-Westernism that could not help but make foreign residents of the Kingdom nervous. In its mildest form it manifested in resistance to the encroachments of global (Western) culture on traditional ways and values. This often became a strident denunciation of the West expressed in terms such as 'indecent', 'degraded', 'fornication' and 'abomination'. The occasional self-critical or pro-Western article did little to balance the picture. The cumulative effect was to create a view of the West and all her people as hell-bent upon humiliating the Arabs and their culture, and destroying Islam.

My response to this rhetoric varied from anger to disbelief. I wanted to tell the readers of the *Arab News* that the West was full of good people committed to social justice for all. That although Muslims living in Europe, America and Australia had their share of problems, they enjoyed rights that could only be dreamed of in most Muslim states. That in this multi-cultural era, most Western leaders scrupulously avoided any statement or action that could be interpreted as anti-Islamic. Above all, I wanted to reassure them: the West is not plotting against you. It doesn't really give a damn about Islam. In fact, although this may hurt your pride, the West is ignoring you.

At the time, before September 11, 2001, this seemed to me to be true.

Flick. The Saudi news. A prince inspecting a new oil facility somewhere in the Kingdom. The director beaming with pride as he guides him around, pointing out the finer features of the installation. The prince smiling benevolently, graciously. The men crowding around hang upon his every gesture.

Crown Prince Abdullah greeting a delegation from Eastern Europe. The Prince, tall and dignified, resplendent in white. The flowing, gold-trimmed brown robe that covers his *thobe* is so fine it is transparent. The entourage he leads is only slightly less splendid than himself. The Europeans wear ill-fitting Soviet-era suits. The scene shifts to the royal *majlis*. At one end of an enormous rectangular room, the gracious Prince and the European leader sit in large gilt chairs of the style unkindly referred to as 'Louis Farouk', exchanging pleasantries. The camera lingers on the pair, then pans around the room. The walls are lined with more of the gilt chairs. Seated in them, Europeans alternate with Saudis. Some are managing to chat, but most sit silently, the Europeans squirming uncomfortable in their heavily creased suits, the Saudis looking relaxed, but infinitely bored.

'Najran incidents have no roots, Prince Naif says.' So read the modest headline in the *Arab News* of April 26, 2000. I read on, intrigued. What had happened in Najran? I wondered. The article was curiously evasive.

Its first paragraph avoided the subject altogether.

Paragraph two repeated Prince Naif's statement that the incident in Najran had no roots or repercussions, and added that it was the first time such an event had occurred in the Kingdom. 'And it has nothing to do with anything else and it has no link with any foreign power. It was mere emotions and sympathy attached with a man staying in the country illegally and who practiced sorcery. There is no other version for it.'

In paragraph three I learned that 'only one security man was killed and five men were injured', and that 'none among the unruly gathering was injured or killed'.

Paragraph four revealed that several people had been arrested, and that many more might be arrested. Prince Naif added that the 'Ismailiyah sect who are living in Najran and Kingdom's southern region are our brethren and trustworthy citizens'.

It was only some weeks later, when Geoff ran into a former student, a young Najrani, that we found out what had really happened.

The Najran region of southern Arabia is home to the Yammi tribe, who are adherents of the Ismaeli sect, an offshoot of the Shia branch of Islam. They owe allegiance to the Agha Khan, direct descendant of the Prophet Mohammad through his daughter Fatima and son-in-law Ali, and as non-Sunnis, they are despised and distrusted by the Saudi religious establishment.

According to our source, the trouble in Najran began when a group of *muttaween* forced their way into an Ismaeli mosque and confiscated some literature. News of the raid spread rapidly. Immediately, between fifty and sixty Yammis rose up in armed revolt. Eventually calm was restored, and the government was able to issue its reassuring messages of brotherhood with the Najranis.

The reporting of the incident in the local press was remarkable not so much for its opacity, but because it appeared at all. Only the need to refute reports in the international media, based on the accounts of some chance European witnesses, had led to its being published.

Flick. The Discovery Channel. A cheetah stalking her prey: a young gazelle. I had become a bit of an expert on cheetahs. They can run faster than any other animal, but not over great distances. They are delicate eaters, and can't stomach any kill more than a few hours old. The natural enemy of the cheetah is the lion. Lionesses go out of their way to hunt out cheetah cubs and kill them. All cheetahs are so genetically similar that they are at enormous risk of being wiped out by disease. But probably the greatest risk facing the cheetah population is that of starvation. They find it difficult to eat with so many cameras trained upon them.

'Who is our press trying to fool anyway?' Dr Nasir Al-Jihani head-lined his *Arab News* article, and went on to complain that every time a government edict was issued, the papers rushed to print it and to express the citizens' delight with it. 'Could it be that these statements are nothing but the creations of newspaper editors who wish to achieve their own personal aims by printing what will please the owners of the papers?' he asked (May 15, 2000).

The *Arab News* approached the authorities with a respect that bordered on toadying (hardly surprising, given that the chairman of its board of publishers was Prince Ahmad ibn Salman), and the Saudi media in general was a tame beast that served the interests of the ruling power elite. Self-expression was permitted within bounds. Institutions could be criticised for inefficiency and other bureaucracic shortcomings, reforms could be suggested. Three areas, however, were strictly off limits: criticism of the royal family, and political or religious dissent.

Official sources urged the press to show restraint in order to protect the image of the Kingdom. But restraint often added up to compliance with the official line, and an absence of investigative journalism.

'Our newspapers have a strange way reporting serious matters. They report on the first day of school by saying that all preparations are perfect in all schools. When any health problem occurs, they assure us that hospitals are capable of dealing expertly with the problem,' wrote one journalist (*Arab News*, August 27, 1999).

'Sometimes it saddens to see your beloved newspaper publishing certain things which smacks [sic] of propaganda,' wrote one reader to the *Arab News* on the occasion of its anniversary (April 26, 2000).

Flick. A local channel again. A line of men, ammunition strapped across their chests, daggers in curved sheaths in their belts, swords raised in the air. Each man had his left arm locked around the waist of the next man in line. This was the *ardha*, a traditional dance performed by Najdi tribesmen to cement their solidarity before a raid. As the drums beat out a steady rhythm, the dancers moved back and forth – but not very much.

Flick. Zee TV, the Indian channel. A cast of thousands dressed in red, yellow and gold, singing and dancing. A lighthearted comedy that had me smiling, though I couldn't understand a word that was said. Thank God for Indian exuberance.

Late in the evenings, the young men of Riyadh flocked to the city's downtown coffee shops to hang out with their friends, to smoke a *sheesha* or two, and to watch sporting programs on satellite TV. There was precious little else for them to do in a city that is notorious for its lack of night life.

In July 1999 the local authorities decided to clamp down on even this form of entertainment with a move designed, they said, to 'protect the morality of young Saudis and to stop them staying up late'. New rules ordered the coffee shops to close by midnight, to restrict TV viewing to the two state-run channels, and to stop satellite transmissions altogether (*Arab News*, July 27, 1999).

You would never have guessed that satellite dishes were illegal in the Kingdom. Installation companies operated openly, advertising both in the press and on billboards, and newspapers carried the daily viewing schedules of the satellite channels. It was the dishes themselves, however, appearing on the rooftops of almost every compound, every labour camp, every apartment building and every villa that signalled just how popular satellite access was. Even the Bedouin out in the desert had dishes installed alongside their black woollen tents.

Where once Saudis tuned in to a restricted diet of wholesome religious or officially disseminated information programs, their TV screens now display CNN, the BBC, and the Movie Channel. Romance, sex, nudity and violence – 'the full bouquet', as the satellite providers describe their services – are now available to Saudis in their homes for the price of a subscription.

The impact of satellite TV on traditional life can only be guessed at, but it is not the Western channels that are causing the biggest shockwaves. That honour belongs to Al-Jazeera, the satellite broadcaster based in nearby Qatar, and known as 'the Arabic CNN'.

Al-Jazeera grew out of a joint BBC–Saudi venture that aimed to provide a satellite news service to the Middle East. The BBC recruited and trained a number of Arab journalists and technicians and the Saudis were contracted to supply access to their Europe-based Orbit satellite for the broadcasts. In 1996 the venture collapsed over censorship issues: the Saudis withdrew their support because the British insisted on their right to include material deemed critical of the Saudi regime. Sensing an opportunity, the Emir of Qatar was able to recruit the BBC-trained staff, and Al-Jazeera was established.

All over the Arab world, viewers have tuned in to the station enthusiastically, and it is not hard to see why. It offers them what they cannot get from their national media – homegrown, Arabic freedom of expression and a robust exchange of views on issues that matter to them.

Al-Jazeera has aired the ideas of both Muslim extremists and of critics of Islam, has explored the issue of women's rights, has canvassed the possibility of peace with Israel, and has questioned the lack of democracy in the Arab world. It has even, to the dismay of its neighbour, put to air interviews with Saudi dissidents, leading the Minister of the Interior, Prince Naif, to complain that it is 'serving up poison on a golden platter'.

Matching the challenge posed by satellite TV to Saudi authority and tradition is the Internet, cautiously introduced early in 1999. Rather than using filters to weed out undesirable sites, the official policy was to ban every site until it had been reviewed by a committee and placed on an approved list. No doubt this tactic had some effect; nevertheless, the general feeling was that the floodgates had been opened. A cartoon from the *Arab News* of the time shows the window of a Saudi house, heavily shuttered and barred. 'Muneera, where are you, my daughter?' calls a voice from inside. Outside, a young woman sits on a flying carpet labelled 'Internet' that has just whisked her clear around the world. 'I'm right here in my room, Mom. I haven't moved an inch!' she replies (October 10, 1999).

I soon had girls in my classes who were enthusiastic emailers and chat group participants, although one reported sadly that when she told her cyber-pals she was Saudi, they refused at first to believe her, and then to have anything to do with her.

Flick. Syrian TV. A full symphony orchestra in white tie and tails playing Beethoven.

Flick. A Gulf channel. A cooking show. A rotund and jolly gentleman demonstrating how to make pancakes.

Flick. A chat show. A female MC talking to unseen callers. Whatever could they be talking about?

My taxi was stuck in Riyadh traffic. In a sentry box nearby stood a soldier in an unfamiliar maroon uniform.

'What is he?' I asked my driver.

The driver didn't know. 'Maybe he is private security guard,' he said.

'So many soldiers; so many different uniforms,' I mused.

'Yes, madam,' the driver replied. 'Too many security men. But please do not worry about these uniforms. We must worry about the other ones.'

'Oh?' I asked, curious.

'Everywhere there are spies,' said the driver, lowering his voice and glancing nervously around.

'What sort of spies?'

'Government spies. *Muttawa* spies. This country is not safe. I will tell you the truth, we must be very careful when we speak. Every time when ten people are together, one of them is a spy.'

At the time I dismissed his comments as paranoia, although

the idea would have accounted for the air of wariness and guarded suspicion I felt so often about me.

Later I learned that he had been close to the truth. According to Middle East scholar Daryl Champion, the Saudi royal family maintains an informal network of informers 'with links to academics, businessmen, tribesmen and other sections of the community to keep on top of grassroots sentiments'. This state intelligence network keeps a close watch on any political expression, including 'jokes about the king and senior princes'.

Expatriate teachers were warned to stay well clear of any mention of politics in their classes, and both Geoff and I experienced the sudden iciness in our classrooms when we strayed too close to a political comment, albeit an innocuous one.

My perception was that for all the outward displays of goodwill – the kisses and hand-on-heart greetings, their courtly expressions of friendship – a deep level of distrust existed amongst the Saudis. The state intelligence network no doubt exacerbates this, creating, in Champion's words, an 'efficient mechanism of regime security: that of an insidious intimidation and fear'.

And yet, the rulers seemed unlikely to have their fingers truly on the pulse of national opinion, surrounded as they were by honour and flattery. Perhaps they should have followed the example of young King Abdullah, newly ascended to the throne of neighbouring Jordan: on several occasions, the press reported, he had disguised himself with a false moustache and beard, and had toured about by taxi to hear what was being said of him in the streets.

Flick. The Hallmark Channel, with a made-for-TV movie. Far too sentimental for my tastes. Besides, I'd already seen it twice.

In his later years, the Kingdom's founder, Abdul Aziz, enjoyed telling the stories of the conquests that had brought him to power. Those who heard him remembered the musicality of his voice, and the eloquent gestures he used to illustrate his tales. They also noted that, with each telling, the details of the stories could change.

According to historian Robert Lacey, Harry St John Philby, British envoy to the court of Abdul Aziz (and father of the notorious British spy, Kim Philby), is said to have once commented on the differences in detail. The King replied that he had 'felt like a change'. This was not so much an indication of any dishonesty on the King's part as it was evidence of his love of story-telling. It is a love shared by his people.

Tell me a story, I would ask my students, and they would fall to the task with relish. Tell me about a journey you have taken, about your childhood, about your grandmother's life, I would say, and the anecdotes would come flowing out.

Expats, too, love to tell tales. Amongst the teachers at KFUPM, the stories were of legendary expats, famous for their quirkiness of character or for their exploits. The tale of one – let's call him John – was a favourite, although not having met the man myself, I could never quite understand why. John was cycling unsteadily back to his apartment, carrying a couple of bottles of homemade wine in his shoulder bag, when he was challenged by the campus security guards. In a panic, he took off across the desert, and the guards gave chase. John was caught, the alcohol was discovered, the police were brought in, and he went to jail before eventually being deported.

With each telling of the story, a detail would be added or changed. 'He was leaving a party at my place,' said one gossip. 'The cheap bastard was taking wine home from a party,' said another. 'He should have left it for his host.' 'He should never have run away,' offered a third. 'That's what got him into trouble.' 'I visited him in jail,' said a fourth. 'He was in a bad way.' Finally someone told me that John was living in Africa, and writing a book that would recount his own version of the incident.

Anecdotes, rumours, gossip, scandal-mongering and exaggeration were major forms of entertainment amongst the expats, and I have no doubt amongst the Saudis too. In the absence of reliable sources of hard facts or objective truth, they crackled through the nation's tea parties like fire through dry underbrush.

Flick. Back to the BBC news. I watched it through, hoping that something had happened since I last tuned in. It hadn't.

A famous story tells of three blind men who are taken to inspect an elephant. The first one, having felt the animal's side, reports that the elephant is 'very like a wall'. The second has grasped the elephant's leg, and says that the beast is 'very like a tree'. 'Nonsense,' says the third, who has a hold on the tail. 'The elephant is very like a rope.'

Although it is rare for outsiders to truly grasp the essence of a foreign culture, one of the great fascinations of travel is to explore the complex strands of truth that make up its otherness. Saudi Arabia, with its reserve and obsessive privacy, was a particularly difficult knot to unravel, made even more difficult for me by the restrictions I faced as a woman. In my attempts to understand, I often thought of the three blind men: I could see different parts of the picture, but the overall pattern eluded me.

I sat at the feet of long-term resident expats to draw on the wisdom of their experience. I scanned the newspapers for stories of life in the Kingdom. I gleaned insights from the women who came to my classes. I picked the brains of taxi drivers. Depending on who I talked to, the image changed. Was Saudi Arabia a corrupt dictatorship headed for disintegration, or a stable and benevolent autocracy loved by its people? Was it a nation of fanatics, or one of peace-loving people of faith? And was King Fahd really addicted to computer games?

I often met people outside my own narrow world of English teachers: medical workers, engineers, businessmen, tradesmen and technocrats. As we listened to each other's stories, it was as though we each carried a single shard from a shattered image, and were desperately trying to fit them together to find out where we were.

Flick. Those damn cheetahs again.

14

ON THE ROAD

The vasty wilds
Of wide Arabia are as throughfares now.
THE MERCHANT OF VENICE, Act II, Scene vii

I t was to have been our big adventure. For the *haj* break, we planned to hire a Land Cruiser and follow the route of the old Hejaz railway. The line was built by the Ottomans in the early twentieth century to carry pilgrims from Damascus to Medina, and was destroyed in the Arab revolt in 1917. Filmmaker David Lean memorably depicted the ambush of one of its trains in *Lawrence of Arabia*. We had heard from friends who had made the journey that it was still possible to see bullet-ridden carriages lying abandoned in the desert where Lawrence and his raiders left them.

We hadn't reckoned upon the effect of the *haj*. Every off-road vehicle in the Kingdom had been commandeered for the trip to Mecca. We considered ourselves lucky to find a small sedan, and resigned ourselves to a far less exciting journey along well-paved roads. Still, it was with a feeling of liberation that we left the suffocating atmosphere of Riyadh behind us and headed north.

Once past the villas, mosques, schools and factories, the landscape settled into steady monotony. We had, by now, become accustomed to the sight of grazing camels, and no longer pointed out the small herds to each other. What towns there were along the way, the freeway bypassed. Only the curling clover-leaf intersections, where roads forked off into surrounding emptiness, interrupted our progress. We passed the time singing our repertoire of songs on a desert theme, or at least the snatches of them that we could remember:

'Midnight at the oasis, send your camel to bed . . . mmm mmm da da da mmm mmm . . .'

At Tumayr we stopped to see the fields where native irises are said to burst into bloom every springtime, but it had been a dry year and we were a few weeks late. Instead of flowers, we found fossilised seashells on the gritty desert floor.

'All day I faced the barren waste, without a taste of water . . . cooool water . . .'

Just before Zilfi we came to the edge of the Tuwaiq plateau, where the highway dropped away through a wide cutting in the massive escarpment. We followed its descent through layer upon layer of sedimentary rock laid down on an ancient seabed. Sparse settlements and black Bedouin tents were scattered across the plain below.

'Oh I'm the sheik of Arabie, the sheik of Arabeeee . . .'

We shared the road with lumbering pilgrim buses, their roofs laden with bundles of luggage and rolls of bedding. 'Mecca or Bust' read the banners tied on their grills, or at least that's what I imagine they said.

'The desert song calling, its voice enthralling, will make you miiiiiiiiiiinnnne . . .'

By late afternoon, I was nervously contemplating the lack of public toilets along the road. The desert offered no chance of concealment, and while it was thinly populated, we were never quite alone. At last we pulled into one of the big roadside complexes that combined petrol station, restaurant, shops and mosque. I followed the women disembarking from the pilgrim buses in the car park, and headed for the rest rooms at the back of the mosque.

Inside, at the long, low water trough, a crowd of young women were jostling to wash faces, hands and feet. Mothers juggled babies and bags of nappies as they waited for a chance at the changing area, or tried to soothe irritable children. Some of the old ladies wore traditional embroidered robes, and had blue tattoos etched on their parchment-brown faces. Except for the children, who gazed at me with frank curiosity, no-one paid me the slightest heed. I tagged desperately onto the end of one of the long queues that had formed outside the four cubicles. Judging from the strained expressions and nervous jigging of the other women in the lines, there had been very few stops on the long road to Mecca.

The road to the north took us towards the town of Buraydah in the Qassim oasis. We had been warned that only maniacs and fools drive on Saudi highways after dark, so Geoff was anxious to get there before nightfall; yet as we approached the town, my nervousness increased. Buraydah is the heartland of the conservative Najd, and the austere home of Wahhabism.

'The genuine Wahhabi country is to the rest of Arabia a sort of lion's den, on which few venture and fewer return', wrote the English traveller W.G. Palgrave in 1865. 'Its mountains . . . the strongholds of fanatics who consider everyone save themselves an infidel or a heretic, and who regard the slaughter of an infidel or a heretic as a duty.'

'Buraydah has the unenviable reputation of being the least hospitable city in Saudi Arabia,' I read in our 1993 guidebook. 'It is the only place in the Kingdom where all foreign women are required to be veiled.' Suitably intimidated, I had myself rigged out in *abaya*, headscarf and dark glasses.

We reached the outskirts just as the last light was fading from the sky, and drove down an endless narrow street lined with the small workshops of glaziers, metalworkers, minaret-makers, carpenters and mechanics. In the commercial centre of town, the footpaths were jammed with sullen-looking Subcontinental men, all standing round with nothing to do and nowhere to go. Not a single woman was in sight.

The Al-Salman Hotel on the far side of town was an overblown five-star palace gone to seed. Although this was peak holiday season, there were few other guests. Thinking that we might head back into Buraydah for a meal, I asked the Egyptian desk clerk if he though my outfit would be suitable for an excursion into town.

'No!' he replied.

We ordered kebabs and rice from room service.

'Is Buraydah a good place to live?' I asked the Indian busboy.

'No!'

In the morning the town seemed less threatening. At least the Indian behind the bakery counter in the small supermarket across the street was glad to see us.

'Welcome, welcome,' he beamed as he plied us with generous samples of sticky baklava still warm from the oven, with sweet cakes stuffed with dates, and with cheese sandwiches. We bought supplies for lunch, and coffee in styrofoam cups, and took them back to the hotel garden with our free samples for a picnic breakfast. As we sat out on the lawn under the palms, we drew a few curious glances, but no-one objected to our presence.

'There's not much to see and do,' said the guidebook, but we decided to take a look around town before heading out.

With its commercial buildings, public parks and tree-lined streets, Buraydah had an air of prosperous civic pride. At its heart stood an enormous new pale brick mosque with soaring square towers, sister in style to our mosque at al Kendi. It was sur-rounded by an expanse of freshly washed paving, and beyond that, a sprawling modern *souk*.

Away from the main street we came across an area of mud-brick houses, some still occupied, most crumbling into ruin. They looked like small fortresses. Their doors were of heavy wood or metal; their thick walls were devoid of windows. Around the edge of each roof ran the familiar stepped crenellations, perfect cover for a defender with a rifle.

'Foreigners are still a slightly unusual sight here so try not to draw too much attention to yourself,' the guidebook said, and I found myself slinking along, trying to disappear into Geoff's shadow.

I needn't have worried. The morning streets were deserted. Only one small boy passed us by. With a look of pure hostility, he spat out *'Kaffir!'* and went on his way. The only other sign of fanaticism that we saw was some vandalism on a naïve painting of a woman dressed Pakistani-style in *shawar kamis* outside a tailor's shop: an angry scrawl had obliterated her face.

As we drove north from the city centre, it fell to me to navigate. As usual, the map in the National Road Atlas bore only the barest resemblance to the labyrinth of actual roads, and, unable to read the street signs, I soon had us hopelessly lost. Geoff stopped to talk to a group of men gathered outside a mosque. Expecting hostility, we were unprepared for their friendly response. One of them climbed into his car and urged us to follow him. He guided us through mile after mile of back roads to the main highway, and then left us there with a cheerful wave and turned back.

Hospitality is such an important element in the Saudi self-image that civic fathers like to build monuments to it. Its symbols are: the deep mortar and pestle used to grind coffee beans; the distinctive Arabian coffee pot with its bulbous base and long spout; the delicate, long-necked vessel used to sprinkle rose water on hands and faces; and the horned incense burner, passed around so that guests can imbue their garments with fragrant smoke. These totems stand blown up to gigantic proportions in traffic islands, in parks, and outside public buildings in towns all over Arabia. Despite its reputation, Buraydah has more than its share.

The very few European travellers who, over the centuries, penetrated deep into the desert peninsula, were as much impressed by the grace and generosity of their hosts as they were by the hostility they encountered.

'Arabia, like the Arabs, has a rough, frowning exterior but a warm hospitable heart,' wrote the Christian missionary Samuel Zwemer at the end of the nineteenth century.

'Bedu hospitality was past belief,' wrote Wilfred Thesiger in 1986, remembering his crossings of the Empty Quarter in south-eastern Arabia forty years earlier. 'We might pass an encampment and a man would kill a camel to feed us, sending us off in the morning having half convinced me that we had conferred a kindness on him by accepting his hospitality.'

Rituals and rules govern the etiquette of host and guest; for example, a stranger can demand three days of hospitality, and guests must always be served ahead of the host's own household. When the nineteenth-century Italian horse dealer and spy for Napoleon III, Carlo Guarmani, was invited to dinner with a group of Sherarat tribesmen, his hosts had to forgo their own meal in order for Guarmani and his Arab companions to eat.

'Often it exasperated me,' wrote Thesiger, 'when . . . my companions fed our scanty rations or gave the little water we had with us to chance-met strangers.' In one memorable incident, someone in Thesiger's party managed to shoot a skinny hare after they had been several days without food. Just as they were about to eat, three strangers arrived at their camp. Thesiger vividly describes his bitter rage as the strangers were served the hare, and his party went hungry again. His companions were simply obeying the code of the desert, knowing that one day their own survival might depend on the generosity of strangers.

Englishman William Charles Doughty, who ventured into Arabia from Damascus in 1876 at the tail end of a pilgrim caravan, was to experience a less welcoming side to Arabian hospitality. In the two years he spent wandering the desert, he was robbed, spat upon, cheated, humiliated, attacked and frequently in fear of his life. He once wrote that he passed just one good day in Arabia, and that 'all the rest were evil'. Doughty's lack of social skills and his obstinate insistence on proclaiming himself a Nasrani (Christian), against the advice of the Arabs who attempted to help him, may have had much to do with his misfortune. However, his journals, written in strangely archaic English, also reveal instances of great kindness and forbearance shown to him.

Of all the vagabond European travellers and adventurers drawn to Arabia over the centuries, Doughty is my favourite. I might admire the audacity of Richard Burton, or smile at the pomposity of Lord Wilfred and Lady Caroline Blunt, or cheer the courage of Palgrave, Lawrence, Thesiger and Stark. But Doughty, a loner and misfit even in his own society, is by far the most eccentric in a stiffly competitive field. For all his ineptness and discomfort, he struck an empathetic chord with me.

Our paths had already crossed. In 1878, Doughty became only the third European to reach Buraydah, which he described as 'a great clay town'. His short stay was not a happy one. At the house of the local emir where he presented himself, he was jostled and robbed. As he walked around the streets, hostile crowds jeered him. When he retreated to the emir's guest house, a crowd followed him and broke the door down, forcing him to take refuge in the harem. 'My sisters, you must defend me with your tongues,' he told the women, and they obligingly went out to confront the crowd. '[The people] are clamouring to the emir for thy death,' said the guard who finally rescued him. 'No Nasrani, they say, ever entered Buraydah.' Doughty left the very next day.

Our journey would take us to the same towns that Doughty had visited more than 120 years earlier. Over the coming days, our path would cross his again and again.

The road from Buraydah to Hail passed through some of Arabia's prime agricultural land. On each side of the highway, lines of sprinklers jetted out a fine rainbow mist as they crept around the Saudi version of crop circles. Where the wheat crop had been harvested, flocks of sheep and goats had been allowed in to graze on the stubble. Beyond the narrow belt of greenery, the desert rolled away to the far horizons. For some 200 kilometres we counted off our progress through the flat landscape by the grain silos that occurred at ten-kilometre intervals, watching them appear as specks on the horizon, grow large, and then disappear behind us.

Eventually the crop circles gave way to desolation. Plastic shopping bags drifted across the highway in front of us, or snagged like blue flowers in the low vegetation. The road was quieter now. The pilgrim buses that had accompanied us yesterday had turned off towards Medina at Buraydah. Now the only ones we saw passed us by in the opposite direction, heading south.

At a lonely wayside petrol station painted a garishly optimistic pink, we stopped to fill our tank and to eat a picnic lunch in the shade of a ruined concrete outbuilding. About us lay the detritus of a long-departed mechanic's trade: old batteries, tyres, bits of rusty metal, engine parts and shattered windscreen glass; and animal bones, papers and more plastic bags, all cauterised in the harsh sunlight.

Closer to Hail, shepherds in Toyota pick-up trucks watched over flocks of grazing sheep, goats and camels. A low range of mountains appeared in the distance, and in the folds of the plain in front of them, palm trees, villages and greenery.

The town of Hail sits in a basin surrounded by jagged red mountains. Now the official centre of the nation's agricultural industry, it was in times past the seat of the powerful al Rashid clan, chief rivals of the al Sauds.

Doughty visited Hail in 1877 after wandering with the Bedouin for several months. He was received warily by the Emir, Mohammad ibn Rashid, who suspected him of spying and was anxious to be rid of him. Allowed to explore the streets of the town, he became the object first of curiosity, then of hostility. When, after three weeks, Doughty had offended almost everyone and shown no sign of moving on, the Emir dispatched his troublesome guest to Khayber, some 300 kilometres and eight days' distance by camel, where the Turkish authorities held sway.

Three months later he was back again, having worn out his welcome at Khayber. The townsfolk of Hail had not forgotten him. 'Now may it please Allah he will be put to death,' was their greeting. In the absence of the Emir, his nervous deputy, afraid of the civil disturbance the Nasrani might cause, allowed him to stay just one night, and next morning sent him off once more to Khayber. In despair, Doughty foresaw a life spent scuttling back and forth between the two cities.

The last thing we expected was to be welcomed to Hail, but as we strolled around, friendly drivers beeped their horns at us and waved, passers-by greeted Geoff with 'Welcome, brother', and shopkeepers invited us in. Admittedly, they were not Saudis, but guest workers from other Middle Eastern countries; still, in comparison to Buraydah, there was a noticeable lightness in the atmosphere. Although the little pleasure garden at the centre of town was sadly neglected, I detected just a trace of Arabian Nights whimsy in its crumbling pavilions, fountains and bowers. There was an air of frivolity, of delight in decoration, that suggested not the desert austerity of the Najd, but the more complex urban culture of the north: of places like Damascus and Baghdad.

'. . . a lot better than it looks from the outside,' was the guidebook's description of the Hail Hotel, so we were well prepared for the shabby rooms with their cheap furniture, broken fixtures, exposed wires and dripping taps. But the staff were friendly, and when we drew back the shutters our window looked out onto a pleasant courtyard filled with date palms and greenery.

Early evening. When we awoke refreshed from our afternoon nap, our thoughts turned enthusiastically to food. We decided to eat at the hotel restaurant. Out in the street, at the main entrance, a waiter stood smoking a cigarette.

'*Marhaba*,' we greeted him.

'*Marhaba*,' he replied, smiling.

'How is it in your restaurant?' asked Geoff. 'Is it a good place to eat?'

'No!' he said, with an emphatic flick of the head.

Perhaps he had misunderstood the question.

'Is the food good?' I asked.

'No!'

We followed his directions around the corner and into the main street, to a fast-food restaurant called Honey. There we ate in the family room, shut away in a private cubicle next to the children's play area. As we tucked into a meal of broasted chicken, coleslaw and fries, the children of the only other family of diners came to stare at us through the door that we had left ajar. We smiled and waved, but they remained wide-eyed and stony-faced until the waiter came and closed the door. Ah well! I was becoming accustomed to seasoning my food with a dash of claustrophobia.

The next day we set out to explore. First we went to Al-Qashalah, the fortress built by King Abdul Aziz ibn Saud as a garrison for his troops after his conquest of Hail. The huge mud-brick building, now a museum, was closed for *haj*, however, and so we set out instead for the smaller 200-year-old Airif Fort, perched high on a hill overlooking the town. Its wooden door was padlocked, but the hinges were so broken that it lay well ajar. We slipped inside.

From the parapets of a large forecourt, we were rewarded with an excellent view out over the palm groves, minarets, clay walls and white block houses of Hail. I snapped a few photographs, then went to explore the small inner courtyard and castle keep. After a while I heard voices, and Geoff calling to me from outside.

The dignified Saudi gentleman who stood beside Geoff was only slightly the worse for wear for having toiled up the steep slope to the fort in the midday heat. He explained that the fort was closed, and that, besides, a permit available only from the Department of Antiquities in Riyadh was needed for us to visit it.

Chastened and embarrassed, we accompanied him down the hill, apologising profusely for the trouble we had caused him. Although we feigned ignorance, we had known all along that entry to Airif would require a permit.

'Madam,' he asked me, seeing the camera hanging around my neck, 'did you take any photographs?'

I confessed that yes, I had, realising suddenly that the town vistas I had been snapping away at probably included sites of strategic importance. He looked at me doubtfully, then tactfully dropped the subject.

At the bottom of the hill we parted. We thanked him for his courtesy, and he wished us a happy journey.

That night, unable to face another meal of broasted chicken, we were determined not to eat at the Honey restaurant. We wandered through the streets looking for an alternative, and asking the friendly locals who greeted us where we might go. They were unanimous – Honey was the only restaurant in town where a woman could eat. We kept walking.

The kebab restaurant was in a dark, quiet street. We peered doubtfully through the dirty window. Not a single customer in the place.

'Botulism palace?' Geoff suggested.

'No family room,' I said. 'They probably won't let us in anyway.'

But as we stood there, the chef tending the spit caught sight of us, and sent his waiter out.

'Please you must eat here,' said the waiter. 'We make you good food. Very good!'

The chef, we saw, was already stirring his coals to life.

We allowed ourselves to be led in and shown to a private cubicle at the rear of the restaurant, where we sat on a greasy carpet, propped up on grimy plush velvet cushions. Previous diners had scratched graffiti into the partition walls.

The waiter appeared with a disposable plastic tablecloth that he spread out with a flourish in front of us. On it he placed small bowls of spiced olives, and dishes of *hummus*, *babaghanoush* and yoghurt laced with cucumber and mint, and flat breads pulled fresh from the grill. Next came a tray piled with skewers of succulent lamb served with a fiery tomato sauce, and bowls of peppery rocket leaves and of sliced ripe tomatoes, and of *fatoush*, the crisp green salad laced with toasted pita bread and dressed with lemon juice, olive oil and bitter sumac.

An hour later we staggered to our feet.

'So, how was your meal?' asked the waiter.

We assured him that it had been perfect.

The journey from Hail to Taima took us through an epic landscape of vast, sweeping plains, of jutting mountains half buried in drifts of sand, of mesas and lava flows and rocks carved into bizarre shapes by the desert wind. It was easy to imagine a Bronze Age army marching through this wilderness en route to a forgotten battle, or to look at the Bedouin encampments that we saw in the distance and see the tents of Abraham.

Doughty had passed through here on his way to Hail in the company of Bedouin tribes. The journey had been a difficult one. Resentful of the burden that his presence imposed upon them, his companions had refused to share their food and water with him, leaving him tormented by thirst.

Geoff, meanwhile, was suffering his own torments. He had an inflamed Achilles tendon, and driving was exacerbating the pain.

It was becoming clear that he would be unable to cope with the hours behind the wheel that our journey required. There was only one thing to do.

Before we came to Arabia, we had promised each other that we would do nothing that would get us into trouble with the Saudi authorities. In the safety of the expat compounds, we had interpreted this vow rather loosely. For me to drive on the open road, however, was quite another matter, even though I recalled that my students had once assured me that, out in the desert, their mothers drove without compunction. I slid behind the wheel, nervously wishing that I had a red and white head cloth to wear as a disguise.

I kept a wary eye in the rear view mirror and another on the road ahead, resolved that at the first sign of a road block or an approaching patrol car I would pull over and change places with Geoff. Fortunately there was little traffic. Soon I was flying along, revelling in my newfound sense of freedom and control. Let other, more daring souls trudge across Europe in the winter snow, or ride a bicycle across the Khyber Pass, or paddle a canoe down the Amazon. For me, driving in Arabia was adventure enough.

Feeling immensely pleased with myself, I glanced into the rear view mirror. There, only about 100 metres away and rapidly closing, was an official four wheel drive truck with a flashing red light on its roof. I gasped, and almost ran our car off the road. The truck passed us by and sped off into the distance, leaving me quivering in its wake. Not a highway patrol car, but an ambulance. I struggled to regain my composure, and drove on.

Our destination that day was Taima. We were going there to see the ruins. For a brief ten years, from 553 to 543 BC, Taima served as the capital of the Babylonian Empire under the Emperor Nabonidus. Today, remnants of the city wall still surround the town. As well, there are ancient fortresses and temple sites, and a well-regarded museum.

In the Old Testament the town is mentioned as a place of refuge.

'The inhabitants of the land of Tema brought water to him that was thirsty, they prevented with their bread him that fled. For they fled from the swords, from the drawn sword, and from the bent bow, and from the grievousness of war.' (Isaiah 21:14-15)

Taima also made a favourable impression on Doughty. 'Delightful now was the green sight of Taima, the haven of the desert,' he wrote, but he didn't linger. His Bedouin hosts owed taxes to the local emir, and they moved swiftly on.

After a jolting 100 kilometres along a narrow, bumpy road through flinty terrain strewn with sharp red rocks, Taima looked like a haven to us too. And yet, from the moment we arrived (with Geoff at the wheel), we faced hostility.

At the Al-Bakr Hotel, we fronted up to the desk with our bags and waited expectantly for someone to check us in. After a while, the desk clerk appeared.

'What do you want?' he growled.

'What do you think?' said Geoff. 'We want a room.'

Ungraciously, he gave us one.

The museum was on the other side of town and, after our long drive, we decided to stretch our legs and walk to it. As we made our way along the main street, every man and boy we encountered clenched his teeth and glowered at us. One actually snarled.

The museum was closed. We peered through the barred gate and through the perimeter fence, but there was little to see, except for a portion of the Babylonian city wall enclosed there. This same wall, however, extended out of the museum grounds and off into the desert behind it. We strolled over to take a closer look.

The wall was impressive in its extent, but instead of suggesting Babylonian glory, it had all the charm of a garbage dump. Up against the crumbling ridge of slate-like rock, we found the carcasses of dead sheep, old engine parts, PVC bottles, rusty cans, and a collection of the ubiquitous plastic supermarket bags.

We had just started back to our hotel when a car pulled up nearby. An Arabian gentleman in white *thobe* and head cloth climbed out, followed by a couple of men in khaki.

'*Salaam alaikum,*' he said, and Geoff, pleased at this chance for human contact, returned the greeting enthusiastically: '*Wa alaikum salaam.*'

But the gentleman was a police officer, and his mission was not a friendly one. He demanded our papers. What he read in them did not satisfy him.

'Why are you here? Where are you staying? Where is your car?'

Geoff explained: we had come to see the museum. We were staying at a hotel on the other side of town. Our car was at the hotel.

'What colour is your car?'

Geoff said it was dark red.

'It is not a white car?'

'No, red.'

'I think it is a white car.'

Geoff, now mightily offended, insisted that it was not.

It was obvious that the small crowd of onlookers who had gathered around didn't believe us. The officer looked sceptical too, but eventually he agreed to let us walk back to our hotel. We strolled off, bemused, pleased that the incident was behind us.

But halfway back, the car pulled in front of us again. 'Where are you going? Where is your car?' demanded the officer angrily. We had walked straight past Taima's main hotel, where he had assumed we were staying. Our explanation failed to convince him, but at last he gestured impatiently for us to walk on.

Fifteen minutes later when we arrived back at the car park in front of the Al-Bakr Hotel, he was waiting for us. 'Now you show me this red car,' he snapped. Geoff, by now totally incensed, slapped the bonnet of our maroon Mitsubishi.

'Here it is. Now are you happy?' He grabbed his keys and threw open the door. 'Take a look,' he fumed. 'Go ahead. I insist.'

But at the sight of the car, all arrogance vanished from the officer's face. Suddenly he looked embarrassed. He backed off, waving his hands apologetically in front of him.

'I'm sorry. It is a misunderstanding, no? I'm very sorry.' He climbed hastily into his own car. 'Please enjoy your visit,' he muttered as he drove off.

'What is wrong with the people in this town?' Geoff, still steaming, said to the desk clerk back inside the hotel.

'They are Bedu,' he replied with a dismissive wave of his hand, implying that they were ignorant desert nomads. But I wondered what the pair of foreigners who had passed through Taima in a white car just ahead of us could possibly have done to so offend the citizens.

The road to Medain Saleh passed through mountains of spectacular beauty. Gigantic boulders piled up around us, cut by great horizontal swathes of black, tan, grey, white and red. Deep gorges filled with drifting sand fell away from the road. Massive folds of sandstone stretched away to the horizon, fading from rust-red to distant violet. In the late afternoon, we came down into a fertile valley that lay in a wide gorge, and turned to the north.

The Nabatean people once laid claim to this valley; in fact, between 100 BC and 100 AD their Empire controlled most of north-western Arabia. A Semitic people, they built their cities astride the major frankincense route that ran from Yemen in the south to Roman Damascus in the north. Medain Saleh was one of these cities. Her people grew rich from the tolls they levied on caravans that passed through their territory. Eventually, however, the Romans established a sea route for their frankincense, bypassing the old trading route. By 106 AD, when the Nabatean Kingdom was absorbed into the Roman Empire, Medain Saleh had been abandoned. Today its ruins are the premier archaeological site in Saudi Arabia. They are spread out over a vast plain studded with jagged rocky outcrops, softly eroded hills and distant mesas: a place of surpassing beauty.

We arrived just in time to present our visitors permits to the friendly police guards at the gate, and to take a brief drive around the site. In the middle of a sandy expanse, a high mesh fence enclosed a level field of rubble and wild grass, all that remained of the thriving markets, temples and dwellings of Medain Saleh. For once there was no hole in the fence for us to squeeze through. Instead we turned our attention to the ridges and boulders that peppered the site. In their soft sandstone faces we made out carved classical facades: the 2,000-year-old tombs of the Nabateans. In the late afternoon light, the rocks were aflame in orange and red.

As the shadows grew long and the distant mountains faded to purple, we set up our tent outside the site in the shelter of an enormous boulder. Around us, the sand was criss-crossed with the tracks of small birds, a camel and a lizard. We watched the sun set in a blaze of gold, and a perfect half moon appear in the sky. The stars came out as we ate our simple meal of bread, cheese and dates. As the night air grew crisp, we lay on our backs and gazed into the heavens.

In the Quran, the ruined city of Medain Saleh is referred to as al Hijr, and serves as an example of the disaster that can befall a people who pay no heed to God's prophets. 'And verily, the dwellers of al Hijr denied the messengers,' reads the text. 'And We gave them Our Signs, but they were averse to them. And they used to hew out dwellings from the mountains [feeling themselves] secure. But torment overtook them in the early morning . . . and that which they used to earn availed them not.' (Holy Quran 15:80-84)

The pilgrim route from Damascus to Mecca once ran close by Medain Saleh and, because they believed that the ancient city was accursed in the sight of Allah, the pilgrims would avert their eyes as they passed by.

In 1876, William Doughty arrived at Medain Saleh travelling in the tail of the Damascus caravan. He became the first European to visit the tombs, and spent three months sketching their columns, their pediments, and the carved griffins, medusas, lions and eagles that graced their facades. He stayed in the small Turkish fort that still stands nearby. In his usual style, he stretched the patience of his hosts to breaking point, seemingly oblivious to the demands that his presence placed upon the garrison. Finally the commander, Mohammad Ali, demanded Doughty's rifle as payment for the food he had eaten, and the two fell to fisticuffs. Soon after, Doughty departed, sans rifle, with the returning Damascus caravan.

We spent just one day inspecting the tombs carved into the golden rocks. Their stories are told in inscriptions chiselled above the entrances, and provided in translation by the Department of Antiquities. 'In the reign of King Ahe who loves his people, Marcus the centurion built this tomb so that he and his family and their sons and daughters could lie here. An eternal curse upon anyone who usurps this tomb.' (I quote from memory, having neglected to copy the text into my diary.) These days the tombs lie empty, their roofs and walls blackened with the smoke from Bedouin campfires.

The Hejaz railway, built to follow the old pilgrim route, runs through the site. The raised embankment that once supported its sleepers and rails is still clearly visible, and a row of fine stone buildings marks the curve of the line where it passed through al Hijr station. The yards are filled with old carriages and rolling stock, still standing where they were abandoned after their last journey, some eighty years earlier. Off to the side in a spacious workshop sits a German steam engine, recently restored. The fort where Doughty lodged is a part of the complex.

It was marvellous to be in such a spectacular place with such a richness of history; better still to have it virtually to ourselves. We could not help but think of Petra, sister city to Medain Saleh, and once capital of the Nabatean Empire. Situated just a little to the north in southern Jordan, the ruins of Petra are both more famous and more magnificent than those of Medain Saleh. They are also visited by some 3,000 tourists per day. Here only a trickle of visitors, all of them expats, were wandering about. We knew that each of them would have gone through the same convoluted process to get there: obtaining a special permit from the Department of Antiquities in Riyadh and another from their sponsor, braving the long journey to the site, to say nothing of the rigours of coming to live in Saudi Arabia in the first place. That feeling of venturing where few had gone before was one of the great attractions of the Kingdom for intrepid expats, and we never experienced it more intensely than at Medain Saleh. When we occasionally crossed paths with other visitors, we greeted each other with smug self-satisfaction.

As we sat eating our lunch in the shade of a gully amongst the tombs, a pair of rugged expats drove up in a cloud of dust, and, leaning out of their jeep, asked us where we were from.

'Australia,' I replied, but the driver waved his hand in annoyance.

'No, where do you live?'

'Ah!' I said. 'We're up from Riyadh. How about y—'

'Did you know, there are tourists here!' he blurted indignantly, then hit the gas pedal and sped away.

And soon we could see for ourselves: a crowd of Germans, flagrantly dressed in shorts and sleeveless shirts, swarming around the site and pointing their video cameras at everything.

We were, to say the least, astonished. Was the Kingdom now granting tourist visas? There had been talk in the press that such a move was being considered as a way to diversify the economy. The idea, bound to offend exclusionary conservative Muslims, had been couched in the vaguest of terms: a possibility at some indefinite time in the future. But here, under our very noses, was evidence that the plans were already being implemented.

After our day at Medain Saleh, we drove into nearby al Ula to look for a hotel. Site of the biblical city of Dedan, and mentioned in both Isaiah and Ezekial as a trading centre, al Ula was described in our guidebook as 'small and nondescript'. It was anything but. The town was dramatically situated in a deep gorge between towering red cliffs, and surrounded by lush orchards of date palms, pomegranate, grape vines and citrus. In the main street, bright sprays of magenta bougainvillea tumbled about the doors and blue-shuttered windows of whitewashed stone houses. The old quarter was a labyrinth of mud-brick dwellings, many still occupied, leaning up against the valley wall. We decided that al Ula was the prettiest town we had seen in all Arabia, and that by local standards the people were friendly enough. At least they seemed untroubled by our presence, and they didn't snarl at us.

It would have been the perfect place to base a tourism industry, if such an industry existed. There was even an up-market motel under construction on the edge of town, and a five-star hotel nearing completion on a rise overlooking it. The only accommodation available to us, however, was the Madain Saleh Guest House. It was in the middle of a major renovation. The inside of the building had been completely gutted, with plaster ripped from the walls and ceilings, carpets torn from the floor, plumbing fixtures wrenched out, and electrical wires poking ominously from the wreckage. We had to negotiate piles of rubble to reach our room, the only one still undamaged. As we blew the concrete dust off the furniture, we considered ourselves lucky to have it.

'Welcome to the Grozny Hilton,' said Geoff.

We had heard from the guards at Medain Saleh that, although the new hotel looked like a building site, its kitchen was already in operation, and that it offered excellent meals. After cleaning ourselves up as best we could in the circumstances, we presented ourselves to the tuxedo-clad head waiter, who showed us to our seats in a cavernous dining room. And there they were again, the Germans, now dressed in tasteful evening clothes and looking very much at home. I called the waiter over.

'Who are these people?' I asked.

'They are a tour group from Germany,' he said, as if it were the most natural thing in the world. 'Guests at this hotel. They arrived by coach last night from Jeddah. We have had many tours like this.'

I felt the winds of change swirl through the room.

For the first eighty kilometres out of al Ula, we followed the route of the old railway, marked by a raised embankment, stone culverts and abandoned way stations. Then our road swung away to the east while the line held its course between ranges of sharp red mountains. But like us, it was headed for Medina, some 300 kilometres to the south.

Our path wound through endless hills of rusty iron. In valleys washed with gravel or swept with sand, we passed Bedouin tents surrounded by herds of grazing camels, sheep and goats. All day long the swirling willy-willies that the Arabs call *djinns* danced across the desert in front of us.

Just before Khayber, we came down onto a sinister-looking plain covered with a crust of black pumice: the lava flow of an ancient volcano. Beneath the branching fissures that crazed the hard surface, deep gullies had formed in the soft, underlying sandstone. We saw the crowns of palm trees and old stone

watchtowers emerging from them as we drove past, and, gazing
down, the occasional glimpse of a small cultivated field.

Old Khayber had once nestled in this labyrinth of valleys. The
town is famous as the site of the last Jewish resistance to Islam
in Arabia. In the time of Mohammad, a thriving community of
some 20,000 Jews lived in Khayber, practising trade and agriculture. The Prophet accused them of scheming with the Arab tribes
who opposed him. In the seventh year of the Muslim calendar,
determined to neutralise this opposition, he led an army of
1,600 men out of Medina towards Khayber. He approached by
night, stealthily. In the morning, the townsfolk woke up to find
themselves besieged. There was no major battle. After one
month and several skirmishes, the town capitulated. Although
Mohammad was merciful to the Jews of Khayber, the second
caliph to succeed him, Umar (634–644 AD), expelled all Jews
and Christians from the Arabian Peninsula.

Like many Arabian towns, modern Khayber sits alongside the
ruins of its old quarters; it is an accretion of nondescript white
buildings at the base of a rusty crag. In the mid-afternoon when
we drove through its main street, the shops were closed and
shuttered, and there was no indication that momentous events
had ever taken place in the vicinity. Still, Geoff decided that, for
historical interest, Khayber was worth a photo. Not a single soul
was in sight as he aimed his camera first up the street and then
down, but as he fired off a final shot of me sitting in the car, an
old man emerged from a shop a little distance away, raised
his fist and shouted at him. Geoff waved politely back, got into
the car and drove off, intent upon exploring the *wadis* of the
old town.

No more than three minutes later a patrol car appeared beside
us and signalled us to pull over. We complied. Geoff got out to
talk to the officers.

'Camera, *jib*!' – give me your camera – they demanded rudely,
and we realised that the old man had reported us.

Damn! I thought. All the photos I had taken in Medain Saleh
were still in the camera. Geoff had the same idea. He stalled, pre-
tending not to understand.

The two officers spoke no English. They angrily demanded the camera again, and pantomimed pulling out the roll of film and exposing it. Again, Geoff stalled.

A driver passing by stopped to translate. After listening to the policemen, he explained in flawless English that they would like us to surrender our camera so that they could remove the roll of film and expose it. Geoff, with exquisite politeness, asked him to tell them that he was unwilling to do this because we had taken no photographs of forbidden subjects. Stalemate.

The policemen glowered darkly at Geoff, who held up the palm of his hand. 'Tell them that I wish to see their superior,' he announced grandly to the translator.

A hasty consultation. 'They want you to accompany them back to the police station,' he told us.

So there we were, in trouble with the law. I was appalled. I imagined us disappearing into a provincial jail cell, never to be heard from again. Geoff, on the other hand, seemed to be enjoying himself. He was determined that our precious photos would not be lost, and determined not to give in to the arbitrary bullying of our captors.

'They're very junior officers,' he said. 'Their standover tactics may work on poor Bangladeshis, but I don't think that we have anything to fear.' I envied him his confidence.

In the police compound on the edge of town, we were ordered to park our car. After a few minutes, a senior officer swaggered over.

'Why you will not give your camera?' he wanted to know.

'My wife does not want to lose her photographs. But we will stay here until they are developed, and you can take the ones you don't like.'

'This is not possible.'

The officer now tried to approach me directly, but here we were on safe ground. Geoff blocked his way, acting mightily offended that he should even think of such a breach of etiquette.

'I wish to speak to your superior,' said Geoff.

'Iqama!' demanded the officer with ill-concealed irritation. 'Papers!' He took them and disappeared back into his office.

And so we waited. An hour later a stir of activity at the entrance of the compound announced the arrival of the sheik. He strolled into the yard in his cool white *thobe* and *ghutra*, graciously accepting the deferential handshakes and kisses of his uniformed men. Geoff walked over to greet him as I watched warily through the car window.

For a while the outcome was doubtful. A frowning sheik asked questions and listened. Geoff answered, explained. A tense group of officers milled around them looking first at one, then at the other, like spectators at a tennis match. And suddenly everyone was smiling. The watching men relaxed and laughed. Hands were shaken. Hands were placed over sincere hearts.

We were sent on our way with apologies and good wishes for a pleasant journey. Out on the road, our desire to explore the *wadis* of Khayber had evaporated. Now we both wanted to put as much distance as possible between ourselves and these sombre, rubble-strewn plains.

'I told you that there was nothing to worry about,' said Geoff, pleased with himself. 'There's no such thing as the law in Saudi Arabia. It's all a matter of how much rank you can pull. Everything is negotiable.'

Medina. Site of the Prophet's Holy Mosque, the second most holy site in Islam. When Mohammad was forced to flee from his native Mecca, he came here. His followers had already converted a large number of the inhabitants, and Mohammad was welcomed as a prophet as well as the leader of the community, a combination of the spiritual and the secular that was to set the pattern for subsequent Muslim societies. In Medina, the foundations of the Islamic Empire were laid down. Islam ceased to be a small, powerless sect trapped in an unfriendly society, and became a mass movement. It was in Medina, too, that the Prophet established the principle of using force to protect and to further Islam: the notion of *jihad*. The year was 622: year one of the Muslim calendar.

Like Mecca, Medina is off limits to non-Muslims, although we were permitted to visit the outskirts of the city. We reached them by mid-afternoon, winding down on a mega-freeway through

crumbling red hills to a buzzing metropolis. Everything we saw
suggested substance and prosperity.

Hungry for luxury, we made straight for the Sheraton. The big
hotel was quiet and deserted. A waiter, dozing at his post, roused
himself to bring us coffee and cakes. A television in the lounge
showed where the action really was: at Mecca, some 400 kilometres to the south, a great swirl of pilgrims was circling the
Kaabah. The *haj* was reaching its climax.

By the strict rules of Wahhabi Islam, praying at the Prophet's
tomb in Medina is the equivalent of saint worship or idolatry.
This does not stop some of the faithful from making the journey
to the Holy Mosque, and many choose to cap off their *haj*
pilgrimage with a visit to the city.

'Tomorrow we will be busy,' said the waiter. 'When the *haj* is
over, many, many pilgrims will come here.'

After our taste of indulgence at the Sheraton, we set off to
find accommodation more in tune with our budget. The Ouyen
Hotel at the base of Mount Ohud was plain, but adequate, and
had the bonus of bringing us close to history. In 624, a Muslim
army camped on the other side of the mountain was defeated by
a force of pagan Meccans who circled round behind it to
surprise the defenders. It was to be Mohammad's last defeat,
one of very few.

For dinner we enjoyed the incongruous pleasure of a slap-up
Chinese banquet in a stylish restaurant fitted out with rosewood
dragon screens and red-tasselled lanterns. Later, as we headed
back to the Ouyen, I caught a glimpse from the freeway of the
Holy Mosque, its floodlit minarets and dome glowing a subma-
rine green in the distant darkness.

The next morning, the area behind the mountain had been
transformed into a giant livestock market teeming with sheep
and goats: on sale for sacrifice on this last day of the *haj*. We
headed past them on the freeway. At an intersection signed
'Airport and Qassim' in one direction, and 'Medina City Center
– Muslims Only' in the other, we took the road less travelled.
Further out we passed tent villages set up to accommodate
returning pilgrims, and thanked our stars that we were one day
ahead of them.

The road back to Buraydah ran straight through desert, mountains, lava beds and *wadis*, past scattered herds of live-stock. Around the small settlements we passed through lay graveyards of ruined cars, their twisted hulks rusting slowly in the sun. Desolate looking petrol stations dotted the highway, each encompassing a mechanics workshop, a tiny mosque, and a whitewashed concrete café with 'Turki Restaurant' painted crudely on its side. We stopped at one to buy food and petrol.

'How long have you been working here?' I asked the young Sudanese who served us.

'Seven years,' he replied.

'This is a very lonely place,' I said.

'Yes, it is so very, very lonely.'

We ate out in the garbage-strewn desert under a scrawny acacia clipped high from below by grazing camels: the only shrub for miles around.

Now that we were back on a busier road, Geoff had taken over all the driving. As we ticked off the kilometres, we reviewed our journey. In many ways, it had not been an easy one. The simple matters of obtaining food, lodgings and even a woman's lavatory had been fraught with difficulty. Our contact with the locals had been fleeting and superficial at best, and we had often been made to feel unwelcome.

On the other hand, no-one had tried to fleece us, or persuade us to visit their uncle's shop, or to ride their camel, or to buy their trinkets. The Saudis had remained proudly, disdainfully aloof, and that was surely preferable to the calculated sycophancy that tourism engenders in more travelled places.

Best of all, in the vast open spaces of the northern deserts, far from the rules and restrictions of the cities, we had experienced an expansive, exhilarating sense of freedom. We were even more than a little chuffed by our run-in with the police of Khayber, or at least, Geoff was. He had saved our roll of film, had not caved in to bullying, and had gained insight into the way things work in the Kingdom. Later a Saudi friend was to congratulate him on his handling of the camera incident. 'You did exactly the right thing,' he said. 'Now you are learning to be a real Saudi.'

We felt as if we had graduated.

That evening, when we rolled back into Buraydah, the town held no terrors for us.

And what of Doughty? By 1878, he had been wandering in Arabia for almost two years, shunted from the jurisdiction of one unwilling desert potentate to another. His hosts had been loath to accept his presence, but wary enough of the European powers to preserve his life. His diaries reveal a tale of constant hardship, misery, humiliation and danger, and more than a little foolhardiness on his part.

His last journey took him from Unayzah, twin city of Buraydah, south towards Mecca with a camel caravan transporting butter. As on his other journeys, the Nasrani soon became the object of hostilities. His companions, who regarded him as unclean, refused to share their water with him. At a *caravanserai* on the outskirts of the holy city, Doughty found himself in the midst of an angry crowd, face to face with a fanatic armed with a knife who declared: 'He shall be a Muslim!'

'Only say . . . thou art a Muslim, it is but a word to appease them,' urged his companion from the butter caravan. Doughty refused.

He was rescued by the intervention of an old Negro slave from the household of the Sherif of Mecca, who told the crowd to 'remember Jeddah bombarded! And that was for the blood of some of this stranger's people.' (The British navy had indeed recently shelled Jeddah in retaliation for the murder of a British sailor.)

To his dismay, Doughty was placed into the care of Salem, the fanatic who had threatened to kill him, and sent off to Taif. Along the way, they fought over possession of Doughty's only remaining gun, which he had revealed in a moment of fear. Now deprived of his weapons, and defenceless, his survival and eventual arrival in Taif was nothing short of miraculous.

'The tunic was rent on my back, my mantle was old and torn; the hair was grown down under my kerchief to the shoulders, and the beard fallen and unkempt,' he wrote. 'I had bloodshot eyes, half-blinded, and the scorched skin was cracked to the quick upon my face.'

And yet, to the disgust of Salem, the Turkish commander of the town made Doughty welcome, and treated him with kindly respect. After four days, he rode to Jeddah and boarded a ship for India.

As Geoff and I drove back towards Riyadh, our thoughts, too, were of departure.

15

MAASALAMAH

Arabia and the Arabs are now astir.
GERALD DE GAURY, Arabia Phoenix

I've always been fascinated by the great 'what ifs' of life. What if we had decided to stay in Arabia? It's almost as though I have left a part of myself there: a part that lives on, evolving through that alternative choice into a different version of me. Perhaps in another reality I'm still living in Riyadh, grown rich by now in my insights into Arabian ways, possessed of all the wisdom of the old hand. I can almost hear myself intoning to some neophyte: 'Well, when you've been in the Middle East for as long as I have . . .'

We could have stayed. Arabia was not without its attractions. We had friends there. We were enjoying the expat social scene. Australia seemed to hold an uncertain future for us.

But Riyadh, never an easy place to live, was becoming especially irksome. Suddenly the *muttaween* were everywhere, riding a wave of repression. They had even invaded the Diplomatic Quarter, where they were busy harassing and bullying the foreign residents.

The golden-voiced *muezzin* who had summoned the faithful to prayers was gone from the al Kendi mosque, replaced by another with a harsh and grating tone. The imam's sermons, broadcast over speakers mounted high in the nearest minaret, grew longer and louder and more and more angry. As they blasted in upon me, they irritated me to distraction.

By late April, the heat was returning. Day by day, relentlessly, the mercury was rising. The air reeked of baking dust. When I ventured outside, it roasted my face and seared my lungs. My feet and my hands swelled up. Sweat trickled down my face and my chest and back, then dried to a salty crust on my skin in the parched air. My *abaya* clung to me in a rapture of static electricity. When I peeled it off in the cool darkness of my hallway, it fizzed and crackled with sparks of blue lightning, and my hair stood on end.

I thought of the long, monotonous months of heat to be endured, and dreamt of fog and of great, soaking drops of rain. One summer in Arabia had been interesting, much as the experience of an earthquake or hurricane or some other natural disaster might be interesting – once. I had no desire to try it again.

We could have signed up for another round. The extra income would certainly have come in handy. But we were tired.

The constipated atmosphere of Riyadh had gotten to me. I was bored, dispirited. It wasn't enough that society demanded me to be circumspect and constrained: I was starting to censor myself. My mood carried over into my English classes. Once such a delight, they were now flat and lacking in all spark. Try as I might, although I spent hours fretting over lesson plans, I could not resuscitate my enthusiasm. I got through each class mechanically. I lost confidence. The demanding young women I confronted in the classroom grew restless. They expected their English lessons to be fun; God knows, they had few other opportunities for it. They had little patience with a droopy teacher who was unable to deliver. I felt as exposed as a stand-up comedian in front of a hostile audience, and despaired. Poor me. Poor students!

After almost four years in the Kingdom, Geoff had had more than enough too, although his dissatisfaction manifested in anger. Once he had been entertained by Saudi offhandedness. Now he took it personally. He told the dean that he might leave when his contract expired. He expected to be thanked for his faithful service, perhaps persuaded to stay on.

'Huh,' said the dean. 'We can get plenty more staffs.'
It was the final straw.

We had to make one last trip back to Dhahran to wind up our affairs and to arrange exit visas through Geoff's original sponsor, KFUPM. This time, we decided, we would make the journey by 'luxury bus'. A three-hour sprint across the desert brought us to the Gulf just as the last glow was fading from the evening sky. After our year in the oppressive atmosphere of Riyadh, we saw al Khobar in a new light.

Along the corniche, palm trees were waving in a gentle sea breeze. The pink and green fluorescent tubes that marked the driveways of the petrol stations gave them a jaunty, holiday air. I stepped out of the bus into a blanket of humidity, and instantly relaxed. Suddenly Riyadh and its tensions seemed a world away.

At our favourite restaurant, the fish were still darting about in their tanks and the waiters were still wearing bright Hawaiian shirts. They smiled as we came in and welcomed us back. How could I ever have imagined that al Khobar was straight-laced or threatening?

When we turned on the lights in our old apartment at Ferdaws, gangs of cockroaches scuttled out of sight. The floor was covered with squads of dead ones, victims of the Maintenance Department's periodic insecticide blitzes. Apart from the wildlife and the layer of dust everywhere, all was exactly as we had left it nine months – an eternity – ago. We made up the bed and collapsed into it. It felt like home.

The following morning Geoff went up to the *jabal* to begin collecting his exit stamps. Before we would be allowed to leave, he had to obtain clearance from Educational Aides, Recreation Center, Faculty Affairs, Medical Center, Payroll Division, Telecom. & Elect. Maint., Admin. Affairs, Security, Library Affairs, Housing & Office Serv., Dept. Head, Registrar, Faculty &

Personnel Serv., Dir. Gen. Housing & Off. Serv., Dir. Gen. Fin. Affairs, and finally, general approval. The process had been known to take days, weeks or even months.

I set to work cleaning up the apartment in preparation for the housing inspector's visit, then wandered off to renew old acquaintances.

All over Ferdaws women were packing; preparing for perma-nent departure, a new posting, a return to their homelands, or a summer of travel. All except Marie. 'We can't afford a holiday,' she said. 'We'll be here for the summer.' She was, as always, busy. Now her living room doubled as a classroom where she con-ducted English lessons for private students. 'We really need the money,' she said. 'This year both the children will be away at boarding school, and it's so expensive.' Despite her positive attitude, Marie was doing it tough.

At Katy's, small children were still charging in and out, and women were still dropping by to reclaim them, to borrow and return items, or simply to chat. Katy, too, was in the midst of packing. She would be moving to the Emirates after the summer break, where her husband had secured a post at another univer-sity. It had been a good year, she reported. The arts club, despite difficulties with the authorities and power plays within, had finally come together, and several recitals involving both men and women had taken place in the recreation centre. 'It's been really difficult,' she said, 'but wonderful to work with Saudi musicians and artists, and to see them with an outlet for their work. There's so much talent out there.'

Soon I was swept up into the familiar, female ghetto that was Ferdaws, with its clashes, its carping and its warmth. I had missed its swirling social currents.

Some of the women had been to so many farewell functions that they confessed themselves to be quite partied out, but when one of the Arabian faculty wives threw a farewell party for Katy at her villa in Doha, we all went along.

At the rear of the mansion, tables had been set up beside the clear waters of a large swimming pool. A team of servants was at work in the gazebo preparing a feast for us as we sat out under the bright moonlight sipping tea, chatting and listening to the sinuous throb of Arabic music. When the women rose to dance, their movements were relaxed, sensuous and mildly flirtatious.

Some of us had brought cameras with which to take farewell photographs. Our hostesses were reluctant to be included until they realised that we would all soon be leaving the Kingdom. 'That's all right then,' said one, 'no-one will see them,' and they all joined in the posing.

At the end of the evening the Saudi women made their final farewells: courteously to those who, like me, were still outsiders, but for Katy, who had made such an effort to get to know them, with warmth, affection and sadness.

With nothing left for me to do in Dhahran, I headed back alone to Riyadh to complete my packing. Geoff delivered me to the bus, so I had no problems getting on board: it was clear that I had his permission to travel. At the other end of my journey, I hired a taxi to take me to al Kendi. As we drove through the night, I thought back to my first night in Riyadh, and how impossible such a simple act would have seemed to me then.

Geoff stayed in Dhahran to finish obtaining his clearance stamps, to sort out his salary entitlements, and to reclaim his possessions – his wristwatch, his spare clothing, even his lunch – from the campus housing officers who had somewhat pre-maturely repossessed our apartment. All this he accomplished successfully, and was able to join me a few days later.

Most of our friends in Riyadh had already left for the summer. By the end of May, we were ready to follow them.

Until the very last minute, Geoff was convinced that some-thing would happen to prevent our departure. His greatest fear was that the ghost of our old car, the rusty Honda that had seized up a year earlier, would come back to haunt us. He had never been confident that the mountain of paperwork required to officially dispose of it had been completed satisfactorily, and knew that a mistake could be grounds for detaining us in the Kingdom. As we waited at the check-in counter at Riyadh airport, he fretted anxiously, but I felt in my bones that nothing could go wrong. I had just downed several glasses of fine French wine at our farewell luncheon. I was already flying.

And in the end, I was right. When we presented our exit papers, the immigration officer checked our records on his computer, and then broke into a sunny smile as he stamped our passports and wished us well.

We flew to Bangkok, where Geoff took the necktie that had given him such faithful service in the classrooms of Arabia and placed it gently on a Buddhist street shrine. My *abaya* ended up in the rubbish bin of our hotel room. I like to think it was retrieved by a thrifty Thai maid.

Melbourne in midwinter. Short, dark days. Grey skies, cold winds and drizzle – bliss! We promised each other that we would never complain about winter again, and set about re-establishing our lives.

Our old neighbourhood had changed. The public housing at the bottom of the street was now home to immigrants from the Horn of Africa and the Middle East. At our local supermarket, Eritrean women did their shopping draped in brilliantly coloured *hijab*. At the *halal* butcher's down the street, I saw Gulf women in full blackout, veils and all. I wondered how my city looked through their eyes. What, for instance, would they have made of the billboard advertisement in which a larger-than-life, almost naked model smiled seductively down upon passers-by, inviting them to admire her lingerie?

My lifestyle didn't change much. I didn't take to drink or drugs or indulge in wild affairs. Freedom was something that I expanded into gradually, feeling my way around. Small things were important: an hour spent browsing in a good book shop, a night at the movies, a glass of wine with my lunch in a sidewalk café, the spectacle of young men and women happily spending time together. For months Geoff and I would exchange conspiratorial glances, congratulating ourselves on our new sense of liberty.

Just over a year after we returned, on a morning in September, we awoke early, for some reason unable to sleep. Just after five a.m. Geoff flicked on the radio. An Australian journalist was filing a report from a phone booth in downtown Manhattan. 'I understand that you're not far from the Twin Towers site,' said the announcer. 'Can you tell us what you can see?' The journalist replied in a shaky voice that she couldn't really see anything through the cloud of brown smoke and dust that was billowing out of the wreckage and blanketing the area. 'If you've just tuned in,' said the announcer, 'we have suspended normal programming to bring you live coverage from New York . . .'

Perhaps we should have seen it coming. Suddenly all the anger, all the accusations of anti-Islamic conspiracies, all the anti-Western vitriol that I had heard and read about in Arabia came flooding back to me. At the time, I had found it disturbing, but rarely alarming. Perhaps, like the rest of the world, I just hadn't been paying enough attention.

If the attacks on New York and Washington brought terrorism into the heart of the West and caused a swift reorientation of attitudes, they had just as dramatic an effect on the Saudis.

True, some rejoiced that the US had got its come-uppence. Even moderates expressed the hope that, through their experience of tragedy, the Americans would learn compassion for the sufferings of the Palestinian people. Others suggested that the attack had been a Zionist plot, designed to discredit Arabs and Muslims. A rumour circulated on Al-Jazeera TV gained ready credence. It said that not a single Jew had died in the collapse of the World Trade Center, because, forewarned, they had all stayed home that day. Many Saudis, however, were profoundly shocked by the events of September 11 and by the fact that their country had spawned so many of the perpetrators.

When I was in Arabia, despite my awareness that what I was witnessing was the result of explosive social change, I somehow had the illusion that the society was static, even stagnant. Yes, there were mutterings about the instability of the monarchy, about economic stresses and about social pressures for reform, but nothing seemed urgent. The same discussions had been going on for twenty years or more with little result. I believed that the al Saud regime would go on running the country, that the reform process would grind on ineffectually, even that the bubble of my own little expat world would endure.

September 11 and the War on Terrorism has changed all that. A combination of external and internal pressures has meant that real change is now not just more likely, but inevitable. The direction that this change will take, however, is far from clear.

I became an avid Saudi watcher, scouring the local and international press for articles about the Kingdom. Happily, the *Arab News* had upgraded its website, making it possible for me to read up to the minute news and commentary from within the Kingdom.

At first I was optimistic that the forces for liberalisation would prevail. Belatedly, there was talk of genuine political reform. The Crown Prince promised a more participatory form of government to his subjects. Dissidents who had once been imprisoned or exiled for their views were given permission to discuss the formation of a civic society. One hundred of them signed a paper calling for an elected council and delivered it to the Crown Prince. Even women were making progress, having finally been given the right to have their own ID cards.

In March 2002, a fire in a girls high school in Mecca that claimed the lives of fifteen young students became the catalyst for open criticism of the *muttaween*, who had prevented the girls from escaping the building because they were not wearing *abayas*. When it also emerged that the building had been grossly over-crowded, substandard, and leased for many times its market value, the public outcry against a complacent and corrupt administration was unprecedented.

Evidence of a new openness could be seen in a wave of foreign journalists reporting from the Kingdom on such previously sensitive subjects as dissent, youthful rebellion, poverty and even drug addiction. As they filed their stories, all their talk was of a new era of reform. No doubt this was the image that the Royal House of al Saud wished to project as it attempted to ride out the storm of change.

In attempting to bring about change, however, the al Sauds must still overcome the resistance of the religious establishment. It is evident that the old pact between the princes and the Wahhabis is a serious impediment to progress, and yet it would be foolish to underestimate the depth of conservatism in the Kingdom, or the power of the fundamentalists.

In the final analysis it is neither the current secular leaders nor traditional religious leaders who will determine the nation's future, but the masses of young Saudis who even now inject an element of volatility into the equation. Unless their energies can be integrated and their aspirations realised, their discontent will provide a fertile recruiting ground for religious fanatics offering easy answers and passionate commitment.

It would be all too easy to see our two worlds, East and West, lined up for an apocalyptic clash of civilisations. This is an image that many on both sides of the divide are keen to cultivate.

Most Westerners remain profoundly ignorant about Islam, the Middle East and the Arabs. We have indulged in stereotyping and oversimplification. We have ignored the complexity and the diversity of the East. We have shown ourselves to be indifferent to the pain and aspirations of her people. At the same time, we have been complacent in face of their hostility to us.

Our failure to engage has been matched and exceeded by Eastern views of the West; views based in a rhetoric of hatred, ignorance, suspicion and intolerance. The Arabs have found it easier to blame the West for the backwardness, corruption, repression and stagnation that besets their societies than to engage with it themselves.

September 11 was a watershed moment for both sides. Ironically, it now appears that al Qaeda's successes have roused the West from its complacency, and transformed her into the enemy that they had previously only imagined. Perhaps that is what al Qaeda desired. My own fear is that by our actions in the Middle

East – our failure to unravel the Israeli–Palestinian knot, our participation in the 'coalition of the willing' – we will create the enemy of our own nightmares. That we will undermine and isolate those who are calling for genuine social reform and for a more tolerant and pluralistic interpretation of Islam.

There are those, both Western and Muslim alike, who suggest that al Qaeda and its radical offshoots are engaged not so much in a war against the West, but in a war for the soul of Islam. That their main objectives are to overthrow the House of al Saud and to reclaim holy Arabia for themselves. That, like the Wahhabis who inspired them, they will crush dissent and reform Islam in their own image.

I think of the young Saudi women I knew – their kindness, their sense of fun, their hopes for the future – and pray that the fanatics will not succeed.

At first, when expatriates became the target of occasional sniper attacks or car-bombings in the year after September 11, 2001, the Saudi authorities were loath to attribute blame to anti-Western elements within the Kingdom. They insisted that the victims were alcohol bootleggers caught up in a Mafia-style turf war with rival gangs. Several were arrested, and the authorities were able to present signed confessions in which they admitted their guilt. The prisoners, under threat of execution for their alleged crimes, protested their innocence and insisted that their signatures had been obtained under torture. Most expats believed them.

The May 12, 2003 suicide bombings of Western compounds in Riyadh, which took thirty-five lives, left no-one in any doubt as to what was really going on. Whether as revenge for Western actions in the War on Terror or in pure hatred of non-Muslims, militants are determined to rid Islam's holy heartland of infidels.

The victims of the explosion at Riyadh's al Muhaya compound on November 8, 2003 were not Western expats, but non-Saudi Muslims enjoying the affluent and relaxed atmosphere of Western-style compound life. This attack signalled that it is not only infidels in the firing line of the fanatics, but also Muslims deemed to have lapsed from purity.

The Saudi Government has belatedly moved to round up militants and to seize their substantial caches of weapons and explosives. In response to pressure from the Americans, they have started to cooperate on measures to cut funding to terrorist organisations, and to crack down on firebrand preachers. No one knows how effective they have been, nor the extent of the problem.

The Australian Government's latest travel advice for Saudi Arabia recommends that non-essential travel should be deferred, and that Australians living in the Kingdom should consider leaving. Those who remain are advised to exercise extreme caution, particularly in commercial and public areas known to be frequented by foreigners.

We keep in touch with the expat friends we made in Arabia. Many have moved on, but some remain. In their emails and letters they are guarded in their comments: it is wise to be circumspect when the authorities censor private correspondence.

These friends stay close to home, and venture into town only reluctantly. Our old camping companions have curtailed their trips to the desert because they no longer feel safe there. One teacher swears that he has seen a triumphal gleam in the eyes of his students. Another says that, under a brittle politeness, things are tense. The old-timers, as usual, keep a low profile, and report that things are much as they have always been.

GLOSSARY

The lack of a standard for transcribing Arabic words into English makes spelling them a matter of some difficulty. I have opted to use the simplest form that adequately conveys the sound of the words. I have tried to observe each person's preferred spelling of their name, or else the printed version that I most commonly saw.

abaya	black cloak worn by Gulf women
ardha	Saudi tribal dance
babaghanoush	a dip made from roasted eggplant and sesame paste
baklava	Middle Eastern sweet pastry
baksheesh	a gratuity or tip
Bedouin	the nomadic, tribal people of the Arabian desert, locally known as Bedu
biriyani	a dish of rice steamed with spiced meat or vegetables
caravanserai	an inn on the pilgrim or trade route
dawa	a centre for the promotion of Islam

dhoti (Hindi)	length of cloth worn as a garment by Subcontinental men
dhow	a wooden sailing boat
Eid Al-Fitr	three-day festival that marks the end of Ramadan
emir	prince, ruler
fatoush	a green salad laced with dry bread
ferdaws	paradise
fi	is there . . .? Do you have . . .?
foul	a dish of stewed fava beans served with various accompaniments
ghawa	spiced coffee brewed from green coffee beans
ghutra	red and white chequered head cloth worn by Saudi men
Hadith	a saying attributed to the Prophet
haj	the pilgrimage to Mecca; the month in which it takes place
hala	modesty
halal	slaughtered in accordance with Islamic rites
haram	forbidden
Hejaz	the western region of Arabia

hijab	modest women's clothing, as decreed by Islam
hummus	a dip made from chick peas
iftar	the sunset meal that breaks the fast during Ramadan
ihram	the simple robes worn by pilgrims
imam	a Muslim scholar or leader
iqaal	a rope headdress worn by Saudi men over their *ghutra*
iqama	internal passport carried by foreign workers
jabal	mountain, hill
jib	give me
jihad	holy war
Kaabah	the shrine in Mecca that Muslims turn towards in prayer
kaffir	infidel, unbeliever
kasir	castle, palace
kebab	meat grilled on a skewer
kabbzah	traditional Arabian dish of rice and stewed meat
khelas	finished, enough
kofta	minced lamb, grilled on skewers

la	no
maasalamah	goodbye; God's peace be upon you
madrassa	Quranic school
mahram	a woman's close male relatives, excluding those she may marry
majlis	a formal reception
majlis hareem	women's formal reception
marat-ammi	mother-in-law
marhaba	informal greeting
mishwak	a stick that is chewed to form a toothbrush
molokia	soup made from a leafy green vegetable of the same name
muezzin	a person employed to call the faithful to prayer
muttawa	a member of the religious police; the plural form is *muttaween*
Najd	the central region of Arabia
Nasrani	Christian (Nazarene)
paan	a preparation of betel nut, betel leaf, spices and lime
qamar-ad-din	a sweet drink made of dried apricots
Quran	the Muslim holy book, believed to be the direct word of Allah

Ramadan	the month of fasting observed by Muslims
riyal	unit of Saudi currency; SR3.75 = US$1.00
salaam alaikum	formal greeting, literally meaning 'may God's peace be upon you'; the response is *'wa alaikum salaam'*, meaning 'and upon you, God's peace'
seraglio	women's quarters, *hareem*
shamal	a hot, dusty northerly wind
Sharia	the Islamic system of justice based on the Quran and the Hadith
shawar kamis	loose trousers and overshirt worn by Pakistanis
shawarma	a sandwich of spit-grilled chicken wrapped in flat bread
Shaitaan	Satan
shebab	bachelor, young man
sheesha	water pipe for smoking tobacco
Shia	a minority form of Islam in which believers trace the lineage of the Prophet through his assassinated grandson, Hussein
shula	flame
siddiqi	my friend; also the name given to moonshine liquor
souk	a traditional market

sumac	a tart Middle Eastern spice, deep magenta in colour
Sunna	the observed practice of the Prophet
Sunni	the form of Islam practised by the majority of Saudis
Surah	verse of the Quran
tabbouli	a salad of parsley, tomato and bulgur wheat
tajine	a stew of meat or vegetables
thobe	the white robe worn by Saudi men
ulema	the ruling council of leading religious scholars
Ummah	the worldwide community of the faithful
umrah	pilgrimage to Mecca taken outside the month of *haj*, also known as the lesser pilgrimage
wadi	canyon or gorge
wasta	expats use the word *wasta* to mean 'influence', or 'connections', but this usage is inaccurate; it simply means 'custom'
yala	let's go
zain	good
Zakat	charity, alms; one of the pillars of Islam
Zam zam	the sacred well in Mecca

AUTHOR'S NOTES

The following notes contain publication details for the various sources used in the writing of this book, as well as further information and clarifications I felt necessary to include.

The unit of currency used throughout is the Saudi Riyal, which is fixed to that of the US dollar at the rate of US$1 = SR3.75. In the interests of simplicity, I have rounded the dollar amounts in my conversions. During my time in Arabia, AUD$1 was approximately equal to SR2.50.

Statistics related to Saudi Arabia are often based on estimates, extrapolations and assumptions. They can be years out of date and are notoriously unreliable.

Foreword
p.xiii The information on the 2001–2002 attacks on Western expats is drawn from reports in the *Guardian* newspaper accessed through their website at http://www.guardian.co.uk. These include: Pilkington, E. 'Like Dallas policed by the Taliban', July 2, 2002; Harris, P., Pelham, N. and Bright, M. 'Expat Brits live in fear as Saudis turn on the West', July 28, 2002; Sweeney, J. 'Greed and torture at the House of Saud', November 24, 2002. Information on the 2003 incidents was sourced from contemporaneous newspaper reports.

1   The Price of Admission
p.1 The quote, 'Tell me said he . . .' is from *Travels in Arabia Deserta*, by C.M. Doughty, Jonathon Cape and the Medici Society Limited, London, 1926, p.1.

p.5 There was 'no such thing' as a tourist or transit visa when I visited Saudi Arabia; however, the Kingdom is now encouraging tourism of a sort. They welcome wealthy travellers on package tours, and Muslim travellers who wish to extend their pilgrimage visas to visit the holy sites of Islam. Western backpackers need not apply.

2   Paradise

p.20 The recreation centre library at KFUPM was set up by the Americans. Its collection reflects more liberal times in the Kingdom. Since the first Gulf War in 1991, Saudi Arabia has become far more conservative. This trend was reflected at KFUPM when the Saudis took over the running of the university.

p.24 Information on the King Fahd Causeway is from *The Story of the Eastern Province of Saudi Arabia* by W. Facey, Stacey International, London, 1994, p.146.

3   The Gulf

p.39 The quote, 'A hooded Bedouin . . .' is from *Arabia Phoenix* by G. de Gaury, George G. Harrap & Company, London, 1946, p.129.

4   Hard Labour

p.64 According to Alain Gresh ('The world invades Saudi Arabia', *Le Monde Diplomatique*, April 2000) there are five million expatriate workers in the Kingdom. For David Hirst ('Fall of the House of Saud', *Guardian Weekly*, September 15, 1999) the figure is six million. For Roger Harrison (*Arab News*, May 5, 2000) it is seven million, although this figure may include the families of working expats.

The figures '70 percent of the workforce, and . . . 95 percent of the private sector' are from R. Baer's 'The Fall of the House of Saud', *Atlantic Monthly,* May 2003, p.58.

The figure US$18 billion is from S. Liesman's 'Driven to distraction – Saudi women may soon take the wheel', *Wall Street Journal*, Eastern edition, March 1, 1999, p.A1.

The figures on the expatriate elite are from 'Saudi Arabia's foreign workforce', *BBC News*, http://newsvote.bbc.co.uk, accessed June 18, 2003.

Figures on the number of third-world nationals in Saudi Arabia are from Bureau of Democracy, Human Rights, and Labour, 'International Religious Freedom Report', October 26, 2001. However, these figures are unreliable, and I have seen many variants on them.

p.68 The figures US$300 to $1,000 are anecdotal. A letter to the *Saudi Gazette* (February 29, 1999) suggested that the cost could be SR10,000 (US$2,700) or more.

p.70 Information on the abolition of slavery in Saudi Arabia is from *The Kingdom – Arabia and the House of Saud* by R. Lacey, Avon Books, New York, 1982, pp.344–5.

Information on the status of slaves in Islam is from *Race and Slavery in the Middle East* by B. Lewis, Oxford University Press, 1994. Sourced from http://www.fordham.edu/halsall/med/lewis1.html, accessed March 11, 2003.

p.72 Prince Faisal's visit to New York is described in Lacey, op. cit., p.177.

p.74 The Philippines Overseas Workers Welfare Administration pamphlet cited is from 'The Plight of Foreign Workers in Saudi Arabia' by B. Evans, 1999, http://www.geocities.com/CapitolHill/Parliament/3251/spring99/saudi.html, accessed March 11, 2002.

The information on runaways is from Evans, ibid.

p.76 For an example of the documented evidence of international human rights groups, see 'Saudi Arabia – Flawed justice: The Execution of 'Abd al-Karim Mara'i al-Naqshabandi', *Human Rights Watch*, October 1997, Vol.9, No.9(E) at http://www.hrw.org/summaries/s.saudiarabia97o.html, accessed March 21, 2002.

The quote, 'a fraudulent way of avoiding the provisions' is from Evans, op. cit.

5   *Oasis Dreaming*

In this chapter, I have drawn extensively on William Facey's *The Story of the Eastern Province of Saudi Arabia* (op. cit.).

p.84 Information on the Dilmun is from Facey, op. cit., pp.23–30.
   The information on Enki is from *Arab Gulf States* by G. Robison, 2nd edition, Lonely Planet Publications, Hawthorn, 1996, p.73.

p.85 Information on Qatif is from Facey, op. cit., pp.75–89; and from Robison, op. cit., pp.407–8.

p.87 Information on Tarut Island is from Facey, op. cit., pp.83–9.

p.90–91 Information on al Hasa and Hofuf is from Facey, op. cit., pp.67–83.

p.93 The 1950 output of 90,000 litres 'from one well alone' is a figure cited in Facey, op. cit., p.78.

p.94 Information on agriculture and irrigation is from C.S. Smith's 'Saudis worry as they waste their scarce water', *New York Times*, January 26, 2003.

p.95 Information on Ayn Dhil is from *Desert Treks from Riyadh* by I. Thompson, Stacey International, London, 1994, p.28.

p.96 Information on water use in cities is from Smith, op. cit.

6   *Black Bags and Precious Pearls*

p.101 The information sheet cited is 'The Mutawwa: Information and Guidance', Australian Embassy, Riyadh.

p.105 Information on the protest in Buraydah is from Lacey, op. cit., p.369.
   Information on the Dar al Hanan is from Lacey, op. cit., p.365.

p.106 For an account of the 1979 rebel seizure of the Grand Mosque at Mecca, see Lacey, op. cit., pp.478–86.

p.109 The figure of 50 percent unemployment for female graduates is from J. Tamer's 'The limits of job creation', *Arabies Trends*, April 1999, p.37.

The proportion of female expatriate workers cited is from Gresh, op. cit.

p.110 Information on the Olayan Group is from K. Thomas's 'A velvet revolution', *Arabies Trends*, April 1999, p.34.

p.119 Information on women in Oman taking their place in the nation's legislature is from K. Thomas's 'The new Arab woman', *The Middle East*, January 2000, p.43.

7 *Royal Flush*
Robert Lacey's brilliant book, *The Kingdom* (op. cit., passim) was the source for much of the information on Abdul Aziz and the early days of the Kingdom presented in this chapter.

Information on the impact of the oil boom in the 1970s was drawn from *The Saudis – Inside the Desert Kingdom* by Sandra Mackey, W.W. Norton & Company, New York, 2002, passim.

p.121 The quote, 'I realised that the Bedu . . .' is from *Arabian Sands* by W. Thesiger, Motivate Publishing, Dubai, 1994, pp.286–7.

p.122 The figure of 20,000 descendants is from Hirst, op. cit.

p.124 The quote attributed to Abdul Aziz, 'hoarded money never does anyone any good', is from Lacey, op. cit., p.105.

The 'popular story' of Aziz's gold is from Lacey, op. cit., p.238.

p.125 Figures on King Fahd's transport to Spain are from Hirst, op. cit.

The figure of US$800 million for Prince Mohammad's palace was given to Geoff by one of the workers on the project.

The figure of US$2.7 billion for Prince Abdul Aziz's palace is from Hirst, op. cit.

p.126 The figure of 5 percent for the number of nomadic Bedouin is from Mackey, op. cit., p.105.

p.128 Figures on the royal family's cost to the nation are from Hirst, op. cit.

Information on the al Saud's embrace of a Western lifestyle and reliance on US military support is from E. Rouleau's 'Trouble in the Kingdom', *Foreign Affairs*, July/August 2002, pp.75–89.

p.129 For an interesting description of a royal *majlis*, see E. Sciolino's 'Taking a rare peek inside the Royal House of Saud', *New York Times*, January 28, 2002.

Information on King Fahd's reputation is from Baer, op. cit.

Information on the speculation regarding succession is from P. McKeogh's 'Inside the crumbling Kingdom', *The Age,* 'Insight', October 5, 2002, p.5.

p.133 Information on the centennial celebrations was drawn from various editions of the *Arab News*.

8   Heat
p.135 The quote, 'The door finally opened . . .' is from *Honey and Onions – A Memoir of Saudi Arabia in the Sixties* by F. Meade, Sands Books, Riyadh, 1996, p.12.

p.146 Information on Uqayr is from Thompson, op. cit., pp.36–7.

9   Riyadh
p.153 The quote, 'Everything was ruled . . .' is from *Sandstorms – Days and Nights in Arabia* by P. Theroux, W.W. Norton & Company, 1991, p.85.

p.164 Information on Diriyah is from Robison, op. cit., p.329; and from Thompson, op. cit., p.6.

10   Love and Marriage
p.172 Jean Sasson's *Princess* is published by Bantam Books, London, 1993.

The quote, 'Oh Muslim community . . .' is from Sayyid Mujtaba Musavi Lari, *Islam and the Family*, http://home. swipnet.se/islam/articles/family.html, accessed October 20, 2003.

p.176 The story about the groom who switched brides is one that Geoff claims to have read in the *Arab News*.

p.180 The figure of 39 percent first-cousin marriages is from J. Sim's, 'Too close for comfort', *Arab Woman*, October 1999, p.18.

The medical opinion regarding the possible exaggeration of risks of genetic disorder comes from Professor Alan Bittles, foundation professor at Edith Cowan University, cited in Sims, op. cit., p.17.

p.182 I have heard birth-rate estimates ranging from 6 to 6.7. This figure of 6.25 for the year 2001 is taken from the *CIA World Factbook*, http://www.cia.gov/cia/publications/factbook/geos/sa. html, accessed March 21, 2003.

Information on the history of polygamy in Islam is from *Islam* by A. Guillaume, 2nd edition, Penguin, Middlesex, 1956, pp.159–61.

p.185 Estimates on the frequency of divorce are as follows: the figure of 20 percent of Saudi marriages ending in divorce is from S. Peterson's 'In strict Kingdom, Saudi youth shift gears of change', *Christian Science Monitor*, June 13, 2002; the figure of 70 percent of marriages ending in divorce is from Muhammad Omar al-Amoudi, *Arab News*, May 10, 2000.

11 God's Country
The translations of Muslim prayers in this chapter are drawn from various Islamic websites.

The background information on pre-Islam, the history of Islam in Arabia, and Wahabbism is from Guillaume, op. cit.

p.193 The quote, 'If we look around . . .' is from *Islam Beliefs and Teachings* by G. Sarwar, The Muslim Educational Trust, London, 1996, p.13.

p.200 Information on monthly food bills and hospital admissions during Ramadan is from an article by Abdullah Saeed Al-Zahrani, *Saudi Gazette/Okaz*, date unknown, but possibly January 1998.

p.203 The Al-Wahhab quote, 'Mud alone cannot save you . . .' is cited in Lacey, op. cit., p.56.
   The description of Wahhabism as 'sublime minimalism' is from Z. Sardar's 'Mecca', *What we think of America – Granta*, Issue 77, Spring 2002, p.247.

p.205 The quote 'a nice little family business' is from Ian Haig, former Australian ambassador to Saudi Arabia. Interviewed in Melbourne, September 28, 2003.

p.207 Examples of reported 'Islamophobia' include: 'CAIR report highlights growing prejudice against US Muslims', *Arab News*, December 12, 1997; 'OIC seeks UN help for protection of Muslims in non-Muslim states', *Arab News*, April 4, 2000; and 'Muslims in Europe: A case study', *Saudi Gazette*, January 14, 2000.

p.213 Information on strict Wahhabi Islam is from Sardar, op. cit., p.246.

p.214 The imam quoted as saying 'harbour enmity . . .' is Sheik Muhammad bin Othaimeen, cited in N. MacFarquhar's 'A few Saudis defy a rigid Islam to debate their own intolerance', *New York Times*, July 12, 2002.
   Background information on the Kaabah is from 'The Ka'bah: Facts and History', *Crescent Life*, http://www.crescentlife.com/thisthat/kaabah_facts.htm, accessed October 3, 2003.

p.215 Historical information on the *haj* is from *Arabian Travellers* by R. Trench, MacMillan, 1997, pp.11–12 and 23.
   Dr Fouad Angawi's quote, 'The haj is like a war' is cited in E. Sciolino's, 'Muslims feel Sept. 11 chill as Mecca plays it safe', *New York Times*, February 5, 2002.

p.216 Information on the rituals of the *haj* is from Sardar, op. cit., passim and from M. Abdul-Rauf's, 'Pilgrimage to Mecca', *National Geographic*, Vol.154, No.5, November 1978, pp.484–5.

p.219 Information on the international spread of Wahhabism is drawn from A. Alexiev's 2002 article 'Confronting Saudi lies, extremism and subversion for the benefit of all', United States Committee for a Free Lebanon, http://freelebanon.org/articles/a322.htm, accessed February 17, 2003.

p.220 The quote, 'Wahhabism has reduced Islam to an arid list of do's and don'ts,' is from Sardar, op. cit., p.249.

12   *Progress Without Change*

p.223 Crown Prince Abdullah's warning is cited in D. Hirst's 'Saudis strain inside Islamic straitjacket', *Guardian Weekly*, August 12, 1999.

Information on the national budget deficit is from D. Champion's 'The Kingdom of Saudi Arabia: Elements of instability within stability', *Middle East Review of International Affairs*, Vol.3, No.4 (December 1999), http://www.biu.ac.il/SOC/besa/meria/journal/1999/issue4/jv3n4a4.html.

Information on the national debt equaling 100 percent of GDP is from Gresh, op. cit.

The figure of 90 percent reliance on oil for export earnings is from Champion, op. cit.

Information on infrastructure problems is from Gresh, op. cit.

Figures on the national per capita income are from D. Abu-Nasr's 'Teens turn to terrorism and telephone dating', *The Age*, April 18, 2002, p.16; and E. Sciolino's 'Bored Saudi youth take wild side to the street', *New York Times*, February 20, 2002.

p.224 For a discussion of the Kingdom's bid to join the WTO, see R. Dean's 'International Trade', *Gulf Business*, April 2000, pp.37–40.

The total unemployment figure of 27 percent is from Gresh, op. cit.

The figure of 95 percent for women is from *Saudi Arabia: The coming storm* by P.W. Wilson and D.F. Graham, M.E. Sharpe, New York, 1994, pp.254–5.

p.225 The figures on the number of working-age Saudis are from D. Hirst's 'Fall of the House of Saud', *Guardian Weekly*, September 15, 1999; as is the number of Saudis aged under eighteen.

p.227 Information on the impact of the oil boom in the 1970s is, again, drawn largely from Mackey, op. cit.

p.228 The figure of 60 percent of the national budget paying civil service salaries is from Hirst, op. cit.

p.232 The imam's quote is taken from a transcript of his December 3 address that was given to me by a Muslim friend.

13   *The Information*
p.237 Information on King Abdul Aziz's introduction of radio broadcasts is from Lacey, op. cit., pp.243–4.

p.238 Information on Crown Prince Faisal's introduction of television is from R. Azzi's 'Saudi Arabia: the Kingdom and its power', *National Geographic*, Vol.158, No.3, 1980, p.332.
   'It really is a case of mind over body' was an *Emirates Woman* article by P. Westcott, June 1999, pp.21–4.

p.240 Information on the banning of *The Kingdom* is from Lacey, op. cit., p.506.

p.243 The circulation figure for the *Arab News* is for 1998, and is sourced from the *Arab News* website, http://www.arab news.com, accessed December 8, 2003.

p.250 Background information on Al-Jazeera is from M. Dobbs's, September 10, 2001 article 'Qatar TV station a clear channel to Middle East', *The Washington Post EUA*, http://www.mre.gov.br/ acs/interclip2/Diario-WL/Outubro-01/Materias/wpost09a.html, accessed October 6, 2003; as is Prince Naif's quote, 'serving up poison on a golden platter'.

p.252 Information on the royal family's network of informers is from Champion, op. cit.

p.253 Philby's anecdote is from Lacey, op. cit., p.48.

14 *On the Road*
p.258 Palgrave's quote, 'The genuine Wahhabi country . . .' was drawn from Trench, op. cit., p.107.
All guidebook comments on Buraydah are from Robison, op. cit., p.330.

p.260 The quote, 'Arabia, like the Arabs . . .' is from *Arabia: The cradle of Islam* by S. M. Zwemer, Oliphant, Andserson & Ferrier, Edinburgh, 1900, quoted in De Gaury, op. cit., p.98.
Thesiger's quote 'Bedu hospitality was past belief . . .' is from Trench, op. cit., p.7.

p.261 Thesiger's quote, 'Often it exasperated me . . .' is from Trench, op. cit., p.7.
Thesiger's 'In one memorable incident', however, appears in his book *Arabian Sands*, op. cit., p.148.
Doughty's quote, 'all the rest were evil' is from *Arabia Deserta*, op. cit., cited in Trench, op. cit., p.157. (I have relied heavily on Trench for the account of Doughty's travels in Arabia in this chapter.)

p.262 Doughty's quote, 'a great clay town' is from Trench, op. cit., p.154; and 'My sisters . . .', Trench, op. cit., p.156.

p.263 Doughty's quote, 'Now may it please Allah . . .' is from Trench, op. cit., p.153.

p.264 The guidebook description of the Hail Hotel is from Robison, op. cit., p.333.

p.267 Background information on Taima is from Robison, op. cit., pp.397–9.

p.268 Doughty's quote, 'Delightful now was the green sight of Taima . . .' is from Trench, op. cit., p.136.

p.270 Background information on Medain Saleh is from Robison, op. cit., pp.365–71; and Thompson, op. cit., pp.64–7.

p.273 The guidebook description of al Ula is from Robison, op. cit., p.370.

p.275 Historical information on Khayber is from Guillaume, op. cit., pp.48–9.

p.277 Historical information on Medina is from Guillaume, op. cit., pp.38–41.

p.280 The quoted material from Doughty's tale was obtained from Trench, op. cit., pp.160–62.

15 Maasalamah

p.282 The quote, 'Arabia and the Arabs are now astir' is from de Gaury, op. cit., p.135.

p.289 The fire in the girls school in Mecca was reported in the *Arab News* in March 2002. The *Arab News* is available online at http://www.arabnews.com.

Western commentators who have explored the impact of extremism within the Muslim world include Thomas L. Friedman ('War of Ideas', *New York Times*, June 2, 2002), Alex Alexiev ('Confronting Saudi lies, extremism and subversion for the benefit of all', United States Committee for a Free Lebanon, http://freelebanon.org/articles/a322.htm), and Patrick E. Tyler ('A Campaign to Rattle a Long-Ruling Dynasty', *New York Times*, November 10, 2003). Liberal Muslim voices include Ziauddin Sardar (op. cit., and 'My fatwa on the fanatics', *The Observer*, September 23, 2001), Mansour al-Nogaidan ('Telling the Truth,

Facing the Whip', *New York Times*, November 28, 2003), and Malaysian feminist Zainah Anwar, Executive Director of *Sisters in Islam*.

ACKNOWLEDGEMENTS

I am deeply grateful to everyone who assisted me in writing *My Desert Kingdom*. To Diana Haig for her friendship and encouragement, her help with research, and for her sensitive reading of early drafts. To former Australian ambassador to Saudi Arabia Ian Haig and his wife Beverly, who generously shared their memories and insights. To John and Maryanne Bell, who told me what to expect.

Some of our friends and colleagues in the Kingdom, both expat and Saudi, appear in disguise in these pages; whatever colour they add to them is but a fraction of the enrichment they brought to our lives. Of those who have moved on, my particular thanks to Katy and Richard McClane, Ridwan and Yanti Sedgewick, and Yuko and Larry Sinnot.

For making my stay in Saudi Arabia so very much more interesting and enjoyable than it might otherwise have been, I would like to thank the staff and students at the British Council in Dammam and Riyadh, at the Women's Charity Center in Dammam, at the Dhahran Arts Center, and at al Manahil in Riyadh.

The feedback and encouragement I received from Di Websdale-Morrissey's non-fiction writing group at RMIT was invaluable. My sincere thanks to Di and her students: Annette Alafaci, Sally Gudgeon, Shannon Hayes, Ursula Horlock, Adrian Kaye, Chris Kelly, Josh Lefers, Sarah Lowe, Helen Morgan, Carmel Reilly, Mark Richardson and Emma Tinning.

I am grateful to my agent, Bill Tikos, and to Jane Southward and Lydia Papandrea at Random House for gently guiding me through the publication process. Kim Swivel was the best of editors. I thank her for her patience and insight, and for helping me to dig deeper.

Finally, thanks to Geoff, whose story this is too, for sharing the adventure and for taking care of the distracting details of life while I wrote it down.